THE PARENT'S POCKET CHECKLIST

The Parent's Pocket
CHECKLIST

An Essential
Guide to Baby's
First Year

KIM ARRINGTON JOHNSON

Published by Comm Brevity Publishing, Boston, MA

Cover design by Anne Marie Denton
Interior design by Ryan Scheife / Mayfly Design and typeset in the Whitman and Helvetica Neue typefaces
Editing by Sarah Menkedick
Photo and illustration credits are listed at the end of the book.

Kim Arrington Johnson
Visit the book website at www.parentspocketchecklist.com.

Printed in the United States of America
First edition

Library of Congress Cataloging-in-Publication Data
Johnson, Kim Arrington.
The Parent's pocket checklist : an essential guide to baby's first year / by Kim Arrington Johnson.
p. cm.
ISBN 978-0-9891136-5-6 (pbk.)
ISBN 978-0-9891136-6-3 (EPUB)
ISBN 978-0-9891136-7-0 (Kindle)
Series: The Parent's pocket checklist.
Includes index and bibliographical references.
1. Infants. 2. Infants—Care. 3. Infants—Development. 4. Child rearing. 5. Parenting. 6. Parent and infant. I. Title. II. Series.
HQ774 .J65 2015
649/.122—dc23 2014919908

For Brad, Katie, and Lauren

Contents

• • • • • • • • • • •

A Word of Gratitude

First and foremost, this book would not have been possible without the love and support of my husband, Brad.

I am also sincerely grateful for my mom, brother, grandmothers, in-laws, and other family members who believed in me from the beginning. With special mention, I would like to acknowledge my dad, who is no longer with us, but who shared his special insight on life and passion for the written word. I am also thankful for many others who have inspired or contributed to this work: for my early science teachers, especially Mike Shaw, who creatively brought my favorite subject to life in the small town of King, NC; for my obstetrician, Dr. Jane Piness, and our children's first pediatrician, Dr. Diane Halpin, for their brilliant and balanced approaches to their fields; for my go-to helper and collaborator, Audrey Mangan, for her support with all of *The Parent's Pocket Checklist* projects; for my book reviewers, Kristin Busse, Leslie Riesenhuber, and Susanna Visuri, who shared their honest feedback and encouraged me toward the finish line; for my editor, Sarah Menkedick, who challenged me to reveal more of my own story; for my friend and former squadron mate, Natalie "JJ" Caruso, who helped format this project into viable form; for my early proofreading and editing team, Cathy Johnson and Sharon Weller, who taught me grammar rules that I never knew; for my friend and fellow Dukie, Susan Hazard, who helped craft the book's survey; for the hundreds of parents who filled out the survey, provided feedback, or agreed to an interview; for my mom friends, especially my Mothers of Preschoolers (MOPS) group, who helped me keep it together through some long days as a new parent and reminded me that moms are world influencers; and finally, for my children, Katie and Lauren, who bring immense joy to my life and inspire me to be a better person.

Introduction

When I was pregnant for the first time, I wanted to know everything about having a baby. So I read one book after another and hunched over my computer for hours at a time searching for golden nuggets of parenting wisdom. For better or worse, I am part of an information generation, and we like to over-research everything. How can I find the best restaurants, the best schools, the best apps, and the best deals available? I wanted preeminent advice for all things baby. Yet there is a problem with 24-7 access to infinite information—filtering out the junk wastes precious time and having too many choices paralyzes us. Today, a Google search for "baby care" returns over 30 million hits in .3 seconds, while popular websites bombard new parents with pop-up ads, click-through links, and endless advertisements. There is so much information out there that it ceases to be helpful, and truthfully, we're missing out on the richness of life and time spent in relationship with one another, due to our insatiable need to wander about the Internet when faced with the unknown. In this problem lies the inspiration for this book. I wanted to create a crisp, concise guide with only the most relevant information for baby's first year. I wanted to write a baby book so broad, yet so efficient that Dad might actually read it.

To be clear, I had lots of extra time for reading while pregnant and caring for my firstborn. I had recently quit a demanding job and needed an intellectual outlet (that's a euphemism for "I was a total mess.") I had spent my adult life racing from one action-packed environment to another, from the U.S. Naval Academy to flight school to flying in fighter jets (as an F-14 Tomcat RIO and F/A-18F Super Hornet WSO) to business school at Duke to Goldman Sachs to, finally, being at home all day with a baby. While I was thrilled and blessed to be a mom, I was also lonely and disheartened. The unpaid work I was doing was barely valued, and my new boss mostly complained. Time spent with my child was uniquely satisfying, yet it felt unproductive at the same time. Nobody told me that motherhood would be so complex.

Determined to share my findings and not spend naptime discouraged, I created a simple web site and mom blog. The web site was designed to steer expecting parents to "best of" pregnancy and baby information, while the blog covered a breadth of parenting topics. The blog's intent was not to rant and rave or blast other parents for their choices. It was to be brief and informative, yet reflective of me: a warm, yet slightly satirical "moderate mom" who advocates all things eco-friendly, but isn't about to eat her own placenta; who enthusiastically supports breastfeeding, but refuses to call it mommy nirvana; who subscribes to attachment parenting, but encourages independence when the time is right; who believes in vaccines for the good of all, yet questions the effects on some; and who respects the highest levels of research, but understands that parenting is both art and science. I wanted to prove you don't have to parent on the fringe to be interesting. Tiger moms, earth moms, and moms who rage against everything may sell books and blog ads, but good parenting requires balance. Once I started writing, checklists naturally emerged.

I spent my twenties and early thirties relying on checklists in aviation. Checklists helped me sort through complex problems (like an engine fire), and they also helped my fallible memory recall the mundane (such as startup and shutdown procedures). In Naval Aviation, an aircraft's pocket checklist, called the PCL, was so indispensable that it sat in a special pocket in the leg of our anti-gravity suits for fear it would become detached in an emergency or upside-down flight. You never wanted to be in a situation and not know what the PCL had to say. While parenting may not be as fast-paced as flying in a fighter jet, it is loaded with important yet easily forgettable minutiae. For example, a good packing list for air travel with baby could make or break a vacation, while avoiding certain medications or toxins while breastfeeding or caring for an infant could be lifesaving or life changing.

In the world of checklists, just one piece of critical information can alter perspectives or processes dramatically. Airline pilots, doctors, nurses, and construction crews cannot be expected to know every pitfall and remember every step—and neither can parents. When I first started

Last flight in the F/A-18F Super Hornet. Notice the pocket checklist, or PCL, secured in the bottom left pocket of my G-suit.

Inspiration for this book. A closer look at a pocket checklist used in Naval Aviation.

blogging, readers would write to me with passionate responses and concerns: "My son has ADHD, and I had no idea about mercury, lead paint, or artificial food colorings," or "My daughter started puberty at age eight. We never even considered organic eggs and milk. How are we supposed to know all this stuff?" I learned through blogging that modern parents are longing for transparent and plainspoken guidance.

The scientific community and agencies that oversee public health policy do not always excel at being transparent and plainspoken. I believe this lapse in communication has affected the youngest members of our population. Today, parents have to be the EPA, USDA, and FDA, as the laws that regulate over 80,000 new and existing chemicals are ineffective and out of date. Today, a toddler in Washington State is likely to be sipping on a juice box with apples from China because it's cheaper to grow food and manufacture goods halfway around the world than to do so down the street, making choices about what we buy and what we feed our children problematic. Despite medical advancements, we have a silent pandemic of toxins and synthetic foods damaging our children's bodies and brains with increasing rates of autism, ADHD, cancer, diabetes, and other diseases that *may* be preventable. Yet where does a new parent go to see all of these issues laid out clearly?

Experts dedicate their lives to bettering the condition of our children, and this book is based upon their findings and hard work. Yet who can actually read and understand a scientific journal, at least in its entirety? These publications are filled with disruptive in-text citations, big words that no one knows, and all kinds of other intellectual roadblocks, such as background knowledge. It's as if PhDs have their own secret language that only other PhDs can speak. At the other end of the spectrum, these findings, such as pediatric studies and recommendations, reach everyday moms and dads through popular news outlets. In other words, the science is dumbed-down with a political agenda attached, depending on the news source. Don't we parents deserve better?

Many of you might be wondering what a stay-at-home mom has to offer in this area, and to that point, I freely admit that anyone could have written this book. I simply put my nose to the grindstone to develop this material because I firmly believe that parents are not getting the full story. The threat of malpractice suits, legal liability, and reputation risk can send even our most brilliant doctors and scientists into quiet mode, disclaimer mode, or worse, retreat. On the other hand, a mom with nothing to lose can list every ingredient, call out every deceptive company by name, and talk about the controversial subjects that matter most. As a parent, I don't need overwhelming evidence that X causes Y. I just want to know the well-researched possibilities, and then I can decide what to adjust for my family and my child. This is the heart and soul of this book. As a mom, I want to share information with you that has changed my life and could change yours. Just ask any parent of an autistic child how they feel about spreading the word on environmental toxins and healthy, whole foods. This book sets out to honor these parents and more—synthesizing complex information down to a few bullet points, explaining the "whys" behind parenting recommendations, without dumbing them down. I want to spell out in plain language what you need to know and what to avoid during baby's first year and beyond.

This guide is not meant to be a comprehensive manual for baby, including all special circumstances. Rather, *The Parent's Pocket Checklist* (or the PPCL) hits the baby essentials and then goes deeper into the practical side of "How am I going to survive the sleepless nights and maintain my job and relationships and find joy in parenting?" I have tried my best not to get too clinical and boring. Humor and common sense are critical to surviving baby's first year. From this perspective, you might find this guide to be a bit eccentric, especially when compared to other baby books. For example, expect to find sex after baby advice for Dad, ways to look skinnier for Mom, financial tips, a sleep training guide, and baby brain research all under one cover. Nothing is too deep or too superficial for me, as this is the wild combination of things that my husband and I really wanted to know with our first baby. This is how the art and science of raising a child are woven together into these checklists and my own parenting process, which goes as follows: 1) Learn as much as I can from the experts. 2) Combine that with the practical advice of friends, family, and other parents. 3) Filter all critical information from steps one and two and apply it to my own, individual child. This book was written to help support steps one and two; however, only you can implement step three. Good luck!

Now before we get to the lists, there are a few recurring themes throughout the book. The terms spouse or partner and his or her for baby are all used interchangeably, to be inclusive of all families. You will also notice "Practical Tips from Real Parents" segments throughout the checklists—these contain quotes and advice from experienced moms and dads gathered through surveys and interviews conducted especially for this book. Some of the lists also contain overlapping information from *The Parent's Pocket Checklist: An Essential Guide to Pregnancy*, such as the sections for environmental toxins, postpartum depression, and breast-feeding support, since they contain useful information for both books. Finally, expect your PPCL reading experience to feel unusually fast-paced and dense, due to the concise format. Efficiency is the goal. I want to inundate you with hearty advice that can be consumed in about three hours, sparing you 300 hours on the computer researching for baby. Here we go!

BABY CARE

Basic Baby Care

Congratulations! Your baby is finally here. You may have attended a childbirth class, or perhaps you have been nannying or babysitting for years. However, feeding and caring for your own newborn around the clock can be quite a different experience. Here are some essential baby care tips to help you feel more confident as a new parent.

Breastfeeding basics

Skip to the next section for bottle feeding

- ❑ Expect a newborn to nurse every one-and-a-half to three hours, or eight to twelve times a day, for the first few months. Mark feeding intervals from the start time of feedings.

Did You Know?

Baby's Weight Loss after Birth

It is expected that baby will lose between 5–10% of his birth weight in the first five to seven days, as he adjusts to his new world. However, he should be back to his originally plump self within 10–14 days.

- ❑ Get comfortable first. If Mom is not comfortable, baby will not be comfortable feeding. Try to relax, and don't worry about doing everything just right.
- ❑ Hold baby skin-to-skin and guide baby's movements toward your breast. Bring baby to the breast, not the breast to baby, to avoid straining your neck and back.
- ❑ Line up baby's body so that his nose is opposite your nipple. You will be supporting him with one arm and supporting your breast with the other. Gently stroke his lips with your nipple. Aim your nipple closer to the roof of baby's mouth to encourage a better latch.
- ❑ Don't worry if baby only sucks for a short time. Baby's stomach is about the size of a teaspoon, and colostrum is thick, rich, concentrated milk.
- ❑ Recognize a bad latch. If your nipple is flattening, like a duck's bill, you have a bad latch. When baby comes off the breast, your nipple should be round.
- ❑ If baby is sleeping at the breast, break the latch and burp him or switch breasts. If that doesn't wake him, remove all warm blankets and clothes, rub his feet, or change his diaper.
- ❑ Loosely watch the clock while feeding. Newborns may breastfeed for 20 minutes or more per breast. However, baby can typically get all the milk she needs in the first 15–20 minutes of sucking.
- ❑ Alternate breastfeeding positions, especially if you are developing tight ducts. Some feeding positions draw more milk from one side of the breast than the other. Four popular breastfeeding positions are:
  - ▸ *The football or clutch hold:* In this position, the palm faces up supporting the back of baby's head. Mom's arm is pulled back to bring baby's mouth to the breast on the same side as her arm. The football hold or clutch hold can be easier for women who had a C-section (to keep baby's weight off the abdominal incision) or those with large breasts. This position draws more milk from the ducts in the bottom of the breast (three to nine o'clock), which can be helpful for clearing a clogged duct in that area.

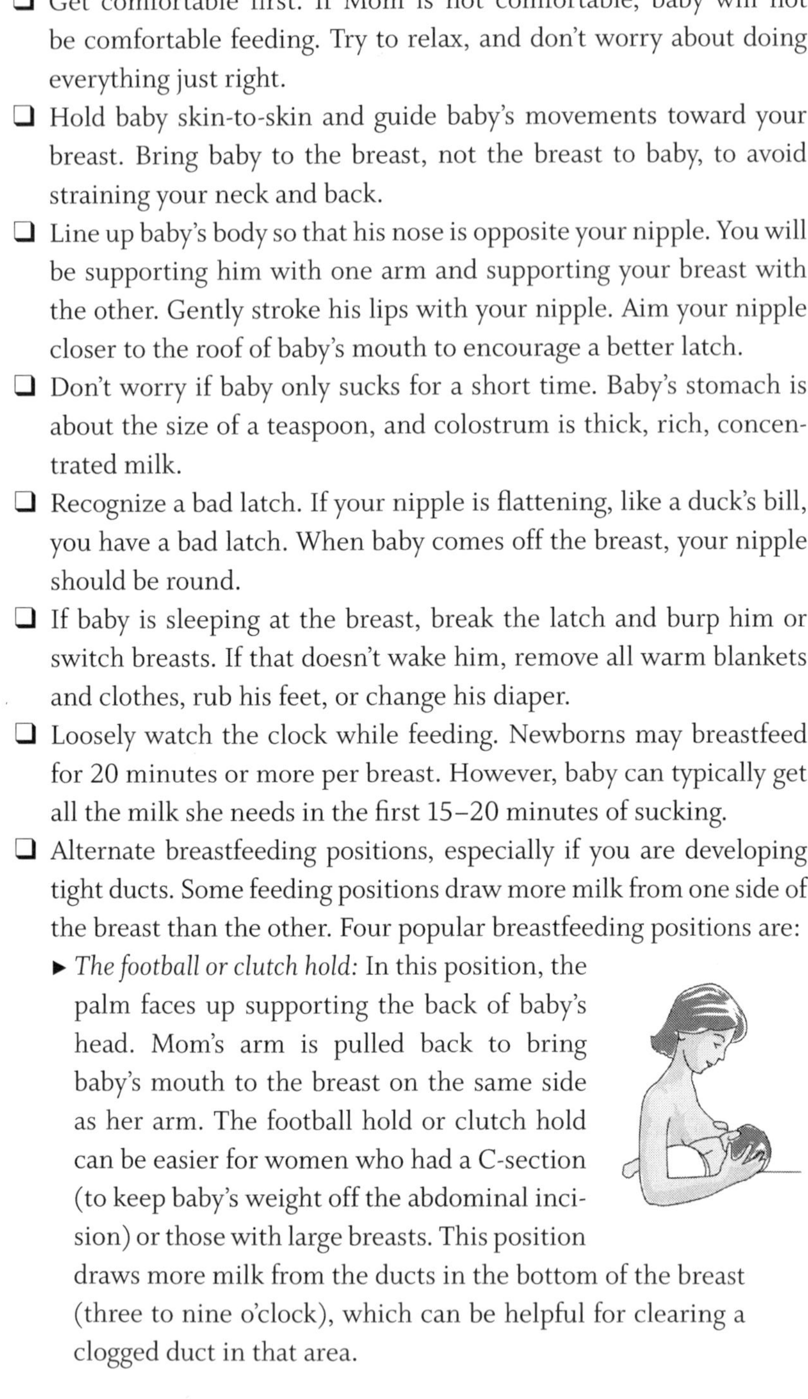

- *The cradle hold:* This classic hold positions baby across the front of the body with baby's head resting in the curve of Mom's arm, feeding on the same side as the supporting arm. This position draws more milk from the top of the breast (nine to three o'clock).
- *The cross-cradle hold:* This variation on the cradle position, also called a transition hold, places baby across the front of the body with the opposite arm supporting baby's head.
- *Side-lying hold:* This position is great for middle-of-the-night feedings, or when Mom simply wants to rest. Use one arm to support baby, keeping her aligned with the breast. Remember to put baby back in her own sleeping space after feeding.

❑ If you have a tight or clogged duct, put a warm washcloth on the sore area before feeding. Let baby feed on the sore breast first.

Safety Alert!

Drinking Alcohol and Breastfeeding

Alcohol does pass from your bloodstream into breast milk. If you drink alcohol while breastfeeding, wait at least three hours to feed after a drink or "pump and dump" your breast milk. Pumping does not clear the alcohol from your system faster, but it does keep your supply steady. If you pump just before drinking an alcoholic beverage, you will have milk to feed during the wait period, or time your drink with one of baby's longer sleep stretches. Drink water to dilute alcohol levels, and definitely don't stop breastfeeding because you want to have an occasional drink. To remove all the guesswork from the process, try Milkscreen test strips for detecting alcohol in breast milk.

- ❑ Wash breasts with water only (no soap) and wear a supportive bra that does not restrict milk flow.
- ❑ For more information on the benefits and challenges of breastfeeding (See: Breastfeeding Support).

The first week: breastfeeding is going well if...

- ❑ Your baby is breastfeeding at least eight times every twenty-four hours.
- ❑ Your baby has at least three to four bowel movements every twenty-four hours by day four (mustard yellow with curds).
- ❑ You can hear your baby gulping and swallowing at feedings.
- ❑ Once your baby latches on, your nipples do not hurt when baby nurses.
- ❑ Your baby is gaining weight. By the end of the first week, you should be making 19 to 30 oz. of milk each day.

Count baby's diapers, if you are concerned he is not getting enough milk.[1]

Age	Mom's milk	Wet diapers every 24 hours	Dirty diapers every 24 hours
1-2 days	colostrum	1-2	green-black tarry meconium
2-6 days	milk comes in	5-6 disposable (6-8 cloth)	at least 3 yellow or green stools
6+ days	milk supply adjusts to baby's needs	5-6 disposable (6-8 cloth)	at least 3-5 loose stools, yellow
6 weeks	milk supply established	5-6 disposable (6-8 cloth)	some have bigger, less frequent stools

Collecting and pumping breast milk

- ❑ Wash hands with soap and water.
- ❑ Wash all pump parts and accessories with hot, soapy water, or use microwave steaming bags. If baby was premature or has health issues, your doctor may require bottle sterilization.
- ❑ Wait three to four weeks before introducing a bottle to avoid nipple confusion, although some choose to have other caregivers feed at night when rest is critical for Mom.

Practical Tips from Real Parents

Introducing a Bottle (with breast milk)

- Try your first bottle around age three to four weeks when baby isn't extremely hungry. He may get upset, if he is starving and Mom is not there to feed.
- Have someone other than Mom give baby her first bottle.
- Tell your spouse to skip any strong cologne when feeding baby. Raid your dirty laundry hamper. Wrap the bottle in a nursing bra to help soothe baby with a familiar, comforting smell.
- Squeeze a little bit of milk on baby's lips and wait for baby to take to the nipple. Be patient. It may take a few tries before baby gets the hang of bottle feeding.
- Make sure that the nipple is a stage 1 or low-flow nipple. Otherwise, baby may get too much milk (and an upset tummy) or become too satisfied with his new quick-and-easy dispensing system. Ideally, you want baby to be comfortable with both the bottle and breast.

- ❑ If employed outside the home, begin storing pumped milk at least one to two weeks prior to returning to work. Breastfeed in the morning, evening, weekends, and days off to maintain your milk supply. Strive to pump three times during an eight-hour shift, or every three hours that you are away from baby (e.g., 10 minutes of pumping during two breaks and 15 minutes during lunch).

Storing freshly expressed breast milk

- ❑ Swirl warmed milk to mix the cream on top with liquid below. Stored milk may separate into layers.
- ❑ Avoid adding warm breast milk to cooled breast milk from the refrigerator.

- ❑ Freeze milk in single feeding portions (2 to 5 oz.). Label bags with a marker before pouring.
- ❑ Lay bags flat to freeze. Use the oldest milk first (first in, first out).

Storage guidelines (for healthy full-term babies)

- ❑ *Room temperature:* four to six hours at 66–78°F (19–26°C)
- ❑ *Cooler with three ice packs:* 24 hours at 59°F (15°C)
- ❑ *Refrigerator:* three to eight days at 39°F or lower (4°C)
- ❑ *Freezer:* six to 12 months at 0–4°F (18–20°C)
- ❑ *Thawed breast milk:* use within 24 hours [2-4]

Bottle-feeding basics

- ❑ Do not use whole milk, goat's milk, evaporated milk, or any other substitute for formula.
- ❑ Sterilize new bottles before first use by submerging them in boiling water for five minutes. Hot, soapy water and air-drying or a cycle through the dishwater should be sufficient for continued use, unless directed otherwise by your child's doctor.
- ❑ Mix formula with filtered tap water. Some parents prefer to boil water for formula for the first six months. However, it is not necessary unless you have a well or non-chlorinated water. Do not use bottled water, if possible, due to concerns of BPA leaching from the plastic. The Environmental Working Group (EWG) gives most brands of water bottles grades of C to F. If you do use bottled water, make sure it is fluoride-free.
- ❑ Wash hands thoroughly before mixing bottles, and mix formula exactly as recommended by the manufacturer.
- ❑ Do not buy expired formula.
- ❑ Do not freeze formula or leave it unrefrigerated for more than four hours.
- ❑ Make a few bottles ahead of time to be used the same day. Store in the refrigerator. Feed to baby within twenty-four hours of preparation.
- ❑ Do not mix breast milk and formula. It changes the composition of breast milk and may concentrate the micronutrients in formula

beyond a level that your newborn's kidneys can handle. Feed baby breast milk first then follow up with formula, if desired.

- ❑ Do not warm formula in the microwave, since it heats unevenly and can lead to burns. Use warm water in a bowl or a bottle warmer for heating.
- ❑ Get baby used to room temperature formula as quickly as possible to ease the burden of chasing down warm water while on the go. In the meantime, a travel thermos can help tote warm water for feedings.
- ❑ Never put a baby to sleep with a propped bottle.

The first week: formula feeding is going well if...

- ❑ Your baby is drinking 1.5 to 3 oz. every two to three hours.
- ❑ You are changing five to six wet and three to four poopy diapers per day.
- ❑ Your baby's stool is yellow to green by the end of week one.
- ❑ Your baby is satisfied after feedings.
- ❑ Your baby is gaining weight at a rate of four to seven ounces per week.

Choosing the right infant formula

- ❑ If baby seems fussy after feedings, take notes and talk to your child's doctor.
- ❑ Talk to your doctor before switching to expensive, sensitive formulas. Formula makers are creating new versions every day for colic, reflux, lactose intolerance, and everything under the sun, mostly to charge a premium. If you have selected a sensitive formula, and baby likes it, it may be because the formula is sweeter. For example, the first two ingredients of Similac Sensitive Infant Formula are "Corn syrup and sugar" (See: Appendix B: Infant Formula).
- ❑ Know the symptoms of an allergy to the protein in cow's milk: vomiting, diarrhea, blood in baby's stool, a rash, and/or abdominal pain.
- ❑ Choose organic formula, if possible, to avoid GMOs, antibiotics, and growth hormones.
- ❑ If your full-term infant must be fed soy-based formula, due to an inherited lactase deficiency (rare) or a preference for a vegetarian diet, choose a non-GMO soy formula, such as Baby's Only Organic Soy Formula, if possible.

Practical Tips from Real Parents

Feeding Preterm Infants (born before 37 weeks)

Premature infants face a higher risk of infection due to an immature immune system. The antibodies and protective live cells in breast milk cannot be found in formula, making breastfeeding even more important for premature babies.

- Even if your baby does not look premature, he is still at risk for more problems than babies born full term. Preemies need breast milk.
- Preterm babies do not eat or feed like full-term babies. They fall asleep at the breast a lot, they have to be wakened to eat, and they may not empty a breast like a full-term baby would.
- If you have a newborn in the NICU (Neonatal Intensive Care Unit), you might want to rent a hospital-grade pump to keep your supply up in the first few weeks.
- My doctor told me to subtract the number weeks of prematurity when thinking about baby's developmental age. This means that if your baby is born at 33 weeks, you should expect her to meet the milestones of a two month old around the four month mark.
- Our twins were born early, and they started out gavage (guh-vahj) feeding—a tube runs through the nasal passage to the stomach—because they both had issues preventing them from getting enough milk. The syringe that fed their tubes contained my pumped breast milk. Don't be intimidated with breastfeeding just because you have multiples: just start pumping. It's worth it, and your babies need it.
- If your babies are in the NICU (I had twins), just bring your hospital pump right up next to them. You don't have to go into another room and then feel torn about where you should be. The hospital staff will support you.
- I quit pumping too early with my eldest daughter, who was born at 35 weeks. I didn't do my homework on breastfeeding, I had a bad attitude about pumping, and I basically let the stress and frustration of our NICU experience overwhelm me. For my next child, who was also preterm, I drank more water, relaxed, and had more self-discipline with pumping because I finally understood the benefits.

Burping

- ❑ Pat baby on her back at regular intervals to help release air swallowed while feeding.
  - ▸ For breastfeeding, burp every five minutes in the first few weeks. This time interval will increase as baby gets older and her digestive system adjusts.
  - ▸ For bottle feedings, burp every half ounce in the first few weeks, then every two ounces as baby matures.
  - ▸ Burp anytime baby is fussy while feeding.
  - ▸ Burp at the end of every feeding.
- ❑ Try multiple burping positions and see what works best.
  - ▸ *Upright:* Baby sits upright over your shoulder.
  - ▸ *Sitting supported:* Baby sits on your lap with one hand holding her chest (palm facing the sternum) and the other hand patting her back gently.
  - ▸ *Across the knees:* Baby lies stomach facing down across the tops of your legs while you are seated with one hand patting the back.
- ❑ Always have a burp cloth handy.

Diapering

- ❑ Expect baby's first stool after birth, called meconium, to be odorless, thick, and tarry in consistency. Meconium, which is sometimes released into the amniotic fluid before birth, is composed of materials that were ingested by baby in utero: mucus, bile, lanugo or tiny hairs, amniotic fluid, water, and other tiny cells. Thankfully, Mom's early milk, called colostrum (pronounced coh-LOSS-trum), has a laxative-type effect during the first feedings to help meconium clear from baby's system.
- ❑ Check bowel movements. By day three or four, they should be brown, yellow, or green (thicker yellow-to-green for formula-fed babies and runny, seedy, and yellow for breastfed babies). Bad colors for stool are red (blood), black (digested blood), and white (blockage in the liver).

- ❑ Always put a clean diaper beneath baby before removing the dirty one.
- ❑ Be sure to let baby's bottom air dry for a moment after using wipes or a wet washcloth. You can also pat with a dry cloth.

Diaper rash

- ❑ To prevent and minimize rashes, change diapers frequently and allow time for baby to have fresh air on her bottom. When baby's urine mixes with bacteria in her stool, ammonia forms that can be harsh against delicate skin. Other factors that can exacerbate rashes are: fragrances and chemicals in disposable diapers and wipes; chaffing from an ill-fitting diaper; and acidic foods such as citrus, berries, and tomato sauces, eaten by a breastfeeding mom.
- ❑ If disposable wipes are too harsh for baby's skin, try a soft cloth and warm water after pee diapers, and warm water and a sensitive soap after poop diapers. Some parents like to keep a spray bottle of natural diaper wash and clean washcloths near baby's changing area.
- ❑ If baby has a bad rash, clean his bottom in a sink or tub after bowel movements. Dry baby's bottom with a soft towel and let it air dry before applying diaper cream and securing a new diaper.

Yeast rash vs. regular diaper rash

If baby gets a beefy red, bumpy rash that lasts more than two to three days and doesn't respond to rash treatments, he might have yeast rash that requires medicine. Yeast rashes occur in both boys and girls. Babies taking antibiotics and moms nursing while taking antibiotics are more susceptible to yeast rashes. If your baby has recently had thrush, the yeast infection that started in the mouth can pass through the digestive system and end up in the warm, moist diaper region. Some women with chronic yeast infections may choose to take an acidophilus supplement, or a probiotic, such as Culturelle or Florastor, to maintain balance of intestinal flora.[5]

Did You Know?

Baby's Skin

Baby's delicate skin is 20–30% thinner and less acidic than adult skin with a surface pH of around 5.5 (the pH scale goes from 0 to 14, and pH factor represents the balance between acid and alkaline.) Look for "skin-neutral" or "pH balanced" baby products, and resist the urge to bathe baby too frequently.

- ❑ If you have confirmed a yeast rash with your baby's doctor, apply a topical anti-yeast or anti-fungal cream, such as nystatin, clotrimazole, or miconazole, or a mild corticosteroid cream. Diaper barrier or rash creams do not relieve yeast rashes.

Bathing

- ❑ Limit newborn bathing to sponge baths until the umbilical cord falls off, around fourteen days postpartum.
- ❑ After the cord falls off, give baby one to two tub baths per week lasting no more than ten minutes. Babies with darker skin should be bathed once a week since they are more prone to dryer skin and skin problems.
- ❑ Before baby's first bath, lay out all of your supplies: a pouring cup, washcloth, cotton balls, baby soap, towel, a fresh diaper, and pajamas. If your home is cold or drafty, you may want to heat the room before bathing. Some babies will love bathing, and some will scream from start to finish.
- ❑ Wash baby gently yet assertively. Dried formula and breast milk can be particularly foul-smelling, if left to hide in baby's skin folds.
- ❑ Never stick a Q-tip into baby's ear. Only clean the outer ear area.
- ❑ Do not worry about touching baby's soft spot, or fontanel, when washing her hair. The fontanel can withstand some handling. It did make it through the birth canal.

Eco Tip

Green Soaps and pH

Most adult soaps have a pH factor of 9 to 11, including green offerings such as castile soap. These soaps can strip baby's skin of natural oils, leading to dryness and eczema.

- ❑ Consider folding a soft, thick towel on the kitchen counter, or using a baby bath cushion, to "catch" baby after her bath for drying. Apply baby lotion to moisturize skin when slightly damp.
- ❑ Let baby hang out on a waterproof sheet or towel for some bare-bottom time, especially if he is prone to diaper rashes.

Umbilical cord care

- ❑ Keep the umbilical cord clean and dry.
- ❑ To avoid drying it out excessively, do not clean the area with alcohol.
- ❑ Expect the cord to progress in color from bluish to yellowish green to brown to black before falling off about two weeks from birth.
- ❑ Fold baby's diaper beneath the umbilical cord stump, if possible.

Circumcised males

- ❑ Keep the area clean by bathing in warm water with a baby cleanser. You may notice swelling, redness, or a slight yellow discharge; however, this should decrease as the circumcision heals. This process takes about seven to ten days. You may be instructed by your doctor to apply a touch of ointment to keep the tip from sticking to the diaper.

Uncircumcised males

- ❑ Keep the area clean with warm water and a gentle baby cleanser.
- ❑ Never force the foreskin back to clean the tip of the penis. Gently tense the foreskin against the tip and wash with care.

Care of the vagina

- ❑ To care for your daughter, gently clean the genital area front to back with a soft cloth, using only water. You may see some bloody vaginal discharge during the first few weeks of life, typically caused by hormones from Mom.

Nail filing and clipping

- ❑ Clip and file baby's nails after a bath, or while baby is feeding. Better yet, have someone else clip and file after a bath while baby is feeding.
- ❑ Expect baby to fuss during nail clippings; however, complete your task. You will regret not clipping or filing baby's nails as soon as she makes a giant scratch across her face.

Pacifier use

The American Academy of Pediatrics (AAP) recommends pacifiers during the first year of life, with the following guidelines.[6]

- ❑ Offer a pacifier at sleep and nap times to reduce the risk of sudden infant death syndrome (SIDS), if baby wants to suck beyond what nursing or bottle-feeding can provide.
- ❑ Do not force a pacifier into the mouth, or coat it with any sweet substance.
- ❑ Do not reinsert a pacifier after baby falls asleep.
- ❑ If a baby refuses a pacifier, he or she should not be forced to take it.

- ❑ If you are concerned about nipple confusion, introduce a pacifier three to four weeks after breastfeeding has been established.
- ❑ Do not use pacifiers to replace or delay meals. Offer a pacifier only when you are certain that baby is not hungry.

Tummy time

In 1992, the AAP began instructing parents to put babies to sleep on their backs. Babies have resisted tummy time ever since. Yet not spending enough time face-down is associated with delays in motor skills, such as pushing up, rolling over, crawling, and pulling up to stand. If your baby is miserable during tummy time, perhaps these strategies can help.

- ❑ Offer tummy time when baby is content. This can begin as soon as she is home from the hospital.
- ❑ Get down on the floor with baby. She might feel abandoned if you just leave her to face-plant.
- ❑ Make tummy time fun. Sing to baby, listen to music, and dance while looking eye-to-eye.
- ❑ Distract baby from her discomfort. It's hard to hold your head up, especially when your skull is 25% of your total body length and you spend 95% of your day on your back. Place baby on a colorful mat. Use a mirror, board books, rattles, and toys to distract her from the process.
- ❑ Prop baby up on a nursing pillow or rolled towel, then gradually remove these aids.
- ❑ Try different tummy positions outside of her structured tummy time. Place baby on your chest for rest. Burp baby across your knees. Place baby on an exercise ball and roll back and forth. Fly baby around the house face down.
- ❑ If baby continues to cry during tummy time, put her on the floor for just a few seconds, then increase to minutes several times a day until she works up to a higher comfort level.

Practical Tips from Real Parents

Newborns and Baby Care

- Try not to stress too much over baby's appearance. Newborns can be funny-looking with cone-shaped heads, unruly hair, birth marks, redness, rashes, bruising, baby acne, scratches, and other marks. Most of these are due to Mom's hormones and the birth process, and other than permanent birth marks, should subside in a few months.
- Newborns have some funny quirks. Their eyes are crossed (this should go away in two to three months), their skin peels, they get startled easily, and they get the hiccups a lot. This is all normal.
- Keep baby facing you as long as possible in the stroller, car seat, and front carrier. More bonding will occur if baby can see your face while you talk.
- If you are unhappy with your pediatrician or pediatric practice, don't be afraid to switch.
- Don't schedule your newborn's well-baby visits on Mondays. That is when all of the sick children from the weekend pile into the doctor's office.
- Trust your instincts. Don't let anyone talk you into doing something with baby that makes you uncomfortable, such as supplementing with formula too early or not taking baby to the doctor for an issue. You know your baby better than anyone.
- Do not be so set on advice from books, or the opinions of doctors, that you disregard what you know about your baby.

Practical Tips from Real Parents

Surviving the Days and Weeks after Birth

Now that we have covered the basics of baby care, let me remind you that other people in your new family have needs, too—like you and your partner. To help you survive the days and weeks after birth, I have compiled some tips from parents who have been there and done that, and lived to tell about baby's first year. Welcome to the world of letting go!

Getting Help

- Make sure that you are comfortable with your postpartum help. You do not want helpers whom you must wait on and clean up after.
- Work hard to not be critical of your help. Be as appreciative as you can.
- Be kind and gracious to your mother-in-law if she comes to help after the baby is born. (Note: Many women I have interviewed have mentioned regrets over being snippy, grumpy, obsessive, or generally rude about how their baby was cared for by their mother-in-law after birth. This relationship is inherently complex in every family; however, if your MIL has agreed to stay with you, she is just trying to help.)
- If family help is unavailable and you have multiples or babies with health issues, hire a sitter or night nanny for rest breaks, if budget permits.
- Let a friend set up a meal calendar for you on takethemameal.com. You can select which days you would like meals to come and let others know about dietary preferences, food allergies, etc. This is the best gift ever.
- I had twins, and I nearly lost it after our help left and my husband went back to work. The eat-poop-sleep-clean bottles cycle was grueling and one baby was always crying. Get help and do whatever you must do to survive.

Photo Tips

- Find a great photographer for newborn portraits, or stage them yourself.

- Send yourself reminders to take photos of your little one weekly, if you aren't already snapping away. Print the photos and give them to grandparents as gifts.
- Delete duplicate photos in your photo library. If you end up with thousands of pictures, you will be so overwhelmed that you do nothing with your baby photos. If you have a manageable folder, you will be more inclined to make albums.
- Use an online service to make photo books, such as Shutterfly or MyPublisher.
- As baby gets older, try an app, such as BabyCam (with prerecorded noises like bells, drums, doorbells, and songs), to keep baby looking and smiling at the camera.

Health and Well-Being Tips

- Relax your standards. Ignore the clutter, leave clean clothes in the basket, and eat cereal for dinner when you are feeling overwhelmed.
- Be prepared for the blues or postpartum depression, especially if you have experienced previous depression.
- Expect to have postpartum issues if you have perfectionist tendencies.
- While on maternity leave, you may have conflicting feelings about your new life, loving your comfy clothes and cuddling but also wanting to get back to work.
- Try to respect your family and postpartum cultural traditions, but at the same time, express your own needs and desires (to avoid stressful situations later). My mom came to stay with me after my daughter was born and wanted me to observe the Chinese custom of zuo yuezi (this means "sitting the month" in Mandarin). I was fine eating her warm broths and mostly staying inside, but I drew the line with not washing my hair.
- Take regular showers. You will have all kinds of strange smells and fluids coming out of your body after birth. (Note: You also might get pajama soaking "night sweats" due to hormone fluctuations and fluid loss.)
- Watch out for increased pressure on your neck and back from carrying baby and baby equipment.

- Sleep while others watch the baby. If you do not have help, sleep when the baby sleeps. Laundry can be done later.
- Just remember, when your baby is screaming at 12:15 a.m. and you just went to sleep at midnight, this is truly a short phase in your child's life.

Technology Tips

- Try a few fun apps to ease your transition to parenthood.
  - Travel with baby: Baby Monitor
  - Medical for baby: WebMD Baby
  - Breastfeeding (to track feedings): Baby Tracker
  - Breastfeeding (to track pumping): Milk Maid
  - Baby timers and trackers: Total Baby
  - Nighttime feedings: Flashlight
  - Colic: Baby Shusher
  - Photos of baby: Qwiki and BabyCam
  - Public restroom finder (for blowouts or nursing): SitOrSquat

Practical Tips from Real Parents

Your Marriage or Partnership

In *The Girlfriends' Guide to Pregnancy,* Vicki Iovine writes, "Pregnancy brings a man and a woman closer together (Yeah, you and your obstetrician!)" Despite the irony and humor in this statement, the truth is that pregnancy barely scratches the surface of relational challenges that can occur during the sleep-deprived newborn phase. Having a baby can bring out the best and the worst in a marriage or partnership. Time use surveys show that new parents have about one-third of the alone time they had before having children, and a survey of over 7,000 mothers revealed that 46% of participants thought their spouse or partner caused them more stress than their children.[7] My husband and I, too, thought that having a baby would bring us closer together, and it did…at first. Then life happened. Here are some tips for your marriage or partnership collected from experienced parents.

- The best advice that I received after the birth of our first child was to put my marriage first. I had postpartum issues and my husband traveled, and we were living in NYC with no family. I obsessed over caring for our baby, and by the time I went back to work, I had nothing to give to my husband at the end of the day. Not fueling our marriage turned into a big problem.
- Remember that your marriage, not your child, is the bedrock of your family. A baby cannot be placed in that position or the family will crumble.
- Think of your family like a pyramid. You and your spouse are at the top, and everything else flows down to your children (love, how you treat one another, communication style, etc.).
- Want to know what happens when you put your kids before your marriage? Mom and Dad get stressed out and become disconnected, which is miserable, and your kids get more demanding and entitled to your attention, which is also miserable.
- Lack of sleep was merely one issue my wife and I had after our first baby. The bigger ones included postpartum depression, breastfeeding challenges, fighting over chores, and just general conflict about how we should raise our child.
- My husband and I had lots of conflict caring for our baby together. I had read a library of books about babies, and he read nothing (but thought he knew everything). Our baby had colic and reflux and formula sensitivities. That period of our life was not much fun. If I had to do it over again, I would change how my husband and I communicated.
- Expect colic, or your baby crying, to make interactions strained with your husband, as you both try to solve the problem. When this scenario arises, try your best to work together.
- Nobody is immune from marital conflict after baby. Expect some type of relational stress, especially when you are ridiculously tired.
- If you both work full time, sit down and write out a list of household chores with your husband. Otherwise, you will be

doing everything and then wondering why your husband can't read your mind.

- The transition from zero to one child is much harder than one to two children.
- Have an honest discussion about the spiritual direction of your family. If you and your spouse do not share religious beliefs, if one is religious and the other is not, or if you were raised with different religious backgrounds, the subject will come up once you have children, especially if one of you wants the child to be christened.
- Don't expect your husband to suddenly become a 'details guy' just because you had a baby and need help.
- Men are not multitaskers. Having a baby will drive this point home.
- Know that no one person has a monopoly on good ideas for your baby, including Mom. Everyone's input should be valued, although input from parents should come first.
- For Mom: Having the ability to breastfeed does not automatically designate you as the better parent. Take a step back and let Dad care for the baby. He doesn't have to pack the perfect diaper bag. He simply needs space to be a good father.
- For Dad: Take a step forward. Take off your shirt and enjoy skin-to-skin contact. Talk to baby, sing to baby, read to baby, and play on the floor. He or she knows your voice and will be comforted by your presence.
- If you want men to do more chores around the house, sex is your golden key to clean floors.
- The sex argument after baby is tough. I gave my wife plenty of space to heal after her C-section, but then months passed, and we were still not having sex. Maybe it's by design that a woman's body isn't ready for another child, but months without sex stinks for a new dad.
- Connecting with your partner after baby does not have to mean 'date night.' You can just hang out and enjoy being a family together.
- When we get home each day, we share a highlight and a low-light to keep our communication lines open. These comments

have to be specific and in the moment. You can't just say 'My day sucked.' You have to elaborate on something interesting and precise so that your spouse doesn't tune out repetitive comments or complaints.

- Designate a "no screens night," leaving you little option other than to spend time with your partner.
- Create a routine that includes "together time" after baby goes to bed, even if it is simply snuggling on the couch and watching a favorite TV show together.
- Try to say "I love you" every night before turning off the lights. These little words can help ease the stresses and trials of the day.

Division of household chores

There is nothing wrong with a traditional division of labor, and no one can plan and divide every task that comes up. However, with 70% of mothers (with children under age 18) working or looking for work, the division of labor at home must be thoughtfully considered.[8] In assigning tasks, you might want to try this approach: "Whoever cares more about this item wins." If one partner has more time and one cares more about the process, establish mutually agreed-upon guidelines. The following items might be included in a list of household chores:

- ❑ Laundry
- ❑ Ironing
- ❑ Vacuuming
- ❑ Dusting
- ❑ Straightening up the living areas
- ❑ Cleaning the living and dining rooms
- ❑ Cleaning the bathrooms
- ❑ Cleaning the bedrooms
- ❑ Preparing dinner (establish rules, such as "the cook doesn't clean" and vice versa)
- ❑ Cleaning the kitchen

- ❑ Doing the dishes
- ❑ Emptying wastebaskets
- ❑ Taking the trash and recycling to the curb, if required
- ❑ Mowing the lawn
- ❑ Grocery shopping
- ❑ Dropping off and picking up dry-cleaning
- ❑ Short term finances: Paying the bills
- ❑ Long term finances: Managing investments and retirement, taxes (collecting receipts)
- ❑ Sick-child duty and back-up care options
- ❑ Management of care providers
- ❑ Sending cards and gifts to family members
- ❑ Photo taking and organization
- ❑ Travel planning

Crying and Colic

Why do babies cry?

- ❑ They are hungry.
- ❑ They are tired.
- ❑ They have a dirty diaper or a diaper rash.
- ❑ They are too hot or too cold.
- ❑ They have gas, reflux, or other tummy issues.
- ❑ They want to be held.
- ❑ They want more stimulation.
- ❑ They want less stimulation.
- ❑ They are sick.
- ❑ They are teething.
- ❑ They are picking up your anxious or depressed mood.
- ❑ They are responding to a random occurrence: this tag on my shirt is scratchy, someone's hair is wrapped tightly around my finger or penis (this is common), or something is pinching me.

What is normal crying?

Crying is a baby's way of communicating that she needs something, or she needs you. Nearly all babies go through a fussy period of normal crying.

What is colic?

Colic occurs in about one-fifth of all babies. Colic is defined as crying that lasts for more than three hours per day, more than three days per week, for more than three weeks. Remember 3-3-3. There is no single cause of colic.

Common characteristics of colic

- ❑ Crying associated with colic generally starts between two and four weeks, peaks at four to six weeks, and subsides by twelve weeks.
- ❑ Colic screams often begin during or shortly after a feeding.
- ❑ Babies with colic may grunt, strain, or seem relieved by passing gas or pooping.
- ❑ Colic is normally worse in the evening hours.
- ❑ Colic can occur with a fifth child just as easily as with a first child.

Possible colic triggers that you can control

- ❑ **Mom's diet.** Foods passed through breast milk can affect baby, typically two to six hours after exposure. The worst trigger foods are dairy products, coffee, tea, soda, soy products, peanuts, shellfish, chocolate, gas-producing vegetables (peppers, onions, broccoli, cabbage, and cauliflower), acidic foods (tomatoes, citrus, berries), and spices (garlic, chili pepper, curry).
- ❑ **Infant formula.** Talk to your doctor. The AAP does not recommend switching to soy formula for colicky infants, but some babies may be sensitive to certain proteins in milk-based formulas.
- ❑ **Over-feeding with a bottle.** Feedings should be at least two to two-and-a-half hours apart. If feeding takes less than twenty minutes, the hole in the nipple may be too large.
- ❑ **Too much foremilk.** If you are breastfeeding a colicky baby, let baby finish the first breast before offering the second. Foremilk at the beginning of each feeding is more pressurized and gassier and lower in calories and fat. Hind milk at the end of each feeding is richer in fat and under less pressure. Hind milk is typically more

soothing to baby's stomach, and it can be healthier as well, since fat is necessary to metabolize many vitamins.

- ❑ **Medicine.** Medicines passed through breast milk can also upset your baby's digestive system.
- ❑ **Hypersensitivity to stimulation in the environment.** Avoid bright lights and loud or abrupt sounds while feeding.

Possible colic triggers that you can't control

- ❑ An intense temperament
- ❑ An immature nervous system
- ❑ An immature digestive system
- ❑ Acid reflux
- ❑ Increased hormone levels that make people fussy
- ❑ Embryonic and post-natal experiences that altered the enteric nervous system, or the "second brain" in the gut[9]

If your baby won't stop crying, what can you do?

- ❑ Take a few deep breaths and calm yourself first.
- ❑ Take baby outside.
- ❑ Hold and cuddle baby in an upright position. This helps move gas out of the body and reduces heartburn.
- ❑ Rock baby. Rocking is particularly calming and comforting because every step Mom took in utero caused a swinging motion. Rocking also helps baby pass gas.
- ❑ Sing lullabies or make calm "shushing" noises.
- ❑ Give baby a massage with lotion.
- ❑ Bicycle baby's legs to help release gas.
- ❑ Offer baby a pacifier or your pinkie finger for sucking.
- ❑ Swaddle baby in a thin blanket. Make her feel secure and warm.
- ❑ Put baby on her side to move the gas around, then put her on her back to sleep.
- ❑ Try a colic hold or "super baby hold": hold your arm in front of you, palm facing up, and place baby stomach-down on your forearm,

Safety Alert!

Self-Control and Colic

The noise stress from colic, in addition to sleep deprivation, social isolation, and frustration over not knowing what to do, can be unexpectedly intense when compounded over several colicky hours. Know when it's time to take a break.

- Call in back-up help. Ask a friend or family member to help with the baby for a few hours.
- If you are feeling out of control, put baby down in a crib, close the door, and let him cry in a safe place (for no more than a few minutes), while you gather perspective in another room.
- Never shake your baby. Inconsolable crying or colic is a primary trigger for shaken baby syndrome (SBS), a leading cause of child abuse deaths in the U.S. It is estimated that 65–90% of SBS offenders are male.[12]

with your hand cupping the upper chest. Walk baby around the house, flying him up and down like super baby.

- ❑ Put baby on his stomach across your knees while rubbing or patting his back.
- ❑ Wear baby in a sling or front carrier. Sometimes the more baby is held during the day, the less baby will fuss at night.
- ❑ Take baby for a car ride.
- ❑ Turn on white noise for baby. You can buy a small, portable white noise machine, download white noise online, or turn on a fan, hair dryer, or vacuum cleaner to help soothe baby.
- ❑ If painful gas is suspected and you've exhausted this list, try a few drops of over-the-counter anti-gas simethicone. Simethicone is generally considered safe for infants because it is not absorbed into the bloodstream. It decreases the surface tension of gas bubbles to promote flatulence.[10] However, at $8–10 per ounce, parents should carefully assess results. Some studies show that simethicone may produce nothing more than a placebo effect for infants and infant colic.[11]

Practical Tips from Real Parents

Colic

• • • •

- Try your best to keep colic in perspective. This, too, shall pass.
- This is how colic played out in our house: After a long day of caring for our firstborn solo, by 8:00 p.m. or so I would lash out at my husband, "Do something! Why do you never help with the baby?" He would yell back, "Because you won't even let me touch the baby without your permission!" Baby would cry louder. Then we would try a swaddle, a pacifier, a hair dryer, a vacuum, and white noise from an iPod. Hours would pass and baby was still crying. Looking back, yelling at my husband was not particularly helpful. Colic is just something that you have to get through together.
- Colic can affect your marriage months after the crying stops.
- Do not let anyone in the family, especially from an older generation, target your wife as the cause of baby's colic. There is an old wives' tale blaming colic on a new Mom's anxiety that has no scientific base.
- Vacuuming with baby in a sling was our colic cure.
- I held our baby upright, danced around the house, and sang repetitive songs. I think it helped my baby weight come off, too.
- Hold a colicky baby in front of a mirror and let him watch his own dramatic performance. Touch his foot or hand to his reflection and watch him go silent.
- Many friends say their worst colicky babies turned out to be their most motivated kids—a frustrated temperament as an infant may signal a child with extra "get-up-and-go" later.

If baby is four months old, and the colic is not subsiding, consider these possible medical causes:

- **Gastroesophageal reflux (GER):** This is baby heartburn, or stomach acid floating up into the esophagus. If baby spits up after feedings, shrieks like he is in pain, cries mostly after feedings, draws up his legs in pain, and seems better when he is upright, he may have reflux.
- **Food sensitivities:** Keep a log of the foods that may be triggering your baby's colic.
- **Cow's milk sensitivity:** The potentially allergenic protein in cow's milk, beta-lactoglobulin, may affect a breastfed baby when Mom drinks cow's milk.
- **Transient lactase deficiency (TLD):** This is a temporary insufficiency in the intestinal enzyme that digests lactose sugar in breast milk or formula. TLD may improve by adding drops of the enzyme to an infant's breast milk or formula.
- **Formula allergies:** Talk to your doctor. Cow's milk allergy (CMA) is estimated to affect two to three percent of young children. The diagnosis of CMA can be based on a supervised oral food challenge (OFC), or a convincing clinical history, skin-prick test, and measurement of certain antibodies when baby drinks milk-based formula.[13] Following proper testing, a hypo-allergenic or lactose-free formula may help.[14]

Sleep Deprivation Preparedness

Research shows that we are more inclined to endure hardship if we understand why we must face that hardship. Let's take a few moments to examine why short sleep cycles (and parents' sleep deprivation) are necessary for baby's development.

- ❑ **Babies sleep in short cycles for survival.** Short, light sleep cycles give baby the ability to facilitate and communicate basic needs:
  - ▸ *Need for warmth:* baby's skin is thinner than adult skin.[15]
  - ▸ *Proper airflow:* breathing increases with lighter sleep.
  - ▸ *Nutrition:* tiny bellies digest milk within two to four hours.
- ❑ **Babies and toddlers have shorter sleep cycles to ensure proper brain development.** Most of the human brain's nerve cells, or neurons, are formed before birth, and we have more than 100 billion of them! However, many of the connections, or synapses, among those cells are made between infancy and early childhood. At birth, the most developed sections of the brain are the brainstem and midbrain areas, which regulate our basic body functions like eating, sleeping, breathing, etc. At this time, the limbic and cortex sections, which regulate emotions, language, and thought, are fairly primitive. The development of synapses between ages zero and three is astounding, and at peak rate, a toddler may create two million synapses per second.[16] By age three, children have roughly one thousand trillion synapses, which is many more than they will ever need (perhaps explaining the irrational behavior of preschoolers). By adolescence, children will have discarded roughly half of

the synapses developed in earlier childhood. Much of the process of building brain connections and then pruning them down occurs while children sleep.[17]

- ❑ **Babies "learn" while they sleep.** Adults drift off into deeper, inactive, non-REM (non-rapid eye movement) sleep and remain in deep sleep with the brain resting for a ninety-minute cycle before entering short cycles of active sleep. However, babies sleep lighter and smarter, engaging in twice the number of active REM cycles. REM sleep, which is associated with dreaming, maintains a pattern of brain activity that looks nearly the same as that of a brain awake. With blood flow to the brain doubled during REM sleep, the body increases production of nerve proteins, the building blocks of the brain. Expect baby's lightest REM sleep cycles to be between 4:00 a.m. and 6:00 a.m., as she grunts, wheezes, and makes funny noises. Try not to disturb her as she gets smarter.[18]
- ❑ **Your baby does not enter sleep the same way you do.** New parents often get frustrated when their newborn erupts into crying just as he is put into his crib. "But he was just fast asleep in my arms a minute ago," parents say. However, the child was probably still in a state of very light sleep. Sometimes rocking a baby just a few minutes longer can help him enter a deeper sleep, indicated by limp limbs and longer, slower breathing patterns.
- ❑ **Don't feel pressure to get your baby to sleep too deeply, too long, too soon.** Friends and well-meaning family members may likely exaggerate how long their babies sleep, or slept, as newborns. Some might brag that all of their kids were good sleepers, as if that is a badge of honor for parental achievement. However, a child's sleep pattern is much more reflective of her natural temperament and level of satiation, rather than the result of a particular parenting style.

Sleep Guide: Newborn to Age Three Years

Where will my baby sleep?

Now that we have established how important sleep is for baby, let's think about *where* baby will sleep. This issue has become slightly contentious as attachment parenting has become a mainstream method of caring for baby. Let's first define some confusing terms. Bed sharing is physically sleeping next to baby in an adult bed. Room sharing, or co-sleeping, is keeping baby nearby in a bassinet, or his own sleep space for the first months of life. The AAP recommends room sharing or co-sleeping. However, many attachment parent advocates steadfastly disagree and maintain that safe bed sharing occurs around the world. So what is a parent to do?

Only you can determine what is best for your family. However, here is an example of what worked in our home. After researching various sleep arrangements, we chose room sharing or co-sleeping for our own children. During the day, we followed attachment parenting techniques. Yet at night, my husband and I wanted to know that our newborns were safe. We both sleep soundly, and our memory foam mattress makes a large indentation around a sleeping adult, a relative sinkhole for a seven-pound baby. Our bedding is also plush and thick, which is not the case for many non-western cultures. Bottom line: If we slept on a firm floor mat or solid wood platform, as many parents do around the world, I might be more inclined to support family bed sharing. However, since we do not, we chose to keep our newborns next to me in a Pack 'n Play crib for the first two to three months of life.

How much sleep does your child need?[19]

Age	Nighttime Sleep	Daytime Sleep	Total Sleep
1 month	8 ½	7 (3 naps)	15 ½
3 months	10	5 (3 naps)	15
6 months	11	3 ¼ (2 naps)	14 ¼
9 months	11	3 (2 naps)	14
12 months	11 ¼	2 ½ (2 naps)	13 ¾
18 months	11 ¼	2 ¼ (1 nap)	13 ½
2 years	11	2 (1 nap)	13
3 years	10 ½	1 ½ (1 nap)	12

Newborns

Newborn babies typically sleep sixteen to eighteen hours a day, but may sleep as little as fourteen hours. A tight swaddle helps babies feel warm and secure, but avoid overheating. Dress your newborn in a single layer cotton pajama and swaddle with a thin blanket (a thicker swaddle or sleep-sack may be used in winter). In general, dress baby with no more than one more layer than an adult might wear to be comfortable. A full-term healthy infant should not need a hat, unless your home is particularly drafty. Place your newborn to sleep on a firm, flat surface. The AAP states that infants should be placed on their backs until age one. The supine sleep position (on the back) does not increase the risk for choking or aspirating, even for babies with gastro-esophageal reflux, since they have protective mechanisms for the airway. Elevating the head is also not recommended, even for reflux, because baby might slide to the foot of the crib or sleeper, which can affect her breathing.[20] A crib nap is always better than a nap in a car seat, bouncer seat, or swing for maximum oxygen flow. The AAP does not recommend any type of bed-sharing as safe. If you do choose to bed-share, place baby next to Mom—not between Mom and Dad—because mothers have an innate protective awareness for baby. Do not bed share with anyone who smokes, drinks alcohol before bedtime, or is taking medications.[12]

Safety Alert!

Sleep Practices and Sudden Unexpected Infant Death (SUID)

More than 4,500 babies die suddenly and unexpectedly each year (SUID). Of those 4,500, roughly 2,300 are diagnosed as sudden infant death syndrome (SIDS)—the sudden death of an infant less than one year of age that cannot be explained after thorough examination. Other diagnoses for SUID, in addition to SIDS, include suffocation and positional asphyxiation, mostly due to unsafe sleep practices.

SIDS is the leading cause of death for babies one to twelve months old in the U.S. The peak age for SIDS is two to four months, and 90% of cases occur between one and six months old. SIDS is more likely to occur in the winter months.[21] Cut SIDS risk in half by putting baby to sleep on her back on a firm mattress and removing all blankets, sleep positioners, bumper pads, and pillows in the crib. Unaccustomed stomach sleeping increases SIDS risk 18–20 times.[22]

One month

Most infants this age will awaken every two to four hours during the night for feedings. To attempt to lengthen sleep periods at night, feed baby every two to three hours during the day. Establish a routine of daily tummy time and avoid excessive time in car seats to prevent positional plagiocephaly, or a flat head.[20] If your baby sleeps more during the day than night, help her know the difference. Let her sleep in a partially lit room for daytime naps and in a darker room at night.

Two months

Most infants are still waking every three to four hours. Sleep patterns are highly variable, and the duration of sleep is not always related to the amount or type of feeding. Fight the urge to talk or play during nighttime feedings or diaper changes. If your baby is still sleeping when you want her awake, encourage more playtime during the day. To establish a better family schedule, wake baby for a late-night feeding at a time that suits your schedule. For example, if baby goes to sleep at 7:00 p.m. and sleeps until 2:00 a.m., wake baby up to feed at 11:00 p.m. and then put her down to sleep for a 5:00 or 6:00 a.m. wakeup. It may take a few nights or weeks to establish this routine; however, it can be accomplished with consistency.

Four months

Typically, by age three to four months babies have started to develop more of a regular sleep and wake pattern and have dropped most of their nighttime feedings. Somewhere between four and six months most babies are ready for some type of sleep training and are capable of sleeping through the night, a stretch of five to six hours.

Six months

If your baby sleeps nine to ten hours at night, it means he's figured out how to settle back to sleep. If your baby isn't sleeping five to six hours straight, you're not alone. As adults, we all wake up several times each night for brief periods of time, yet we put ourselves back to sleep so quickly that we don't remember it in the morning. If your baby hasn't mastered this skill, he will wake up and cry during the night, even if he's not hungry. Nighttime feedings are usually no longer necessary after six months, though a sick or fussy baby will appreciate a soothing feeding when needed.

Nine months

Infants may resist going to sleep due to separation anxiety, and it is not unusual for a child this age to awaken at night, due to teething or achievement of developmental milestones. By nine months, most babies' sleep patterns are fairly established.[23] After the first one to two hours of deep sleep, your baby will move into a stage of lighter snoozing. This pattern of deep and light may occur up to four to six times per night. During the lighter phases of sleep your baby may open his eyes, look around, and cry for you. If his crying includes whimpers, wait and see if baby can soothe himself back to sleep. If the crying warrants attention, go to baby. Use your preferred sleep training method for deciding whether to pick him up or not. Some parents choose to hold, feed, and rock baby back to sleep, while other parents prefer to reassure baby of their presence without picking him up. If handled properly, this exasperating period of nighttime awakenings should last no more than a few weeks.[5, 24]

Twelve months

Naptime and nighttime may be more of a struggle due to separation anxiety. If this occurs, a favorite soft toy or lovey may help. It is also not unusual for a child this age to awaken at night. At some point between twelve and eighteen months, consolidate daytime sleep to one nap. This can often result in more quality sleep for a one-and-a-half-year-old and can be easier to work into family schedules. Never use television in place of a parent for the bedtime routine and expect that if a child, regardless of age, receives an iPad in Mom and Dad's bed upon waking, he will gleefully wake earlier and earlier for this mesmerizing treat. Television viewing at either end of the nighttime sleep cycle can interfere with good sleep. Poor sleep habits affect a child's mood, behavior, and learning.[25, 26]

Eighteen months to thirty-six months (one and a half to three years)

Your child will be ready to move from a crib to a big bed between eighteen and thirty-six months, depending on your circumstances. If your toddler is climbing out of his crib, you'll need to move to a toddler bed or big bed. With two children closely spaced, don't feel too rushed to move the elder sibling into a big bed, especially if there is concern that he is not ready. You can keep an older sibling in a crib (better sleep for everyone), since the newborn may sleep in a bassinet for several months. If your children are very closely spaced, you may want to borrow another crib. A two-year-old can still be potty trained during the day and wear a diaper at night in his crib.

What is a floor bed or Montessori-style bed?

Some parents choose to skip cribs altogether by putting a Montessori-style bed on the floor. The idea behind a Montessori floor bed is similar to the underlying principles of the Montessori Method—a child should have freedom of movement within a safe environment. With a floor bed, a child exerts his own independence as he moves freely about the room once mobile.

Pros: The floor bed can be a firm mattress that you already own, eliminating the expense of a bassinet, crib, and toddler bed. Many parents cite difficulties with bending over a too tall, fixed-side crib as a reason for a floor bed.

Cons: Your nursery must be meticulously childproofed and getting your child to stay in his bed may require time and patience.

Sleep Training: Putting Baby on a Schedule

This checklist is a view of sleep training from 30,000 feet, devised to help you better understand the lay of the land and assess your own preferences. To help you think about establishing a sleep schedule with your baby, I will first summarize some of the most popular methods for sleep training and then provide a checklist that I believe combines the best practices from all the methods. Make adjustments as needed for your child. Please reference the following mentioned books for a more comprehensive look at infant sleep and sleep training.

What is sleep training?

In a nutshell, sleep training includes both parent education and various levels of leaving baby to "cry it out" (CIO) or not. Sleep training occurs during a time when baby no longer requires nourishment throughout the night; this time or age varies, depending on needs of the child. Here are five major methods of sleep training, which may be applied individually or in combination with one another.

- *Parent education.* Before baby arrives or shortly thereafter, parents learn about infant sleep and how to establish healthy sleep habits.
- *Soothing bedtime routines.* Parents establish bedtime routines that help baby wind down, such as taking a warm bath, reading to baby,

singing softly, saying prayers, rocking, etc. Parents then turn off the lights and may or may not respond to any crying.

- *Scheduled awakenings.* This tactic involves waking baby before she would normally get up on her own, such as waking to feed her at your bedtime. The awakenings get fewer and further between as you progress, until finally they are phased-out altogether.
- *The full "cry it out" method.* Once placed in a crib, parents leave baby to cry herself to sleep without comforting her. This is also known as the extinction method. Extinction sleep training is based on the idea that children have sleep problems because they rely on soothing from a parent to put them to sleep.
- *The modified "cry it out" method.* Once baby is placed in a crib, parents let her cry, reassuring her at regular intervals, such as every five to ten minutes, while patting her on the back and whispering reassurances, without picking her up or removing her from the crib.

Baby Wise

Gary Ezzo and Dr. Robert Buckman first published the book *On Becoming Baby Wise: Giving Your Infant the Gift of Nighttime Sleep* in 1993. The principles of *Baby Wise* encourage a parent-led approach to caring for baby, and the book stresses that family-centered philosophies should take precedence over child-centered ones.[27] A few highlights of *Baby Wise* are:

- Baby is a welcome addition to your family, not the center of your family.
- Parent-directed feedings (PDFs) every two-and-a-half to four hours after baby is ten days old will establish a routine. Baby should be sleeping through the night by seven to nine weeks.
- On-demand, round-the-clock feedings are discouraged, since inexperienced parents may interpret all cries as hungry cries.
- Baby's activities should be separated into feedings, wake time, and sleeping. Keeping baby on an EAT-PLAY-SLEEP schedule will help him learn to stabilize hunger for faster nighttime sleeping and not demand feedings right before bedtime.

- Pacifiers and sleep associations, such as rocking, nursing, or feeding before putting baby down to sleep should be avoided.

Note: *On Becoming Baby Wise* has raised concerns from pediatricians for outlining an infant feeding plan that is associated with failure to thrive (FTT), low milk supply, and involuntary early weaning, due to its rigid schedule and refusal to facilitate feeding on-demand.[28]

Ferber Method

Dr. Richard Ferber, founder and director of the Center for Pediatric Sleep Disorders at Children's Hospital Boston, and author of *Solve Your Child's Sleep Problems*, believes that you can teach a baby to soothe himself to sleep between three and five months of age.[24]

- The Ferber method includes a warm, loving bedtime routine, followed by putting baby to sleep awake. If baby cries, Mom or Dad may begin "progressive waiting," or patting baby on the back in the crib to reassure him, but not picking him up. With consistency, baby should learn that crying means nothing more than a check and will go back to sleep.
- After gradually increasing waiting time intervals (three to five to ten to fifteen minutes between checks), baby should learn to fall back asleep without needing a parent or other soothing sleep associations.
- Ferber stresses moderation with sleep training, stating that his gradual extinction recommendation, or delaying your response time to baby's awakenings, is only a small part of his book and not appropriate for every sleep issue.
- Ferber's method of sleep training, which is controversial with those who oppose all cry-it-out methods, became so well-known years ago that parents described their children as "Ferberized" when they were able to sleep through the night.

Weissbluth Method

Dr. Marc Weissbluth, author of *Healthy Sleep Habits, Happy Child,* offers a popular sleep guide that generally encourages parents to put their children to bed earlier. He also suggests "extinction," or not going into baby's room at all after an appropriate age, because it can be too confusing and cause prolonged crying. Weissbluth's other key points include:

- Sleep training doesn't usually begin until four months or so, though good napping starts at age six weeks.
- You cannot spoil an infant less than three months old, and you should not let a young infant "cry it out." It is more important to build trust and let baby know that you are caring for him or her.
- Babies should not be awake for more than two to three hours at a time until age eight months. Watch your child and put them down for a nap as soon as you see signs of tiredness (drowsy but still awake). If you put a child to sleep at the onset of sleep, there should be minimal crying.
- Bed time should be between 6:00 and 8:00 p.m., even if one parent is working late. Parents typically put their children to bed later than they should.
- Putting baby to bed earlier leads to more net sleep, causing a child to wake better rested, so that he or she naps better.
- Every mother of twins knows that whimpering or low-level crying happens all the time. This type of crying can be safely ignored for sleep training at a proper age.
- Weissbluth differs from Ferber in suggesting that baby may require one or two night feedings up to age nine months. Ferber advises that baby may not require any night feedings by age four or five months.

Happiest Baby Method and the Five S's

Dr. Harvey Karp, author of *The Happiest Baby on the Block*, developed the five S's system to help weary parents calm crying babies and get them to sleep. Dr. Karp often refers to the newborn phase (ages zero to three months) as the "fourth trimester." He explains that in the fourth trimester parents mistakenly put newborns in a quiet room with no swaddle—arms loose and legs flailing. Yet baby just spent the previous three trimesters rocking and swaying in a tight, active, noisy environment with muddled voices and swooshing noises from Mom's fluids. The "Happiest Baby" method attempts to replicate this environment for better sleep. Some babies may need all five S's, while others require only a few to help trigger what Dr. Karp calls the "calming reflex."[29]

- **Swaddling**: Tight swaddling provides baby with the confined feeling and snug support that baby experienced while still in Mom's womb.
- **Side/stomach position**: Place baby either on her left side while holding her, to assist in digestion, or on her stomach while providing support or rocking her. Once baby is happily soothed, put her on her back to sleep.
- **Shushing sounds:** These sounds replicate the whooshing sound made by blood flowing through the arteries and other fluids in and around the womb. Many parents choose to download white noise to their iPod or MP3 player and play it at the noise level of a shower through the night.
- **Swinging**: Every step that Mom took caused a swinging motion for baby in the womb. However, this calming mechanism is suddenly taken away after birth, which is why rocking, car rides, and other swinging movements often help to soothe a fussy baby.
- **Sucking**: Sucking triggers a calming reflex in the brain. This "S" can be accomplished with a breast, bottle, pacifier, or even a pinky finger.

Sears Method and Attachment Parenting

Dr. William Sears, author of more than forty books on pregnancy and parenting, coined the phrase "Attachment parenting" (AP), referring to a parenting philosophy based on the developmental psychology principles of attachment theory. Attachment theory implies that sensitive, emotionally available parents help form a secure attachment with baby that yields positive outcomes for life. The effects of early attachment are foundational to social and emotional health later. Attachment parenting can be summed up with Dr. Sears' seven B's:[30]

- **Birth bonding:** The first few weeks after birth are a sensitive period.
- **Breastfeeding:** This practice promotes biological chemistry between Mom and baby, and it also teaches Mom to pick up on baby's cues and body language.
- **Baby-wearing:** Physical closeness with baby breeds familiarity and security.
- **Bedding close to baby:** Co-sleeping helps busy daytime parents bond with baby. Sleeping within close nursing and touching distance minimizes anxiety and teaches baby that sleep is a pleasant state to enter. Sears believes that bed-sharing is okay, too, in the right circumstances (next to Mom, not with a drinker, smoker, or someone who is medicated, etc.).
- **Belief in baby's cry:** Babies cry to communicate needs, not to manipulate. Responding to baby's cries builds trust.
- **Beware of baby trainers:** Sears believes that watching the clock rather than assessing cues from baby is an "unwise approach," an obvious dig at *Baby Wise*. Rigid cry-it-out sleep training can be convenient for tired parents; however, it establishes a palpable emotional distance between parent and child.
- **Balance:** In your enthusiasm for providing for your child, do not neglect your own needs or your marriage. Notice this is the last of the seven B's.

The Sears sleep method suggests a "no tears" approach over cry-it-out methods. Leaving a child to cry alone in his room is unnatural and cruel. This practice can leave a baby filled with panic and anxiety, causing her to release adrenaline and cortisol stress hormones, which over time adversely affects the developing brain.[31] A parent should develop quiet nighttime rituals and respond to all of baby's requests for food and comfort. The downside to the Sears method is parent exhaustion.

Pantley Method

Elizabeth Pantley, author of *The No-Cry Sleep Solution*, also proposes a no-tears approach, which she thinks is middle ground between the "cry it out" and "live with it" schools of thought. Pantley, an attachment parent herself, addresses all types of parents and reminds them to first be sure that baby has no medical reason for interrupted sleep. Her program could be summed up in these steps: parents should do a safety check, then learn infant sleep facts and information, then create a sleep log for naps and nighttime, and finally, implement a sleep solution based on their recorded log. In her book, Pantley contends that one or two longer naps is better than several cat naps, and she specifically addresses the most common sleep association: sucking to sleep. For younger babies (less than four months old), she recommends a full feeding before bedtime so that baby doesn't wake due to a partial feeding. For older babies, Pantley supports a "Gentle removal plan" for sucking and feeding. Parents can give baby a pacifier, bottle, or breast before bedtime, but they should gradually and continually remove it until baby falls asleep without her crutch.

Kim's sleep training checklist

Adjust for your individual child

My approach to sleep training is a combination of all of the above methods, with cuddling, bonding, and feeding in the early months and encouragement toward sleep independence after four to six months or so. Adjust your schedule for multiples, preterm babies, or babies with other health problems.

- ❑ **Observe baby carefully.** Make sure that he does not have a medical condition preventing him from sleeping.
- ❑ **Watch out for these common infant sleep busters.**
  - ▸ *Poor nap habits:* missing naps or too many naps in a car seat
  - ▸ *Overtiredness:* putting baby to bed too late
  - ▸ *Overstimulation:* watching an action movie with baby before bedtime
- ❑ **Make baby tired.** Encourage active play throughout the day. Get baby out of her car seat and on the floor, even if she cries at first. Establish clear tummy time guidelines for nannies and caregivers.
- ❑ **Establish a good sleep environment.** One key factor in regulating sleep and baby's biological clock is light. Provide a darkened room with a nightlight, using room-darkening shades or blackout

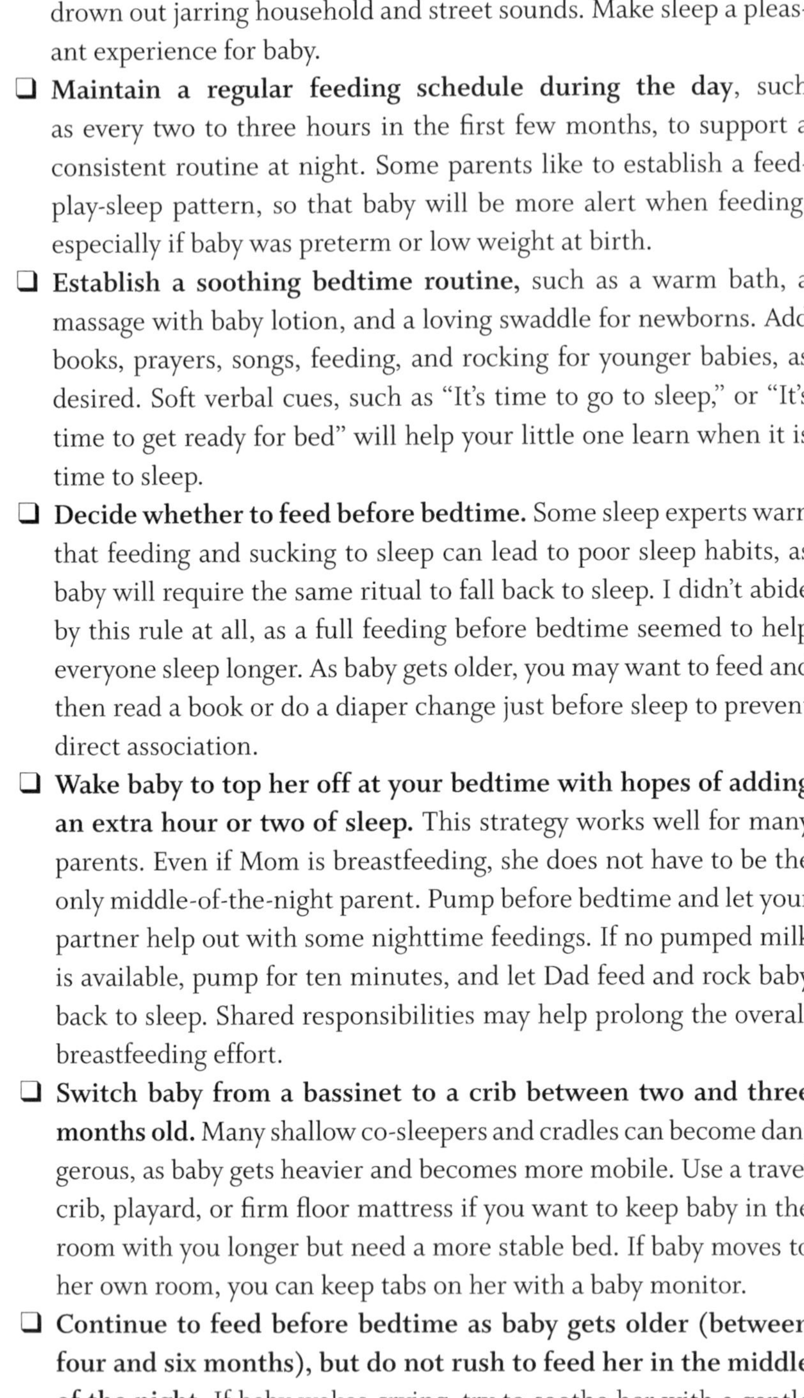

curtains (especially for summer). Play soft music or white noise to drown out jarring household and street sounds. Make sleep a pleasant experience for baby.

❑ **Maintain a regular feeding schedule during the day**, such as every two to three hours in the first few months, to support a consistent routine at night. Some parents like to establish a feed-play-sleep pattern, so that baby will be more alert when feeding, especially if baby was preterm or low weight at birth.

❑ **Establish a soothing bedtime routine,** such as a warm bath, a massage with baby lotion, and a loving swaddle for newborns. Add books, prayers, songs, feeding, and rocking for younger babies, as desired. Soft verbal cues, such as "It's time to go to sleep," or "It's time to get ready for bed" will help your little one learn when it is time to sleep.

❑ **Decide whether to feed before bedtime.** Some sleep experts warn that feeding and sucking to sleep can lead to poor sleep habits, as baby will require the same ritual to fall back to sleep. I didn't abide by this rule at all, as a full feeding before bedtime seemed to help everyone sleep longer. As baby gets older, you may want to feed and then read a book or do a diaper change just before sleep to prevent direct association.

❑ **Wake baby to top her off at your bedtime with hopes of adding an extra hour or two of sleep.** This strategy works well for many parents. Even if Mom is breastfeeding, she does not have to be the only middle-of-the-night parent. Pump before bedtime and let your partner help out with some nighttime feedings. If no pumped milk is available, pump for ten minutes, and let Dad feed and rock baby back to sleep. Shared responsibilities may help prolong the overall breastfeeding effort.

❑ **Switch baby from a bassinet to a crib between two and three months old.** Many shallow co-sleepers and cradles can become dangerous, as baby gets heavier and becomes more mobile. Use a travel crib, playard, or firm floor mattress if you want to keep baby in the room with you longer but need a more stable bed. If baby moves to her own room, you can keep tabs on her with a baby monitor.

❑ **Continue to feed before bedtime as baby gets older (between four and six months), but do not rush to feed her in the middle of the night.** If baby wakes crying, try to soothe her with a gentle caress or a soft lullaby. If you must nurse or warm a bottle, keep the lights low. Shorten nighttime feedings as you progress to night weaning.

- ❑ **If baby is having a hard time returning to sleep, skip middle-of-the-night diaper changes, unless baby has a rash, bowel movement, or a leaky diaper.** If you are cloth diapering with simple inserts and they are soaked, you will need to change them as well. If you must change at night, avoid talking and interacting with baby.
- ❑ **If baby is consistently waking at night, especially after six months old, you may want to break the cycle with gentle sleep training.** Put baby to bed early between 7:00 and 8:00 p.m. When you know that baby's needs have been met, lay her gently in the crib. Pat her with reassurance and let her fuss, checking in as desired.
- ❑ **If baby is inconsolable, cuddle and rock her for a few minutes and put her back to sleep.** If you must nurse or feed, keep it short and sweet.
- ❑ **Consider having Dad reassure baby if night weaning is a goal.** Do not expect night weaning to be successful during times of transition, travel, or sickness.
- ❑ **If your child is still waking frequently after twelve months, let her sleep with a favorite soft toy or blanket**. Experts agree this should be safe since the risk of SIDS decreases after twelve months.
- ❑ **Enjoy the quiet, peaceful moments with your baby.** In a busy and frenetic world, some of your most precious memories of bonding with your newborn will occur in the middle of the night.

Diaper Download

Conservative baby cost calculators estimate that parents spend about $72 per month on diapers and $20 per month on wipes. This means that keeping a child in disposable diapers until three years of age will cost roughly $3,312, and this does not include prices for eco-diapers, night time diapers, or pull-up training pants. Everyone can see why diaper companies are working around the clock to keep children in diapers well into preschool. Knowing this information, you can expect plenty of helpful advice about potty training in my toddler book; but for now, we can all benefit from taking a deeper look at the economic incentives behind diapers and the impact of disposable diapers on the environment.

Diapers in landfills: out of sight, out of mind

The EPA report on Municipal Solid Waste (MSW), a riveting read, points to the same conclusion every year. We are one seriously wasteful nation, and disposable diapers are the third largest consumer item found in landfills behind food and beverage packaging and newspapers. Here are some other alarming diaper statistics, which might encourage you to begin potty training sooner rather than later:

- Diapers represent 30% of non-biodegradable waste in the U.S.
- Disposable diapers generated 7.2 billion pounds of garbage in 2012—the weight of one billion newborn babies.[35]

Did You Know?

The Diaper Industry

- Diapers are big business: By 2017, the global baby diaper industry is expected to reach over $52 billion.[32]
- In 2012, Pampers became Procter and Gamble's largest and first global brand to generate over $10 billion in annual sales.[33]
- Oligopoly alert! The diaper industry is pretty much cornered by two companies: Procter and Gamble (PG) and Kimberly Clark (KMB). These two companies account for the majority of disposables sold in the U.S.
- Pampers and Huggies premium brands represent the leading edge of diaper research and development, and PG and KMB have a chubby leg up on competitors because they can borrow technology from other divisions which require disposable absorbent materials. For example, PG owns Pampers, Tampax, Always, Charmin, Bounty, and Puffs brands, while KMB owns Huggies, Depend, Poise, Kotex, Cottonelle, and Kleenex brands.
- Many private label diapers are simply older styles made by PG and KMB. For example, Luvs are made by PG for a target market who prefer a more affordable, older-style diaper without an elastic waistband, and Huggies' manufacturer KMB makes Costco's Kirkland diapers.
- Final random diaper fact: 60% of people who buy beer also buy diapers, especially on Friday evenings after work. It is not by accident that beer and chips are often placed near diapers in the supermarket, increasing sales for all products.[34]

- At least diapers break down eventually, right? Well, not really. Disposable diapers, sometimes called 'sposies in cloth circles, take 450 years to decompose. That means if William Shakespeare had worn 'sposies (including trendy, tan-colored eco-diapers), his poopy diapers would still be in tact in a landfill today.[36]

Delayed potty training

- In the 1950s, 97% of children were potty-trained by 36 months. Today, just over 50% of children are trained by 36 months. The biggest factors which have led to parents potty training later are: initiation of toilet training at a later age, presence of toileting refusal with stool, and frequent constipation.[37]
- Diaper manufacturers have profited greatly from delayed potty training in the U.S. Training pants and pull-ups are particularly big money-makers. Pull-ups not only generously extend the consumer life cycle, but they are also 35% more expensive per unit—about 15 cents more per diaper.

Other sneaky diaper practices

- **Opaque pricing:** Diaper manufacturers do a masterful job of making per diaper cost comparisons just about impossible. They put odd numbers of diapers into various packs and sizes, allowing only the customer with a calculator to come up with a per diaper cost.
- **Product placement:** Baby stores, such as Babies R' Us and Buy Buy Baby, intentionally make you walk past high profit margin baby gear to get to the diapers and baby food. Marketers know that tired, frazzled parents just might grab an over-priced high chair on the way to the diaper section.
- **Buying diapers and more in online stores:** Online retailers use similar techniques. Popular baby web sites, such as Diapers.com, are hoping that you will pay $50 more for your car seat because you are pleased to have diapers on your doorstep in one or two days. Diapers.com, which was acquired by Amazon in 2010, is not a price leader in diapers or baby gear because their value is in fast shipping.
- **Taking advantage of loyal customers:** Diaper companies know that once parents choose a diaper brand, they generally stick with it. So while newborn diapers are priced very competitively, the pricing quickly ramps up for bigger sizes. For example, the price for a single newborn diaper from The Honest Company is going to be right in the middle of the pack between mainstream and eco-brand diapers. This company is smartly and aggressively offering

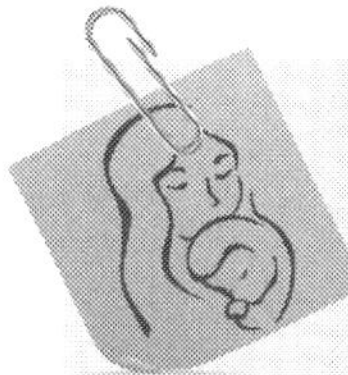

Going Deeper

Donating Leftover and Unopened Diapers

Most people aren't trying to decide whether they should buy gingham or bloom-styled diapers. In 2013, a heart-breaking study found that three in ten low-income mothers cannot afford diapers for their children at all. Federal assistance programs, such as WIC and food stamps, do not cover the cost of diapers, as they do for infant formula. Moreover, many families living in poverty are forced to purchase expensive diapers in convenience stores, due to lack of transportation. Many also do not have washing machines for cloth diapers, and most coin-operated laundromats do not allow the laundering of cloth diapers. Babies and toddlers cannot participate in day care and early childhood education without diapers (students who attend early childhood education are 2.5 times more likely to go on to higher education), and parents cannot go to work without child care.[38] You can help by donating leftover and unopened diapers to your local food bank or pregnancy center. Visit the National Diaper Bank Network to find a center near you. Many facilities will take partially opened packs.

free trial kits, stylish bundles (with dahlia flowers, plaids, and little rocker skulls), and lower prices for newborn diapers to hook new parents. However, as baby grows out of newborn sizes (typically in a few weeks), the prices shoot up. By sizes three to six, Honest Company is leading the pack as the most expensive mainstream brand, charging $.40–.88 per diaper, depending on the size and type of diaper. Honest offerings at Target stores aren't any cheaper ($.47/diaper for size 3, $.51/diaper for size 5, and $.74 for a 4T/5T training pant). I commend Honest Company for being a legitimately eco-friendly business, but c'mon! Those prices average out to roughly $5 per day or $5,500 for three years, and all that bundling is just plain deceptive—making it hard to figure out per diaper cost. The Honest Company "free trial" kit also costs $6 for shipping and handling and signing up for it automatically enrolls you in a monthly subscription service, unless you cancel within seven days. I call these practices less than honest.

- **Deceptively marketing eco-diapers:** Before you walk out of Whole Foods with your brown eco-diapers thinking that you are saving the planet, consider this statement from the Seventh Generation web site: "All disposable diapers, including Seventh Generation's, rely on man-made materials to deliver the high-level performance that parents expect of modern diapers. These materials are mostly petroleum-derived and are not renewable, which adversely impacts the environmental footprint associated with these products." Companies newer to the eco-diaper scene, such as Bambo Nature, The Honest Company, gDiapers, and Nature Babycare all use Super Absorbent Polymer (SAP), just like Pampers and Huggies. Most SAP used today is petroleum derived. For more information about disposable and cloth diapers, including my specific brand recommendations (See: Appendix C: Diapers).

Starting Solid Foods

• •

The AAP recommends that babies be exclusively breastfed for the first six months of life. Most healthy babies will not need additional foods until that time. Some parents choose to introduce solid foods between ages four and six months, or when baby shows signs of readiness, while others may delay solids to eight or nine months.

Age four months or older

Signs your baby may be ready to start solid foods:

- ❑ Baby is at least four months old with good head control and the ability to sit up supported.
- ❑ Baby shows interest in watching others eat.
- ❑ Baby's tongue-pushing reflex has subsided.
- ❑ Your pediatrician gives the okay to start solid foods.

Signs your baby may not be ready to start solid foods:

- ❑ Baby is four to six months, doing well, and sleeping through the night on formula or breast milk alone.
- ❑ Baby cries or turns away from your attempts to feed solid foods.
- ❑ Baby spits out cereal or food given to him, beyond the first few feedings.
- ❑ Baby cannot sit up by himself supported, such as in a high chair.

Did You Know?

Concerns about Rice Cereal and Arsenic

Just a few years ago, doctors recommended rice cereal as an infant's first food because it was the most hypoallergenic cereal. However, in 2012 *Consumer Reports* published an article about the contamination of rice cereal entitled "Arsenic in Your Food," and the FDA launched its own investigation into the arsenic content of rice and rice products. The cause for alarm was due to a problem within our own domestic food supply, as a large portion of the cotton belt in the U.S. south has been converted to rice production. Cotton fields historically received arsenic-based pesticides, and once those fields are flooded to make rice paddies, the arsenic floats right into the crop. The AAP advises parents to feed their infants a variety of first foods, including vegetable purees and cereals made from grains other than rice, to reduce exposure to environmental toxins in any single food.

Four months

Cereals: single-grain cereal, such as oatmeal cereal

- ❑ If baby is thriving on breast milk or formula only, there is no need to feed cereal at four months. At this age, baby should be nursing or feeding roughly four to six times per day with six to seven ounces in each bottle.
- ❑ If you choose to start solid foods, mix a single-grain cereal with breast milk, formula, or water. I recommend starting with oatmeal, since it is sweeter. This should also alleviate concerns about arsenic in rice cereal. Moreover, I would not fret about introducing baby to the "industrial food complex" with boxed cereal. This iron-fortified food is milled to the finest grain, and you will use it for a short time. All of baby's other foods, such as vegetables, fruits, and meats, can easily be homemade. If you choose not to use prepared cereal, puree a lean meat for iron.

- ❑ Use your finger as baby's first spoon. It is soft and just the right temperature. Then work up to a utensil.
- ❑ Give cereal once per day. Some pediatricians recommend morning feedings, so that if baby is allergic to a food, the digestive upset should wear off by the end of day. As a mom, I prefer evening feedings, hoping that baby will feel more satisfied and sleep through the night.
- ❑ Feed one tablespoon the first day, increasing to three tablespoons per serving. Your baby's first cereal will be soupy and mostly liquid.
- ❑ Wait three to five days before introducing a different type of cereal.
- ❑ Be patient. Baby is learning the feeding process, and it can be messy. He may only ingest a very small amount. Solid foods should be considered "an extra" to breast milk or formula at this point.

Five months

Vegetables: sweet potatoes, squash, carrots, green beans, peas, avocados

- ❑ Puree your own vegetables with filtered tap water, or use "stage 1" prepared foods. Food pouches are handy for travel; however, they are typically sweeter than homemade blends.
- ❑ Add plenty of water when pureeing steamed vegetables and fruits at home. This will help baby digest foods more easily.
- ❑ Introduce new foods one variety at a time. One serving is typically two to four ounces (one-half to one full jar). Wait three to five days between each food. Note any allergic reactions: severe gassiness, red rash on the face, red rash around the anus, diarrhea, runny nose, watery eyes, and/or vomiting.
- ❑ Don't be too rigid with insisting that baby eats green vegetables first. Breast milk is naturally sweet, and baby's tongue has more sweet buds than others, explaining why a jar of green beans may not be a gourmet hit. Sweeter veggies, such as sweet potatoes and carrots, often work best for first feedings.
- ❑ Once baby has mastered her eating routine, feed her a variety of foods. Evidence is growing that exposing infants to many different types of foods may reduce the risk of food allergies.

Six months

Fruits: apples, pears, bananas, prunes, peaches, berries, apricots

- ❑ Puree steamed or cooked fruits in a blender. By six to eight months, some infants are eating two small meals per day. A typical schedule may include one meal of cereal and pureed fruit in the morning and one meal of pureed vegetables in the evening.
- ❑ Consider introducing frozen plain bagels or teething biscuits, especially if baby is experiencing teething pain. Let baby practice gnawing, chewing, and eating independently.
- ❑ Introduce water in a sippy cup. Give water with solids to aid digestion. Let baby practice drinking independently.
- ❑ If your baby is constipated from her new diet, add a small amount of pureed prunes, pears, or apricots to her cereal. If your infant's stools are runny, consider a more binding fruit and cereal combination, such as bananas and oatmeal.
- ❑ If baby develops a new, unexplained diaper rash, assess the acidity level of fruits introduced. Pears are a low acid fruit, while citrus, berries, and prepared fruits with ascorbic/citric acid added can affect sensitive babies.

Seven to twelve months

Meats: turkey, lamb, chicken, pork, beef
Beans/legumes: lentils, chick peas, black beans, pinto beans
Processed dairy products: cheese,
yogurt (plain or Greek style), cottage cheese
Other protein sources: salmon, tofu, eggs

- ❑ At this age, blend baby's favorite proteins and veggies together and try seasonings. Stage three prepared foods are also okay, although the meat ones are disgusting. Taste for yourself.
- ❑ Baby is now typically eating two to three meals per day.

- ❑ Typical formula or breast milk intake at this time is 24 oz. or three to four feedings per day, roughly 50% of baby's caloric intake.
- ❑ Be careful not to fill baby up with too many snack foods while preparing healthier foods. If baby is fussy while you are steaming her food, try handing her a toy and not a handful of puffs.
- ❑ Feed baby blended meats in stages. Lamb and turkey are easiest to digest, followed by pork and chicken. Beef is the most difficult to digest.
- ❑ Allow plenty of soft, finger foods. Anything that can be compressed between your baby's thumb and forefinger is the appropriate size and consistency. Fresh, ripe fruit and soft, steamed veggie pieces are significantly cheaper than pouches of baby food.
- ❑ For convenience, feed baby ripe avocados and bananas, which require no prep. You can also use frozen organic vegetables, with a longer shelf life, to ease your shopping burden.
- ❑ For on-the-go snacks, try organic puffs, O-shaped cereal, freeze-dried fruit, and yogurt melts broken in pieces. Cut up blueberries and finely grated ripe fruits are also a favorite snack.
- ❑ Continue to give water in a sippy cup, especially when finger foods are introduced. Hand baby his own spoon for distraction while you feed him healthy foods.
- ❑ Do not feed your infant hot dogs, grapes, nuts, seeds, popcorn, raw fruits and vegetables, or peanut butter, as these foods may cause your child to choke.
- ❑ Consider taking a CPR and first aid for choking class for infants through the American Red Cross. If a class does not fit into your busy schedule, watch an infant choking and CPR video online.

Starting solids: AAP guidelines for introducing allergenic foods

There is a reason for confusion with this issue. In 2000, the American Academy of Pediatrics (AAP) issued guidelines stating that parents should delay the introduction of milk and dairy until age one, eggs until age two, and peanuts, tree nuts, shellfish, and fish until age three. Then in 2008, the AAP retracted their position stating there was not enough evidence to support a delayed introduction of allergens since food allergy prevalence remained on the rise. Beyond that, there were no specifics offered. In January 2013, the American Academy of Asthma, Allergy and Immunology (AAAAI) with AAP input issued the following official recommendations for infant feeding:

- ❑ Do not delay the introduction of allergenic foods, such as wheat, cow's milk dairy, eggs, nuts, and fish, as this may actually increase risk of food allergy or eczema.
- ❑ Once an infant is older than four months and has tolerated several non-allergenic foods, such as oatmeal, sweet potatoes, carrots, bananas, apples, and pears, parents can proceed with the introduction of more allergenic foods, one food at a time. Allergenic foods should be given every three to five days to help isolate triggers of an allergic reaction. Ideally, allergenic foods are to be introduced at home, rather than at day care or a restaurant.
- ❑ If you are pregnant or lactating, you do not have to avoid foods such as milk, eggs, and peanuts, since no protective benefit against food allergy has been found.
- ❑ Cow's milk or whole milk should not be added to a child's diet until age twelve months.

Starting solids: serving tips

- ❑ Once you have blended baby's food, put a small portion of the contents into a separate feeding bowl. Do not feed baby from the blender container.
- ❑ Strain baby's first purees through a metal strainer, such as a flour sifter, if you are not using a high-powered or professional grade blender.
- ❑ Do not heat baby food in plastic, due to the leaching of chemicals. Use small glass prep bowls or ramekins for heating and re-heating.
- ❑ Serve food no warmer than body temperature. Test for temperature on your wrist before feeding.
- ❑ Add flavorful seasonings to baby's food, but there is no need to add salt or sugar.
- ❑ Do not sweeten baby's food, especially with honey or corn syrup, which can cause botulism or food poisoning.

Did You Know?

Concerns about Nitrates and Homemade Baby Food

Has someone told you not to feed baby homemade carrots cooked at home and only to feed them what comes in a jar because of nitrates? This issue needs some clarification. Nitrates are a chemical found in water and soil, and the nitrate reaction of concern is called methemoglobinemia, a rare form of anemia that most often occurs when formula is mixed with water containing nitrates, particularly well water (usually due to synthetic fertilizer runoff). Some vegetables also contain nitrates, such as beets, carrots, green beans, spinach, and squash. Therefore, AAP guidelines state that parents should not feed nitrate-containing vegetables to babies *under three months old*. To note, the age restriction occurs before the age recommendation for starting solid foods. Therefore, do get your well water tested and make sure that the nitrate concentration is less than 10 ppm, but do not choose jars of prepared foods over fresh foods after age three months.

- ❑ Store unused portions in the refrigerator. Use within two to three days. Do not feed your infant food left out of the refrigerator for more than two hours.
- ❑ Make large batches of homemade baby food at night or on weekends. Pour homemade purees into ice cube trays, freeze, and transfer cubes into an airtight freezer bag. Fruits and veggies can last six to eight months as frozen cubes, while meat, poultry, and fish can last one to two months.
- ❑ Use a brush to clean blender blades. Harmful bacteria can be present in old food particles and may contaminate other foods.
- ❑ If baby's messy feedings are driving you crazy, seek help from convenient products: a handy bib, a floor mat, a cordless sweeper, or a bowl with a suction cup. Try a fun novelty spoon to hand baby, so that he will not swat at your spoon during feedings, such as a Nuby Sound Bites spoon, or a pair of chopsticks for kids.

- ❑ Breastfeeding mothers who work outside the home often find that feeding solid foods may be easier for a caregiver to do during the day. Then Mom can focus on breastfeeding during the evenings and at night, making mealtime simpler while keeping up Mom's milk supply.

JUST FOR MOM

(Dad should read, too)

Breastfeeding Support

If you have read The Parent's Pocket Checklist: An Essential Guide to Pregnancy, *this section will be a refresher with some additional information.*

If everyone seems to agree that breast milk is the ideal nutrition for babies, then why is this topic so controversial? To better understand the sensitivities involved, let's take a closer look at breastfeeding issues for women today.

Women are working more hours outside the home than ever before, yet the pressure to breastfeed has skyrocketed, especially when compared to previous generations. Today, breastfeeding initiation rates are 79%, up from 24% in the early 1970s.[39] Today, a tax deduction exists for breast pumps and other supplies (formula supplies do not qualify), while photos of breastfeeding celebrities appear in the same news feeds as major world events—first, a stand-off in the Ukraine, followed by Gisele Bündchen lounging in her bathrobe, nursing her baby with a glam squad in attendance. This is all great news for babies, but a working mom pumping in a storage closet or small back office with co-workers snickering outside may sense that certain expectations for breastfeeding are unrealistic. Let's dive into the full spectrum of breastfeeding, including the good, the bad, and the bumps in the road, because understanding the complex nature of this topic may help us all better achieve our goals.

Benefits of breastfeeding

Breast milk is made especially for baby. It is easier to digest than the protein in cow's milk, and it helps fight disease. Colostrum, also called "liquid gold," is the thick, yellow breast milk that you make during pregnancy and just after birth. This milk is rich in nutrients and antibodies that protect your baby for life. Colostrum changes into mature milk by three to five days after birth, and this milk has just the right amount of fat, sugar, and protein to help baby grow. Formula cannot match the precise chemical makeup of human breast milk.[40] For a closer look at infant formula ingredients and shortcuts companies take for cheaper ingredients (See: Appendix B: Infant Formula).*

Breastfeeding provides instant, healthy food, without bottles to sterilize or warm at night. It is also less expensive than formula feeding and beneficial to Mom. Formula and bottle supplies can cost over $1,500 per year, whereas breastfeeding is nearly free (though most women will probably need a breast pump.) Moreover, breastfed babies are sick less often, which can lower health care costs. Breastfeeding is also linked to a lower risk of certain diseases in women, including postpartum depression, breast cancer, ovarian cancer, and Type 2 diabetes. Other studies link breastfeeding to higher IQ, lower rates of osteoporosis, and less postpartum bleeding.[41, 42]

Common breastfeeding challenges

Truthfully, I have hardly met a nursing mom who didn't have breastfeeding challenges, and more often than not, low milk supply (not over-supply) is a major concern. Common issues such as sore nipples, inverted nipples, and problems with baby's latch can all lower milk supply. A good latch occurs when baby's mouth covers more of the areola above the nipple than below, like a fish kissing a wall. A bad latch can lead to a cycle of frustration, which adversely affects the overall breastfeeding effort; a bad latch causes sore nipples, Mom is edgy with sore nipples and baby is not gaining weight, so Mom or Dad panics and supplements with formula, which contributes to further low milk supply. Repeat. Some babies need supplementation during that initial low milk supply period. However, if this happens to you, please seek help from a lactation specialist.

---

* For a fascinating comparison of exactly what is in breast milk vs. formula, see this project conducted by students at Douglas College: http://www.bcbabyfriendly.ca/whatsinbreastmilkposter.pdf

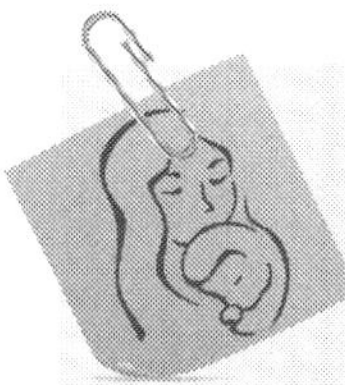

Going Deeper

Challenges with Breastfeeding

I am a passionate breastfeeding advocate. However, there are legitimate challenges to overcome, especially in the beginning. Three days after the birth of my first child, my breasts became so engorged with milk I thought they were going to burst like water balloons. My doctor joked that I had turned into Dolly Parton overnight, and my husband tried to lighten the mood by touting me as our family's prize jersey cow. I was not amused. The more I pumped to relieve the pressure, the more milk I produced. Yet when I didn't pump, my ducts clogged and mastitis ensued (mastitis is inflammation of breast tissue due to infection, engorgement, or clogged ducts). Our baby couldn't begin to drink the milk I was producing, and she struggled to latch on to my fire hose. My nipples were cracked and stinging, and I had cold cabbage leaves hanging out of my bra for relief. There were no glamour-shots posted online of my breastfeeding experience. Thankfully, family and friends helped me get over the breastfeeding hump.

Breastfeeding for preemies, multiples, or babies with health issues

Breastfeeding can be particularly difficult with preemies, multiples, or babies with health issues. If your baby is whisked away to the Neonatal Intensive Care Unit (NICU) immediately after birth, try not to worry about the guidelines for breastfeeding within the first hour. Pumped breast milk can be fed through a tube, and nursing isn't the only form of bonding. Bonding starts long before your baby is born. One study found that not only could three-day-old infants recognize the smell of their mother's amniotic fluid, but that smell was soothing prior to experiencing pain, such as a heel prick.[43] Another study found that newborn babies less than three days old prefer their mothers' voices to those of strangers.[44]

Did You Know?

Break Time Laws for Nursing Mothers

The Patient Protection and Affordable Care Act ("Affordable Care Act") amended section 7 of the Fair Labor Standards Act ("FLSA"), requiring "employers to provide reasonable break time for an employee to express breast milk for her nursing child for one year after the child's birth each time such employee has need to express the milk. Employers are also required to provide a place, other than a bathroom, that is shielded from view and free from intrusion from coworkers and the public, which may be used by an employee to express breast milk." This breastfeeding break time requirement became effective when the Affordable Care Act was signed into law on March 23, 2010.

Breastfeeding and working moms

Some women find that breastfeeding is easier than expected at first, but then meet challenges after returning to work. For example, leaking breast milk on a t-shirt at home is not exactly the same as drenching a silk blouse during a meeting at work. Some new moms may also be concerned about time allowances for pumping during the workday. Yet many do not know that federal regulations are on their side.

Getting over the hump: troubleshooting tips

Surveys often cite "lack of support" as a catch-all reason why women give up on breastfeeding, so let's flesh out a few common scenarios and provide some troubleshooting tips and solutions.

Lack of role models

Problem: New mothers often get information about breastfeeding from pamphlets and online resources, which can be ineffective compared to live role models, such as family and friends who have breastfed successfully.

Solution: If you want to breastfeed, seek the help of trusted friends and family members who have been successful breast feeders.

Generational differences

Problem: At birth, a new mom's own mother may be ambivalent about breastfeeding. She didn't breastfeed, and you turned out fine (breastfeeding rates in the 1970s and 80s were 25–35%).

Solution: Assure your mom that you respect her decisions and ask for her support. Invite her to be present when you talk with a lactation consultant.

Lack of partner support

Problem: In some families, fathers may feel uncertain about breastfeeding. How will Dad bond with baby? How will his partner work outside the home and breastfeed? How much household work will shift to him due to breastfeeding? How will breastfeeding affect the couple's sex life?

Solution: Prenatal education with fathers has shown to enhance breastfeeding support remarkably. One study from an urban university obstetrics practice showed a breastfeeding initiation rate of 74% among mothers whose partners attended a two-hour prenatal intervention class (led by a peer-educator), compared to a 41% rate among control groups without the class. Teach your partner about breastfeeding.[45]

Mixed messages about breastfeeding in the media

Problem: If you peruse popular op-eds, you might come across cynical headlines about breastfeeding, such as "The Breastfeeding Myth," "Booby Trap: Myths about Breastfeeding," or "The Case against Breastfeeding." In the last article, the author states, "it was not the vacuum that was keeping me and my 21st-century sisters down, but another sucking sound." Personally, I don't get it. If you are going to rant and rave and spread cynicism about something, pick a better subject.

Solution: If you want to breastfeed successfully, surround yourself with positive and encouraging messages about breastfeeding.

Misperceptions about low milk supply

Problem: Fifty percent of women rank "insufficient milk supply" as the number one reason for stopping breastfeeding.[46] New mothers are often discouraged by the common misperception they are not producing enough milk for their baby when they actually are producing sufficiently. No one has explained the physiology of lactation.

Solution: Visual cues may help new mothers conceptualize just how much milk a baby needs per day in the first weeks of life, which is not that much. See the chart below.

Visual cues: size and volume of a newborn's stomach

DAY ONE	DAY THREE	ONE WEEK	ONE MONTH
Size of a Cherry	Size of a Walnut	Size of an Apricot	Size of a Large Egg
5-7 ml or ½ tsp.	22-27 ml or .75-1 oz.	45-60 ml or 1.5-3 oz.	80-150 ml or 2.5-5 oz.

What if you just can't breastfeed?

Some mothers simply cannot breastfeed or breastfeed exclusively, due to physical ailments, emotional limitations, medications, employment, and other factors. Know that good parenting is more important than breastfeeding. Your baby needs a healthy mom. So, if you are experiencing difficulties and you choose to give up breastfeeding, make lemonade from lemons and embrace the positives of formula feeding. Formula can be easier to feed on the go, with no worrying about nursing in public. With formula, you know exactly how much baby is eating and your schedule is not directly tied to baby. Other caregivers can also feed baby at night.

Breastfeeding checklist

- ❑ **Learn as much as you can about breastfeeding.** Dad can benefit from an overview, too. Some popular breastfeeding resources are:

- Online instructional videos: These videos demonstrate breastfeeding techniques better than any book.
- La Leche League International online information portal (http://www.llli.org/nb.html) or telephone hotline 1-800-525-3243 from 9:00 a.m. to 5:00 p.m. CST.
- The KellyMom website at www.KellyMom.com
- Books on breastfeeding (See: Appendix E: Recommended Resources).

❑ **If you are struggling in the first two weeks of breastfeeding, know this is normal.** Ninety-two percent of participants in a recent study reported at least one major breastfeeding concern in the first week. The top three concerns included difficulty with infant feeding, breastfeeding pain, and milk quantity.[47]

❑ **Overcome early breastfeeding discomfort with tenacity and a sense of purpose.** The initial pain and discomfort of breastfeeding should subside in two to four weeks. Nursing can be relaxing and peaceful once established.

❑ **Overcome work schedule challenges with compromise.** No one says that baby must be 100% breastfed, especially after Mom returns to work. Try to keep breastfeeding and supplement with formula if needed. For example, breastfeed at night and in the morning and have a care provider feed pumped milk supplemented with formula during the day. Pump what you can at work. Assess your baby's feeding situation one day at a time and keep going as long as you can.

❑ **Talk to your doctor about contraceptives and breastfeeding.** Birth control pills with combined progesterone and estrogen are linked to changes in milk content and low milk supply. Progestin-only contraceptives, including "minipills" and Depo-Provera, are generally the preferred hormonal birth control for breastfeeding women.[48]

❑ **Know that hormonal contraceptives are not your only birth control options.**

- *Nonhormonal methods:* male and female condoms, diaphragm, copper intrauterine device, cervical cap, vaginal sponge, spermicidal cream or foam

Practical Tips from Real Parents

Breastfeeding

- Relax! You and baby are learning how to do this thing called breastfeeding at the same time.
- Know that breastfeeding is kind of like childbirth. When you talk to other women, they often remember the end result and forget the struggle it took to get there.
- Feed as soon as you think baby is hungry (when she first starts rooting or turning her head and opening her mouth) and she will suck with less vigor.
- Apply lanolin or nipple cream around the clock to help with cracked or bleeding nipples.
- Express a tiny amount of breast milk on your nipples after feeding and rub all around the feeding area. Breast milk has antibodies that will speed up the healing. Go braless to air dry.
- Try a thin nipple shield if baby is having problems latching and you are too sore to continue. It really helps!
- Try these things for soreness and nipple pain: Booby Tubes gel packs (these go in the microwave for heat or the freezer for cool relief), Lansinoh Soothies gel pads, lanolin cream, and cold lettuce or cabbage leaves.
- If you are struggling to feed, have a lactation consultant come to your house or attend a La Leche League meeting.
- Use a support pillow to breastfeed, or else you will be hunching over baby uncomfortably for as long as you feed.
- Breastfeeding is rough on your back and neck. Your head is always looking down and you are curled up around baby to get in the right position. Make sure that you stretch and look up while feeding to minimize the strain.
- If you have clogged ducts frequently, try taking lecithin, a natural food additive, to reduce the stickiness of the milk.
- If your baby continues to struggle with a good latch, have your pediatrician check to see if he is tongue-tied or has a physical reason why he can't extend his tongue. The doctor can clip

the frenulum, or webbed place under the tongue, to help with feeding.

- If you have big breasts, make sure that you pinch or squeeze your nipple each time to help baby latch on. Also, don't worry if baby's nose is buried in your breast a little bit. He can still breathe since the nose tip usually extends further than the holes.
- If you are trying to store up pumped milk for returning to work, pump in the morning when you have the most milk and during baby's naps or longer feeding stretches.
- Rub olive oil on your breast pump flanges (the things that look like trumpets), if they are chafing you. Also, make sure the flanges are the right size for getting the most milk.
- Contact your child's pediatrician and your doctor to get treatment for thrush. Dump any pumped milk that may be infected. (Note: Thrush is a common yeast infection that can be shared between Mom and baby. It looks like white patches of cottage cheese in baby's mouth and pink, flaky spots on mom's nipples.)
- Don't trust the rhythm method or breastfeeding for birth control if you want to guarantee you will not get pregnant, especially if you are supplementing with formula. You will be fertile before you get your first period.

- *Hormonal methods:* progestin-only contraceptives, combination progestin-estrogen contraceptives
- *Lactational amenorrhea method (LAM):* if you plan to breastfeed six months or longer, feed your baby 90% to 95% of his food intake from breast milk, and breastfeed every four hours in the day and every six hours at night, you can have a protection rate close to 98% for your first six months of breastfeeding.[49]
- *Permanent sterilization:* vasectomy for a man, tubal ligation for a woman

Breastfeeding: Nutrition and Infant Food Sensitivities

- [ ] **Talk to your doctor about continuing your prescription prenatal vitamin with DHA while breastfeeding,** though it may contain more iron than needed. Breastfeeding women should take some type of regular multivitamin with 100% of the recommended dietary allowance (RDA). Make sure that you are getting 500 mcg of folic acid.
- [ ] **Talk to your doctor about taking supplements.** For example, if you take a calcium supplement, you may not know that calcium supplements from natural sources, such as oyster shell or bone meal, can be high in mercury. Vegans may need a vitamin supplement that contains vitamin B12.
- [ ] **Drink plenty of water.** The average breastfeeding woman produces 25 ounces (750 to 800mL) of breast milk each day and needs to replenish fluids. If plain water is too bland, add slices of lemon, lime, or cucumber. Prioritize milk and sparkling water over juice and soda.
- [ ] **Eat foods high in omega-3 fatty acids (DHA and EPA),** such as wild salmon, anchovies, herring, sardines, walnuts, flaxseeds, tofu, and kidney and pinto beans. The AAP recommends 200 to 300 mg of omega-3 fatty acids per day, which is equal to one to two servings of fish each week.[50]
- [ ] **Eat a variety of different foods.** This should change the flavor of your breast milk and help baby accept various solid foods in the future. It also reduces your exposure to chemicals in certain foods.

Did You Know?

Gluten-Free and Breastfeeding

Popular books, such as best sellers *Wheat Belly* by cardiologist William Davis and *Grain Brain: The Surprising Truth about Wheat, Carbs, and Sugar – Your Brain's Silent Killers* by neurologist David Perlmutter, have helped to lead a mainstream gluten-free movement, maintaining that gluten and excess carbohydrates lead to inflammation in our bodies and brains. However, lactating non-celiac women on a gluten-free diet should talk to their doctors. Many gluten-free products are made with unenriched grains and starches that can be loaded with calories and short on vitamins and minerals.

- ❑ **If you are diagnosed with celiac disease, talk to your doctor.** Strive to breastfeed your infant through baby's gluten introduction; it may decrease his or her chance of acquiring celiac disease. Note: Celiac disease is a digestive and autoimmune disorder that can damage the lining of the small intestine.
- ❑ **If you are a non-celiac on a gluten-free diet "just because," talk to your doctor.** Without proper monitoring, a gluten-free diet can leave you depleted of B vitamins, iron, calcium, zinc, and fiber. For example, breads made with tapioca, rice, and other gluten-free flours are typically not fortified. Fortified breads and cereals are some of the top sources of B vitamins for women in the U.S. This group especially needs vitamin $B_{9,}$ also known as folic acid or folate, to prevent birth defects.
- ❑ **To maintain a gluten-free diet, focus on good sources of gluten-free foods to boost potentially deficient areas.**
  - *Sources of gluten-free fiber:* beans, quinoa, ground flax seeds, berries, sweet potatoes with skin, nuts, kale, chia seeds, broccoli, and prunes
  - *Sources of gluten-free iron:* beef, poultry, liver, non-GMO soy/edamame, lentils, green peas, spinach, and amaranth
  - *Sources of gluten-free calcium:* milk, hard cheese, yogurt, fortified milks (almond, soy, etc.), and green leafy vegetables

- *Sources of gluten-free B vitamins:* meats, leafy greens, nuts, seeds, beans, quinoa, GF oatmeal, brown rice, enriched products (Rice Chex, etc.)
- *Sources of gluten-free zinc:* poultry, beef, liver, dark turkey meat, pecans, pumpkin seeds, beans, and brown rice

Food sensitivities while breastfeeding

Exposing baby to various flavors is a good thing, and research shows that an infant's palate is shaped in utero and through breastfeeding.[51] Amniotic fluid and breast milk are naturally flavored by the foods that Mom eats, just as the taste of dairy milk is affected by cows grazing on garlic and onions. With that, don't be too quick to diagnose every gastrointestinal upset as a food sensitivity. More often than not, baby's immature digestive system is the culprit. Think about it–children in India or Korea or Peru aren't any more colicky or fussy than babies in the U.S. because they are exposed to curry, kimchi, and peppers. Nevertheless, if baby is consistently uncomfortable after eating, you may consider restricting the following foods for a few weeks:

- ❑ soy products
- ❑ coffee, tea, soda, and chocolate
- ❑ peanuts
- ❑ shellfish
- ❑ gas-producing vegetables, such as peppers, onions, broccoli, cabbage, and cauliflower
- ❑ acidic foods, such as tomatoes, citrus, and berries
- ❑ strong spices, such as garlic, chili pepper, and curry

Elimination diet

If baby is still uncomfortable, you may want to go cold turkey (literally) and try an elimination diet. An elimination diet consists of the least allergenic foods in each of the major food groups. Be forewarned: this diet is seriously bland, and after a few days, you may find yourself screaming for Thai green curry and chicken enchiladas. Here are a few staples of an elimination diet:

- ❑ turkey
- ❑ lamb
- ❑ potatoes
- ❑ sweet potatoes
- ❑ rice
- ❑ rice pasta
- ❑ pears
- ❑ zucchini
- ❑ yellow squash

If baby seems to be doing better, gradually add the following healthy foods: apples, bananas, avocado, asparagus, carrots, rolled oats, yogurt, kefir, chicken, and wild salmon.

Breastfeeding Grocery List

Eating a healthy diet while breastfeeding is just as important as during pregnancy. Friends may also tell you that breast milk has a way of meeting baby's nutritional needs, even when you are not eating perfectly. However, when you don't get the nutrients that baby needs, your body draws from its own stores or reserves. Therefore, you should continue to take your prenatal or a multivitamin while breastfeeding, and talk to your doctor about supplements for calcium, Vitamin D, and DHA, if your multivitamin does not have the AAP recommended values for breastfeeding women (calcium = 1000 mg, vitamin D = 600 IU or micrograms, DHA = 200-300 mg per day).

Here is a helpful breastfeeding grocery list. The most nutrient-packed choices are listed at the top of each food group (left to right).

Colorful vegetables *(select a few and mix them up each week)*

- ❑ sweet potatoes
- ❑ bell peppers
- ❑ broccoli
- ❑ avocados
- ❑ winter squash
- ❑ tomatoes
- ❑ artichokes
- ❑ carrots
- ❑ cauliflower
- ❑ beets
- ❑ green peas
- ❑ asparagus
- ❑ Brussels sprouts
- ❑ summer squash
- ❑ parsley

Dark green, leafy vegetables

- ❑ spinach
- ❑ kale
- ❑ Swiss chard or collard greens

Colorful fruits *(select a few)*

- ❑ blueberries
- ❑ blackberries
- ❑ raspberries
- ❑ strawberries
- ❑ cantaloupe
- ❑ kiwi
- ❑ papaya
- ❑ mango
- ❑ bananas
- ❑ oranges
- ❑ grapefruit
- ❑ apples
- ❑ cherries
- ❑ pineapple
- ❑ watermelon

Dried Fruits

- ❑ apricots
- ❑ raisins
- ❑ figs

Whole grains

- ❑ quinoa
- ❑ fortified cereal (Total, All-Bran)
- ❑ oatmeal
- ❑ 100% whole wheat bread
- ❑ whole wheat tortillas or pitas
- ❑ whole grain or protein-fortified pasta
- ❑ brown rice
- ❑ whole grain crackers
- ❑ baked chips

Beans

- ❑ lentils
- ❑ non-GMO soy/ edamame
- ❑ chickpeas/ garbanzo
- ❑ black beans
- ❑ pinto beans*
- ❑ kidney beans*

Lean meats and proteins *(remove the skin and fat before cooking)*

- ❑ beef (95–98% fat free)
- ❑ pork
- ❑ chicken breast
- ❑ lamb
- ❑ tofu*

Dairy products *(you don't need whole fats for rich breast milk)*

- ❑ low fat Greek yogurt
- ❑ low-fat milk, with vitamin D and DHA
- ❑ soy or almond milk (with calcium)
- ❑ cottage cheese
- ❑ string cheese
- ❑ cream cheese

Fish and seafood **Mayo Clinic list*

8 to 12 ounces, approx. 2 meals per week

- ❑ wild salmon*
- ❑ anchovies*
- ❑ herring* (Atlantic)
- ❑ sardines*
- ❑ trout
- ❑ shrimp (wild North American)
- ❑ pollock
- ❑ canned light tuna
- ❑ canned salmon

Eggs

- ❑ eggs fortified with omega-3 acids

Nuts, seeds, and popcorn

- ❑ walnuts*
- ❑ almonds
- ❑ pumpkin seeds*
- ❑ sunflower seeds
- ❑ ground flax seeds*
- ❑ popcorn
- ❑ peanut butter (natural)

Beverages

- ❑ calcium-fortified orange juice
- ❑ 100% fruit juice
- ❑ sparkling water

Baking and condiments

- ❑ whole wheat flour
- ❑ organic ketchup
- ❑ all fruit, low sugar preserves

*Foods high in Omega-3 fatty acids (DHA and EPA)

Anxiety, Depression, and Postpartum Depression

If you have read The Parent's Pocket Checklist: An Essential Guide to Pregnancy, *this section will be a refresher with some additional information.*

In surveys and interviews for this book, I have been overwhelmed by the outpouring of passion surrounding the topics of depression, postpartum depression, and general anxiety after birth. While feelings about the postpartum period have been described to me in a multitude of ways (i.e., *I was in a fog after my baby was born; I was a nervous wreck worrying about my newborn; my energy level and libido went to zero; I really lost my mojo, etc.)* a common thread remains the same. The complexity and intensity of emotions—the highs, the lows, the guilt, and the extreme expectations—involved with motherhood is typically beyond anything most women have ever experienced.

In my observations, the following compounding factors are making today's mothers even more susceptible to anxiety and depression than previous generations:

- *Parents are older when they have their first child:* Caring for a helpless human being after years of independence and self-discovery can be a major adjustment for anyone, but especially for Mom, who is culturally expected to pour herself into her offspring.
- *More "I":* In general, our society has become more individualistic. Life is more about the "I" and less about the "we." We're a selfie generation, yet when we put ourselves at the center and become obsessed with the extent of our own possibilities, any type of setback

can be devastating. Parenting naturally draws the focus away from self and self-pursuit, which can lead to a disruption of the "I" called depression, meaning that we have failed relative to our own goals.[52]

- *Less "we":* When our grandparents struggled with life transitions, they generally had their spiritual faith, extended family, a tighter-knit community, and a cohesive nation to provide comfort and support. This social safety net has all but eroded in the last few decades.
- *Intersection of career and motherhood:* Today, a record share of new moms are working and are college educated—66% of women with a child under age one have at least some college, compared to 18% in 1960.[53] Women are now 33% more likely than men to earn college degrees by age 27, and women are earning the majority of degrees awarded. While this academic success is terrific for women's resumes, a great deal of stress and anxiety can occur when one is confronted with choices between career and raising children.[54]

What is depression?

Depression is more than feeling sad, blue, or down in the dumps for a few days. Depression is having despondent, empty, and anxious feelings that do not go away and affect your ability to function. Depression affects families, relationships, work performance, and day-to-day activities.* One in ten Americans have depression at some point in life. The rate of depression for women is twice that of men, regardless of race or ethnicity.[55]

Depression typically results from a combination of factors rather than a single cause. Stressful life events such as the death of a loved one, loss of a significant relationship or job, abuse, neglect, or poverty can trigger depression. Areas of the brain involving mood, memory, and decision making can be physically and chemically altered by a strong physiological response to a stressful event.

* For an illustration of how depression looks day-to-day, see the World Health Organization's video called "I Had a Black Dog, His Name was Depression" found on YouTube.

What is postpartum depression?

About 80% of postpartum women experience some form of the baby blues, while 15% have postpartum depression (PPD).[56] Change is stressful, and the combination of biological, hormonal, and emotional changes after childbirth can pack a powerful punch.

- *Biological changes:* Postpartum women have endured physical pain from childbirth and considerable changes to their bodies after months of pregnancy. Some women are disappointed that certain changes such as stretch marks, stretched skin, decreased breast uplift, and belly fat may never return to a pre-pregnancy normal. Postpartum women are also sleep-deprived, and the lack of rest affects the other body systems.
- *Hormonal changes:* Changing hormone levels can trigger symptoms of postpartum depression, similar to hormone changes that affect a woman's mood before she gets her period. Levels of thyroid hormones may also drop after giving birth, which can exacerbate symptoms of depression (the thyroid is a small gland in the neck that helps regulate how your body uses and stores energy from food).
- *Emotional and psychological changes:* As if there wasn't enough going on in the recovery department, postpartum women must shift emotionally from a period of high anticipation with freedom in their schedule to a loss of anticipation and a more restricted schedule. Mom is no longer the center of attention, and the effects of weight gain (without a baby) can adversely affect her self-esteem. Low self-esteem and social isolation can lead to disconnection from others. Disconnection from others leads to depression.

Disconnection, denial, and depression

Many women feel embarrassed and ashamed about feeling depressed after the birth of a child. A new mom with PPD may refuse to tell family or friends how she is feeling, worrying that she will be seen as ungrateful and self-absorbed, or worse, an unfit mother. Someone with PPD may also be concerned that an employer or co-worker might find out about her depression and view her as unstable. Family and friends with children may offer little empathy because they have forgotten about their own difficulties adjusting to life with a newborn.[57]

What are some differences between "baby blues" and postpartum depression?

The baby blues often go away within a few days or weeks. The symptoms are not severe and do not require a doctor's treatment. If you have baby blues, you may…

- ❑ Feel sad, anxious, or overwhelmed with your new life
- ❑ Have rapid mood swings
- ❑ Cry very easily, or have crying fits
- ❑ Lose your appetite, or eat too much, for a few weeks
- ❑ Have trouble sleeping, even when others are encouraging or allowing you to rest

If you have the following symptoms of depression **for more than two weeks** without relief, you may have postpartum depression.

- ❑ Feeling sad, overwhelmed, and hopeless about your life
- ❑ Crying a lot, or not being able to stop crying
- ❑ Having no energy or motivation to accomplish life's tasks
- ❑ Isolating yourself from family and friends
- ❑ Losing interest in activities that you used to enjoy
- ❑ Eating too little or too much
- ❑ Sleeping too little or too much (beyond normal sleep interruption with a newborn)
- ❑ Experiencing headaches, aches and pains, or stomach problems that don't go away

Postpartum depression can include more severe symptoms, such as:

- ❑ Thoughts of hurting the baby
- ❑ Thoughts of hurting yourself
- ❑ Not having any interest in caring for the baby

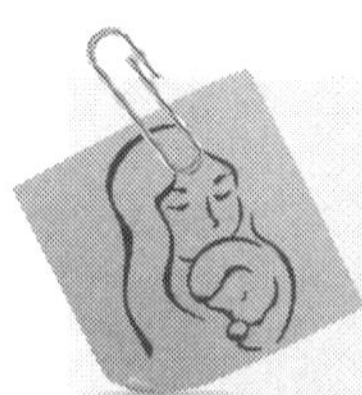

Going Deeper

The Postpartum Paradox

Having a baby is one of life's most joyous and stressful events. This paradoxical relationship may also explain why postpartum depression is often undiagnosed and untreated. I had undiagnosed, untreated postpartum depression. I didn't want to hurt my child, and my world never hit rock bottom. However, I had sad, anxious feelings that did not go away in the days and weeks after birth, and they profoundly affected my marriage and my life.

I loved my newborn wholeheartedly, but the changes to my daily schedule overwhelmed me. I was on a round-the-clock breast-feeding tether that was more demanding than expected, and being in an unfamiliar city left me homebound. Watching my husband pursue his own career and fatherhood with hardly a bump in the road made me resentful. I felt conflicted and crazy. I had longed to be a mom, but my new schedule was exhausting, lonely, and dare I say—boring. So what did I do? I pulled myself up by the boot-straps and poured myself deeper into my new role (I was going to be the best mom ever!) But I was still unhappy. The incongruity between what I thought I was supposed to be and what I actually was triggered a flood of disappointment. I languished in my own mother's guilt: *"You're pathetic, sitting around in your comfy clothes, with your healthy baby, wondering if you'll ever 'have it all.' Most women are already out there doing it all. What are you complaining about?"* I responded by withdrawing from the world.

As far as my doctor knew, I only had "minor baby blues," but I was sputtering on empty. One small spit-up or diaper leak before heading out the door unraveled me, and this is coming from a lady who flew combat missions in Afghanistan and Iraq. The isolation and thankless nature of caretaking had gotten the best of me. By the time I found myself suddenly and mysteriously captivated by the life of Abraham Lincoln (whose melancholy both challenged and fueled him), I knew I was depressed.

Untreated depression can lead to the following risky behaviors that affect both Mom and baby: [58]

- ❑ Out-of-control responses to stimuli, especially crying and noise
- ❑ Neglect of an infant
- ❑ Excessive alcohol use
- ❑ Drug addiction

The recovery period after birth can be *substantially* better for Mom with support from a partner, family, and friends. Although no one can predict postpartum outcomes, families can recognize known high-risk factors. Early identification and preventative measures could alleviate months of suffering for a new mom and the whole family.[59-61] Here is a list of markers collated from several studies on postpartum depression. Read each predictor and think about ways that you might ease potential burdens for yourself or your partner.

- ❑ Previous history of depression
- ❑ Prenatal depression and anxiety (during pregnancy)
- ❑ Recent stressful life events (death in the family, moving, etc.)
- ❑ Lack of relational support from a significant family member or friend
- ❑ Marital dissatisfaction/dysfunction
- ❑ Unplanned pregnancy
- ❑ Child care stress
- ❑ Financial strain
- ❑ Low self-esteem (includes body image dissatisfaction)
- ❑ Perfectionism (high concern over making mistakes)
- ❑ Breastfeeding challenges
- ❑ Difficult infant temperament

Women and rumination

Finally, I would like to offer some thoughts for moms reading this who may be feeling sad or blue, even years after having their first child. There is little doubt that certain depressive disorders (e.g., manic, bipolar, etc.) have biomedical and hormonal components that are more difficult to treat and may require medication. However, the vast majority of standard depression and anxiety, especially for women, could be dramatically improved by changing our habits of thought.

Why do women have depression rates twice that of men? When I first explored this question, I naturally assumed "Well, there are probably hormonal causes with a little bit of oppression and work-life conflict thrown in the mix." Yet study after study has discounted my theories. Work-life conflict? Well, women who work outside the home are actually less depressed than stay-at-home moms. Hormonal imbalances? It turns out hormones are a factor during critical periods, such as pregnancy and menopause, but on average, they do not account for a two-to-one difference. Oppression due to gender roles, less money, and less appealing jobs? Not really. Rich women are twice as likely to be depressed as rich men, and unemployed women are twice as likely to be depressed as unemployed men. Also, men are more likely to be stressed from work than women, yet time wise, work takes up a larger proportion of a woman's day than anything else (other than sleeping). So why do we women suffer so much more?

The answer might be summed up in one word: rumination. Derived from the Latin for "chewing cud" (the process in which a cow chews, swallows, regurgitates, and then re-chews its own food), rumination implies that how women think about problems tends to amplify them. Ruminating, or immersing oneself in negative thoughts like a cow chewing cud and then linking those thoughts back to some unchangeable aspect of oneself, is a recipe for disaster, or at least the blues. Susan Nolen-Hoeksema of Stanford University originated the rumination theory and has spent her life confirming that men do not typically ruminate as women do. In one study, men and women were offered a choice of two tasks when they were sad: make a list of ten words describing their mood (a task focusing on the depressive episode) or rank a list of countries in order of their wealth (a distracting task). Seventy percent of the women chose the ruminating task, describing their feelings and mood, while the reverse percentages were selected by the men.[52] Millions of mental health dollars have supported the idea that if men and women could stop ruminating and explain bumps in the road to themselves in a different light, depression could be lifted for many.

Motherhood and Isolation

During pregnancy I was inundated with stories about the joys of motherhood, and they were mostly true. However, no one told me that I would be so lonely.

Think about these contributors to loneliness and check all that may apply:

- ❑ You have just moved to a new town or a new neighborhood.
- ❑ Your spouse or partner works long hours, travels for work, or deploys for long periods of time in the military.
- ❑ Your family lives far away.
- ❑ You are a single mom.
- ❑ Your friendships have changed now that baby is here.
- ❑ Your friends without kids visited you in the first few weeks. However, now it is hard to find time to get together.
- ❑ Your best friend is still single, or struggling with infertility, and now she is struggling to be your closest friend.
- ❑ Intimacy with your spouse is different, and you are not really in the mood for sex.
- ❑ Your spouse is still acting like a child, even though he now has a child.
- ❑ You are feeling let down by life as a stay-at-home mom.
- ❑ You are on maternity leave for the first time, and you crave adult interaction.
- ❑ Your boss and team at work are treating you like you are a million miles away, and your reputation has been diminished just for having a child.

- ❑ You just had twins or multiples, and the care routine is never ending. Getting out of the house is not worth the hassle.
- ❑ Your baby was born prematurely, and you can't take her out and expose her to germs for two to three months.
- ❑ You tend to avoid people when you don't feel good about yourself due to weight gain and other insecurities.
- ❑ You feel ashamed that you are depressed and lonely, and you are not in the mood to be around others.

Whatever your circumstances, introversion, introspection, and even periods of loneliness are okay. However, there are ways to get ashore from your island. For some, going back to work may be the best outlet for reestablishing community. For work-from-home moms or stay-at-home moms, coping with the social isolation of motherhood can be a more arduous journey, requiring you to put yourself out there in order to connect with others.

Connecting with others

This applies to dads, too

- ❑ Get out of the house at least once per day.
- ❑ Get up, get dressed, and put on makeup in the morning. You will feel more like getting out if you are prepared to do so.
- ❑ Establish a weekly schedule and assign chores to a specific day, such as laundry on Monday, story time on Tuesday, play group on Wednesday, bathrooms on Thursday, and errands on Friday.
- ❑ Try a child care swap with another parent. Set up a regular schedule (i.e., you can watch Jake for four hours on Wednesdays, and I will watch Sarah at the same time on Thursdays).
- ❑ Find an hourly day care center for days when you need to get things done without interruption.
- ❑ If you have a sitter or nanny while you work from home, use a small portion of that time to socialize and address your personal needs, if possible. Have coffee with a friend or invite a friend to work out. It just might add more to your productivity later.

- ❑ Join a postpartum support group at your local hospital or community center.
- ❑ Join a local play group. Search "mom group Boston" or "play group San Francisco" to find active groups nearby. Meetup.com and TheBump.com can direct you to smaller groups within your area.
- ❑ Join a local listserv, or web-based parenting community. Here are some of the larger listserv parent groups across the country. Search your local address for smaller groups.
    - ▸ *San Francisco:* Golden Gate Mother's Group, Parents' Club of Palo Alto and Menlo Park (PAMP)
    - ▸ *Los Angeles:* Peachhead
    - ▸ *San Diego:* San Diego Parent
    - ▸ *Seattle:* Madrona Moms, Green Lake Moms, NE Seattle Moms
    - ▸ *Portland, OR:* Urban Mamas
    - ▸ *Colorado:* Colorado Moms
    - ▸ *Oklahoma City:* Oklahoma City Moms
    - ▸ *Washington DC:* DC Urban Moms and Dads
    - ▸ *Washington DC/NoVA suburbs:* Mothers of North Arlington, DullesMoms
    - ▸ *Philadelphia:* Main Line Parent, Philly Parents' Circle
    - ▸ *Boston:* Garden Moms (Big Tent), Boston Mamas, The Moms Club of South Boston, Somerville Moms
    - ▸ *Brooklyn, NY:* Bococa Parents
    - ▸ *Park Slope and Brooklyn, NY:* Park Slope Parents
    - ▸ *Lower Manhattan, NYC:* Hudson River Park Mothers Group
    - ▸ *Lower East Side, Soho, Chinatown, and downtown, NYC:* Bowery Babes
    - ▸ *Chicago:* Chicago Neighborhood Parent's Network
    - ▸ *Miami:* Moms Miami
    - ▸ *Dallas/Ft Worth:* Dallas/Ft Worth Moms
    - ▸ *Austin:* Austin Mamas
- ❑ If you are a fitness fan, try a new exercise class or invite a friend for a stroller walk.
- ❑ Visit a local gym or YMCA that offers child care.
- ❑ For group weight loss, join Weight Watchers or Jenny Craig.

- ❑ For those exploring faith or looking to connect with their cultural group, consider joining a Bible study with child care, Mothers of Preschoolers (MOPS) group, Mom to Mom group, Jewish moms group, Catholic moms group, Desi moms group, Mocha moms group, Chinese network for moms, etc.
- ❑ Try a community center's or church's parent's day out (PDO) program for a break.
- ❑ Go to your local library for story time.
- ❑ Sign up for a Gymboree or mommy-and-me-type movement and music class.
- ❑ Start a project during naptime and share it with others: put together a scrapbook of your travels, construct a photo album of your baby, or start a blog.
- ❑ Look online for part time work at flexjobs.com or momcorps.com. Contact a non-profit or small start-up to see if you can help part-time, especially if you do not require healthcare coverage and other costly benefits.
- ❑ Start your own home business, sell your crafts on Etsy, and be proud of your work. Don't let anyone belittle you as any type of mom (i.e., a Pinterest mom, competitive crafter, etc).
- ❑ Start selling a product that you like, such as jewelry, makeup, skincare, children's products, etc.
- ❑ Consider taking a night or online class if loved ones can support it.
- ❑ Set aside quality time each day to spend with your child, and you will feel better about your sacrifices.

Motherhood and Weight Gain

I am really sorry to share this news: extra baby weight, or weight gain due to pregnancy, is just one of the many weight-related issues for new mothers.

- ❑ **Watch out for stress eating.** Trying to balance work, personal aspirations, and family is stressful. Sleeping in three-hour increments at night is stressful. Being at home all day with a baby is stressful. Overeating is a common response to stress.
- ❑ **Limit your grazing.** You, too, will find yourself eating like your child—a little bit here and there. Through the dinner hours, you may nosh on some snacks while making baby food, then finish baby's leftovers, then sample ingredients as you cook dinner, then eat your own meal, and then top off the evening with nibbles of something sweet as you clean up the dishes. Oh, dear. The grazing adds up.
- ❑ **Avoid processed foods.** New moms gravitate towards prepared foods because they are low on energy and short on time. There is laundry to fold. The house is a mess. It is more convenient to grab higher-calorie processed foods than to prepare and cook whole foods.
- ❑ **Do not let breastfeeding justify too many extra calories.** I have a theory that breastfeeding moms rationalize too many calories because they have been told repeatedly that they are "working out" by breastfeeding (a myth) and burning 500 extra calories per day. Yet most do not account for the cumulative time spent sedentary

in a chair breastfeeding when they might otherwise be active. If a newborn nurses eight to twelve times a day for twenty to forty-five minutes, a new mom is sitting still for five hours per day! Secondly, it is a natural response to eat more when you think you are burning calories, and 500 calories is less than you think (500 calories = just under one cup of shredded cheddar cheese). Any woman could take that down in a few handfuls.

- ❑ **Know that your body naturally retains fat stores for breastfeeding.** Your body is like a squirrel. Instead of hoarding nuts for winter it stores fatty tissue during pregnancy to support breastfeeding, which can make that last five to ten pounds really difficult to shed.
- ❑ **Find creative ways to exercise.** Head to the gym at night or during your lunch break. Push baby for a long walk after dinner, or work out to a DVD in the morning. You and baby are up early anyway.
- ❑ **Embrace a little vanity.** Motherhood makes you more humble and less vain, and it feels good. The world does not revolve around you, and you are no longer obsessed with your looks. However, a little bit of vanity can be a good thing, promoting healthy eating, exercise, and a wink and a smile when you see yourself in the mirror.
- ❑ **Ask for support.** Tell your husband or partner that you need his support for eating healthy foods and exercising. Establish clear guidelines, such as no bringing snacks to the couch after 8:00 p.m. and no meat-lovers pizza. You need his help to lose weight.

How to Dress Skinnier After Baby

- ❑ **Give me a V for V-Necks.** Show some skin up top. A long V-shape will draw eyes up and away from your midsection, butt, and thighs. V-necks, such as camisoles, sweaters, dresses, cardigans, and tees, are your postpartum friends.
- ❑ **Stick with a single hue.** You don't have to go into mourning wearing all black after baby. Charcoal grey, chocolate brown, and midnight blue can slim your frame, too. Wearing a single color or similar tones with flattering accessories up top can elongate your body.
- ❑ **Wear simple dark jeans** in a straight leg for average body types, or boot cut styles for curvier, pear-shaped figures. Avoid chunky pocket embellishments and low riders.
- ❑ **Bring on the accessories.** Long necklaces can create a narrow line in the center of your body away from hips, while a colorful purse can keep you from looking like a cat burglar in your favorite all-black ensemble. A vibrant scarf may be just what you need at work to conceal a bounteous bust line.
- ❑ **Support the girls properly.** Want to pack on the pounds instantly? Try wearing an ill-fitting bra that pushes your breasts together like two rising Panera Bread loaves, adding extra weight up top. If nursing, look for cleavage-reducing styles that will not constrict milk production.
- ❑ **Match your shoe color to your leg.** In winter, pair black, opaque tights with black boots, or pumps. In summer, wear a beige or nude skin-tone pump or sandal. With jeans, find a denim-colored shoe to extend your leg line.

- ❑ **Wear heels and pointed toe shoes.** Heels push your feet up and off the floor, making you appear taller and your legs longer. A pointed toe creates the same illusion, elongating the line from thigh to toe. Rounded or squared toes make your legs look stumpy.
- ❑ **Wear your hair up.** Up-dos slim the face and accentuate the neckline. Shoulder-length hair can add the look of weight, or bulk, squaring out the face.
- ❑ **Baggy is not better.** Properly fitting clothing is essential. Extra material adds bulk. If you have plateaued with losing baby weight, do not sit around waiting to fit back into your old jeans. Buy clothes that fit you now and make you feel good about yourself.

BABY ON THE GO

Diaper Bag

• • • • • • • • • • • • •

Label your diaper bag with your name and phone number in case it gets lost or left behind. Parents with young children are easily distracted.

Five essentials for the minimalist

- ❑ Wallet
- ❑ Keys
- ❑ Cell phone
- ❑ Diapers/wipes (and a wet bag for cloth diapers)
- ❑ Bottle or sippy cup with formula, breast milk, or water
- ❑ *Epi-Pen, or an epinephrine auto-injector (for treatment of acute allergic reactions), if required

Diaper bag

For daily use:

- ❑ Wallet
- ❑ Keys
- ❑ Cell phone
- ❑ Diapers/wipes (and a wet bag for cloth diapers)
- ❑ Bottle or sippy cup with formula, breast milk, or water

- ❑ Small bottle of hand sanitizer (limit your use of antibacterial products)
- ❑ Small bottle of sunscreen, if season requires
- ❑ Formula dispenser with pre-measured formula, if formula feeding
- ❑ Nursing cover, if breastfeeding
- ❑ Thin burp cloths (1–2)
- ❑ Changing pad (the travel pad that comes with most diaper bags)
- ❑ Change of clothes and socks (in a collapsible, reusable bag)
- ❑ Small plastic bags for dirty diapers (e.g., recycled fruit and veggie bags from the grocery store)
- ❑ Pacifiers (with a cover or in a container)
- ❑ If eating solids, baby food and a spoon or a baby food pouch
- ❑ A collapsible bib
- ❑ Finger-sized snacks (O's cereal, wheat bread pieces, blueberries, puffs, etc.)
- ❑ Small toys
- ❑ Baby books (soft ones that crinkle and have sensory stimulation)
- ❑ Water and snacks for Mom and Dad
- ❑ *Epi-Pen, or an epinephrine auto-injector (for treatment of acute allergic reactions), if required

Car Travel with Baby

Items such as a travel high chair, a nursing pillow, and even a bottle warmer might seem like bulky over-packing at first. However, if you have space in the car, prioritizing all things eating and sleeping may help baby stick to his routine.

Sleeping

- ❑ Pack 'n Play or travel crib
- ❑ Sheets for Pack 'n Play or travel crib (2)
- ❑ Swaddle blankets, or a wearable blanket (1–2)
- ❑ Favorite stuffed animal, lovey, or blanket
- ❑ Thin, light paper books for bedtime stories
- ❑ Baby monitor, if desired
- ❑ iPod and portable speaker, if desired
- ❑ Night light, if desired

Baby clothing

- ❑ Pajamas, shirts, pants, playsuits, shoes, and socks for duration of trip
- ❑ Special clothes for church, holidays, or photos, such as tights, hair bows, shoes, and bow ties
- ❑ Cold weather: coats, jackets, hats, gloves, winter bunting, stroller sack
- ❑ Warm weather: light jacket, sun hat, sun shirt, bathing suit, swim diapers

Diapering

- ❑ Diapers for the duration of your trip (8–12 per day, depending on baby's age)
- ❑ Wipes, at least one large pack for your suitcase and a travel pack for the diaper bag
- ❑ Travel changing pad
- ❑ Diaper cream (expect diaper rashes while traveling, due to distractions and other caregivers changing baby)

Bathing

- ❑ Baby washcloths (2–3)
- ❑ Baby soap or shampoo in a small travel bottle
- ❑ Small bath toys for older babies and toddlers

Health and grooming items

Put in a reusable bag

- ❑ Thermometer
- ❑ Infant pain reliever for older babies (if you bring it, you won't need it)
- ❑ Saline drops and a suction bulb, if desired
- ❑ Nail clippers and files
- ❑ Baby lotion, if desired (in a small travel bottle)
- ❑ Hair brush, if desired
- ❑ Cold weather: lip balm or cream for chapped lips and faces
- ❑ Warm weather: baby sunscreen

Feeding

- ❑ Nursing pillow with slipcover, if desired
- ❑ Burp cloths (3–5, depending on length of stay)
- ❑ Breast pump and accessories, if breastfeeding. Don't forget this item, even if you don't pump much at home. Babies are notoriously

finicky eaters while traveling, and you don't want painful clogged ducts or mastitis to ruin your trip.

- ❑ Formula, if formula feeding
- ❑ Bottles
- ❑ Bottle warmer, if desired
- ❑ Bibs (2)
- ❑ Feeding spoons (2–3)
- ❑ Extra sippy cups
- ❑ Extra pacifiers, if required
- ❑ Booster seat, or travel high chair (if you have room and want to enjoy a meal)

Playing

- ❑ Small toys, such as a favorite hanging toy, spatula, teether, etc.
- ❑ Small tactile books
- ❑ Bouncer seat, if desired (for hands-free hanging out)
- ❑ Front carrier, if desired

Just for mom

- ❑ A regular purse (for outings without baby)
- ❑ Nursing bras (day and night)
- ❑ Nursing pads
- ❑ Nursing cover and nursing friendly clothing

Just for the car

- ❑ See: Diaper Bag Checklist.
- ❑ Small towels, tissues, hand sanitizer, extra diapers, and a bag of wipes that stays in the car for nose wiping, hand cleaning, and messes
- ❑ A small ditty bag of hanging toys, soft books, teething rings, spatulas, and other items for entertaining baby. Swap toys out when baby gets fussy.

- ❑ Small books to read, if there is an additional passenger to read from the back seat
- ❑ A battery pack for pumping milk in the car, if desired
- ❑ A structured, thicker blanket (to be used as a sun shade for the window, changing mat, and blanket for warmth)
- ❑ A DVD player, or iPad, if desired for long trips, especially to occupy older children while baby is sleeping

Car travel considerations

- ❑ Your first road trip with baby will take longer than you expect. Add extra time for unplanned surprises (like diaper leaks and car sickness) and unexpected stops (to comfort inconsolable crying).
- ❑ Try not to push ahead further if you suspect baby has had a bowel movement. Diaper rashes and travel go hand-in-hand, and it is better to change dirty diapers proactively than to arrive at your destination with a rash that will make baby uncomfortable for days.
- ❑ If your baby sleeps well in the car, plan your travel around naptime, or bedtime. Plan gas stops when baby is awake, even if the tank is not empty.
- ❑ If given a choice in routes, select the one with the most highway miles for sleeping.
- ❑ Keep your diaper bag, extra clothing, snacks, bottles/sippy cups, and toy bag accessible when packing the car.
- ❑ Buy or borrow a rear-view baby mirror to check on baby if you are driving a long distance alone.
- ❑ Bring relaxing music or audio books to pass the time for you and help baby sleep.

Air Travel with Baby

To carry on the plane

- ❑ **Diapers.** One for each hour in transit, plus extras in case of delays
- ❑ **Wipes.** A large travel pack for diaper changes and food-covered hands and mouths
- ❑ **Diaper rash cream.** Babies often get diaper rashes while traveling.
- ❑ **Diaper changing travel pad.** Use these for public changes. Airplane lavatory tables that fold down from the wall are tiny and probably haven't been cleaned in months; they're cold, too.
- ❑ **Small reusable wet bags or Ziploc-type plastic bags.** A must-have for soiled clothes, sticky feeding spoons, and other wet or dirty items.
- ❑ **Sanitizing wipes.** Use sanitizing wipes to clean the area around baby, including arm rests and tray tables, especially if traveling September through March (80% of colds occur during this time). If traveling alone, or with an older sibling, you will have to do this step once baby is seated on your lap.
- ❑ **Small bottles of hand sanitizer.** Airports are a place where antibacterial use makes sense. I suggest alcohol and fragrance-free brands for babies.
- ❑ **Blankets.** Bring two thin receiving blankets for multiple uses: to lay baby on the seat, cover baby, cover yourself while nursing, shade baby from sunlight, or use as a play mat during long layovers.
- ❑ **Washcloths.** Bring two for hand and face-washing.
- ❑ **Tissues.** Children have runny noses year round, and pressure changes may trigger the sniffles. Grab several paper towels and tissues on

your first visit to the lavatory and add them to the back of the seat pockets for spills, spit-up, and runny noses.

- ❑ **Extra pacifiers.** Air travel is not the time to fret about excessive pacifier use. Bring extras.
- ❑ **Something old, something new.** Bring familiar small toys, thin paper books, and a soft lovey or stuffed animal that feels like home, plus new inexpensive toys to distract baby with novelty items.
- ❑ **Air travel toys.**

  Toy suggestions for younger babies:

  - ▸ A colorful hanging toy with arms to chew, such as Freddie the Firefly or a Manhattan Toy Whoozit
  - ▸ A favorite noiseless hand-held toy, such as a Manhattan Toy Winkel
  - ▸ A favorite teething toy or spatula, such as Sophie the Giraffe or Baby Banana Bendable Toothbrush
  - ▸ A soft, crinkly book with hanging things to chew and textures to manipulate

  Toy suggestions for older babies and toddlers:

  - ▸ Airplane books, such as *Airplanes* by Byron Barton, *Airport* by Byron Barton, or *Amazing Airplanes* by Tony Mitton and Ant Parker
  - ▸ Finger puppets, or a collapsible hand puppet, such as Elmo, animals, etc.
  - ▸ Small cars or tiny dolls
  - ▸ A roll of colorful tape and paper
  - ▸ Stickers, stickers, and more stickers
  - ▸ Thin paper books to read
  - ▸ My First Touch and Feel Picture Cards by DK Publishing
  - ▸ Silly Putty, or something similar, to keep little hands busy
  - ▸ A travel-size magna doodle
  - ▸ Crayola Color Wonder books with mess-free markers
  - ▸ An iPad or tablet with toddler apps, or a DVD player—don't count on the in-flight entertainment system (the programming is often too mature for the younger crowd)
- ❑ **Clothes, socks, and shoes.** Bring one to three clothing changes, depending on the length of the flight, especially if baby spits up often. Leaks and spills will happen with greater frequency, as baby

Keep It Simple

Ten Favorite Baby and Toddler Apps for Travel

We will discuss 100 reasons why screens are bad for young children later. However, the simplicity of carrying one entertainment device for air travel is undeniable. Here is a list of my favorite baby and toddler apps for travel:

- Scribble
- Baby Sign ASL
- Elmo Loves ABCs
- Bubbles
- Toddler Cards
- Nighty Night
- Peekaboo Barn
- Fish School
- Monkey Preschool Lunchbox
- Endless Alphabet

squirms in your lap, spits up while in motion, or squeezes her food pouch into a spinach-pear food geyser. Put each of baby's outfits into individual bags so that you don't have to hunt for small socks. Better yet, choose pants with feet attached to avoid the sock game altogether.

- ❑ **Formula, water, or juice**. You want to keep baby swallowing during the climb-out and descent phases of the flight. Put pumped breast milk in a bottle to "back-up" breastfeeding babies, as some babies may not do well on the breast due to distractions. You can use water after six months.
- ❑ **Baby food and snacks.** The TSA web site states "Medically required liquids, such as baby formula and food, breast milk and medications are allowed in excess of 3.4 ounces in reasonable quantities for the flight. It is not necessary to place medically required liquids in a zip-top bag. However, you must tell the transportation security officer that you have medically necessary liquids at the beginning of the screening checkpoint process." Check www.tsa.gov for updates.

- ▸ *For younger babies eating solids:* Food pouches are great for travel.
- ▸ *For older babies sitting up*: puffs, yogurt melts, Cheerios, or anything to get your child chewing during cabin pressure changes.
- ▸ *For toddlers*: bags of cut veggies (cucumbers, carrots, red peppers), chilled cut up grapes, pretzels, raisins, peanut butter crackers, apple wedges dipped in lemon juice, and hard boiled eggs for breakfast. You want non-sugary snacks. No granola bars with chocolate chips; they make a huge mess when held in hot little hands.

- ❑ **Extra bottle or sippy cup**. Pack extras for a long trip.
- ❑ **Breast pump**. Babies can be finicky eaters while traveling, which can lead to clogged ducts. If you have a cross country or international flight, consider putting all things feeding-related into your breast pump bag for convenience as a carry-on.
- ❑ **A travel nursing pillow**. Consider using an inflatable travel nursing pillow for longer flights.
- ❑ **Baby saline nose solution and a suction bulb, if baby has a cold**. Prevent leaks by packing medicines and toiletries in reusable toiletry bags or plastic bags.
- ❑ **Sling or front carrier**. This is great for hands-free boarding after your stroller is gate-checked, especially if you are traveling alone with baby. Younger babies may also enjoy staying warm and cozy in a sling while you are sitting in the seat.
- ❑ **Car seat**. Many parents check car seats in with their checked luggage, and there is no extra charge, although the handling can be rough. Cover car seats with a travel bag and place an address tag on the bag handle, or bring your car seat on board for safety.
- ❑ **Collapsible stroller**. Use an inexpensive yet sturdy umbrella stroller for longer trips that do not require a lot of stroller use at your destination. However, for a trip to a city with walking as your main mode of transportation, bring your favorite stroller. Just make sure to cover it with a travel bag with the wheels strapped down inside. Pick up a gate check stroller tag at the desk just prior to boarding.
- ❑ **Snacks and an empty water bottle for you**. If traveling alone with baby, you may not have time for a food stop during a short layover.

Avoid dehydration and cries for a drink by filling water bottles after security and prior to boarding.

- ❑ **Extra shirt for you**. Baby's inner ear is extremely sensitive and enduring a long flight with spit up or vomit on your shirt is no fun. Trust me.
- ❑ **Use mesh packing cubes or ditty bags, if you travel often.** We use Rick Steves' mesh packing cubes and small camping bags. The see-through bags keep items separate, yet together inside of a bigger bag. The ditty bags help gather toys and small items as they are used in the airplane seat.
- ❑ **Cell phone and charger**. Don't get distracted, leaving it plugged in at the airport or on a seat during a layover.
- ❑ **Headphones**. If you need these for a DVD player or iPad, make sure they are kid-friendly. Many babies and toddlers will pull headphones off, or out of their ears, and then fuss because they can't hear. Don't bother with earbud headphones that have thin, rubbery covers. Your child will toss them on the floor and then try to eat them.
- ❑ **Diaper bag**. I prefer to transfer my diaper bag into a rolling carry-on backpack because it hurts my back to carry a child on one arm and a shoulder bag on the other. When traveling alone with the kids, I roll my "everything bag" with one hand and push the stroller with the other.
- ❑ **Special treats**. These include emergency items that can be brought out for catastrophic meltdowns: cookies, stickers, a new toy, a special movie, and my favorite air travel treat for cabin pressure changes–lollipops. YumEarth Organics make lollipops with no artificial colors and real fruit extracts.
- ❑ *__Epi-Pen__, or epinephrine auto-injector, for treatment of acute allergic reactions, if required.

Air travel considerations

Infant ticket or no ticket?

Many travel guides suggest that you buy a separate seat for your infant, and some airlines will offer a discounted rate. However, why not take advantage of a free seat? I do suggest that you try to make friends with airline employees and request a seat change for a full row, if the plane is not full. If this doesn't work, wait until you have boarded the plane. Introduce your child to the flight attendants and ask someone to switch seats, if a good trade is available. Book an aisle seat, if you are alone with a lap infant so that you can get up more easily for diaper changes and walks down the aisle (you cannot have two infants in your lap.) Car seats and boosters must be placed in window seats, since passengers cannot climb over a car seat to exit a row for safety reasons. A bulkhead seat can help prevent active babies and toddlers from pulling down tray tables and kicking the seat in front of them. Bring a birth certificate if there is any doubt that your child is under age two. All children, regardless of age, must have their own passport for international air travel.

What about turbulence?

This is a valid concern. The best way to protect an infant or toddler in turbulence is to bring a car seat and secure it in a separately purchased seat. Toddlers who meet the weight minimum of 22 pounds can use an FAA-approved restraint system, such as CARES. If an infant is in your lap during turbulence, make sure that you hold her upright (to avoid hitting her head on the arm rests), preferably with your infant facing you and your hands protecting her head.

When to plan your flight?

Flights earlier in the day are less likely to be delayed. With a younger baby, you might consider booking a flight during sleepy times—a red-eye international flight may not be so bad if baby sleeps most of the way. With toddlers and preschoolers, I would suggest morning flights, if possible. If you must schedule a layover with baby, don't make it a rushed one. You will have to wait for your stroller leaving the first plane, transit, possibly feed and change baby, and then check your stroller back in at the next gate. Always leave extra time when traveling with children.

How to prepare?

Prepare children for air travel by involving them in the trip planning, including babies. Before your trip, read books about airplanes. Visit a local airport and teach them about flight. A nine-to-twelve-month-old can go "Whoosh!" with his hand in the air and get excited about flying. If you anticipate a long layover, check the airport diagram for any children's play areas.

Car seat, or no car seat?

If you need a car seat at your destination, you have three options: check it in with your checked baggage (at no charge for lap infants), check it in at the gate (to avoid rough handling), or have baby use her car seat while sitting in a paid seat. We always look for creative ways to obtain a car seat at our destination to avoid the extra hassle at the airport—by adding car seats to rental car purchases or borrowing seats from family and friends.

What to wear?

Dress comfortably; however, that doesn't mean that you should roll the kids out of bed wearing house pants and slippers. People are more likely to be helpful if you and your children are dressed respectably.

What must go through security?

Your baby carrier and other items, such as a folded stroller, car seats, and baby's favorite stuffed animal must pass through security.

When to board?

If there are two caregivers, you might consider sending one aboard early to ensure plenty of room for your carry-on luggage, wipe down the area with sanitizing wipes (especially for a young baby) and set up for takeoff (placing snacks, books, and sippy cups in the seat pockets for the climb out), while the other adult stays back at the gate. Babies and toddlers will appreciate the extra time to crawl, walk, play, and explore the airport, as a young child should not be expected to sit for hours without needing to move around. If parenting solo, I would board early to set up and get everyone comfortable with his or her surroundings.

To breastfeed on board, or not?

Everyone wants to see a woman's breasts until they're feeding a baby, and then it's indecent, right? This topic seems to make the nightly news at least once a year as a flight attendant is blasted for asking a mom to cover up while breastfeeding. After reading several airline policies, it seems that most are supportive of breastfeeding during flight. However, some ask for "discretion and a sense of modesty" to keep passengers in the close confines of the plane comfortable. I recommend a nursing cover and your easiest access nursing shirt to make this a non-issue.

Taxi, or no taxi?

When traveling to taxi-friendly cities you ideally want to have a car seat. A seat belt can restrain an infant carrier quickly and easily. However, if you are not traveling with a car seat at all, it is within the law to ride in a taxi with a child on your lap at your own risk (e.g., In New York, "liveries, taxis, and public transportation buses are exempt from the occupant restraint law"). It is generally accepted that a child, regardless of size, is better off wearing an oversized seat belt than being held in a parent's arms. Never put a seat belt over you and a small child. Expect that a front carrier with a baby will break and detach easily, even in a low-speed crash. If you are traveling in NYC, Philadelphia, or Washington DC, try Uber Family, which offers car seats in Uber vehicles.

Products for Frequent Travelers

When selecting travel gear for children, prioritize the items that can be used for several years over items used just for baby.

Travel gear

Car seat and stroller gear

- ❑ **J.L. Childress Gate Check Bag for Car Seats** *($16)*. If you are checking your car seat at the gate, this bag provides inexpensive grease protection. If you are checking your car seat as luggage and want a thicker bag with great reviews, try the **J.L. Childress Ultimate Car Seat Travel Bag** *($45)* or the **J.L. Childress Wheelie Car Seat Travel Bag** *($45)*, which rolls on two small wheels.
- ❑ **J.L. Childress Gate Check Bags for Strollers** *($14–18)*. The umbrella size is for compact umbrella strollers, and the standard/double size is for larger single or double strollers. The bag's bright red color should help call attention to your gate-checked stroller during baggage handling. If you are planning to check your stroller into checked baggage, you may want to purchase a more durable bag such as the **J.L. Childress Standard & Dual Stroller Travel Bag** ($35).
- ❑ **Traveling Toddler Car Seat Travel Accessory** *($14)*. This inexpensive strap attaches your car seat to a carry-on suitcase, creating a rolling stroller/suitcase combo for parents who would otherwise

have to drag a car seat through the airport. Some parents do this with the car seat straps themselves. For parents concerned about straining their luggage with straps, try the **GoGo Kidz Travelmate** *($75–90)*, which sits your car seat on a small rolling platform.

- ❑ **Travel stroller.** If you travel often, you will want a compact, lightweight stroller that can handle rough baggage handling.
  - ▶ *Best inexpensive umbrella stroller:* **Babies R Us** *($20)* and **Cosco** *($20)* umbrella strollers are solid inexpensive options for occasional travelers.
  - ▶ *Best lightweight multi-purpose stroller:* **UPPAbaby G-LITE Stroller** *($160–180)*. Weighing 11 pounds, it is one of the lightest and most durable full-size strollers on the market. If you desire a full recline, try the **UPPAbaby G-LUXE**.
  - ▶ *Best travel system for travel pros:* **Mountain Buggy Nano** *($200)* is a light, compact travel system at 13 pounds. The stroller folds into its own satchel that fits in an overhead compartment. It also doesn't require adapters for many popular infant seats and can be used up to 44 pounds, or approximately four years of age.

  - ▶ *Most innovative travel stroller:* The **Doona Car Seat** *($500)* is the world's first age 0+ infant car seat with integrated wheels (the wheels literally pop out of the bottom of the seat.) Certified as both a car seat and stroller, Doona is great for travel in a taxi or your own car with no need to carry a heavy seat or place it in a separate stroller or frame.

Safety gear

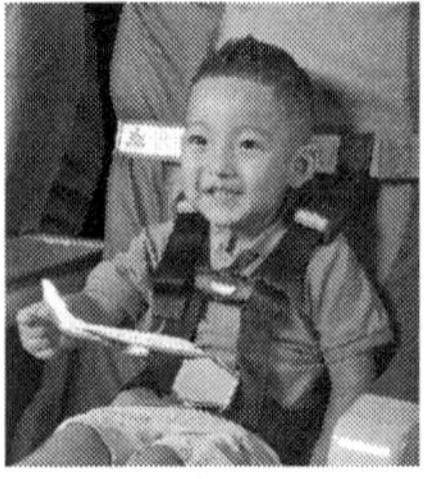

- ❑ **Kids Fly Safe CARES (Child Aviation Restraint System) Airplane Safety Harness for Children** *($75)*. If you fly often, you may want this product for your toddler. CARES is the only harness-type child aviation safety restraint certified for travel by the FAA; it also weighs one pound and fits in a small purse. The CARES system is a belt and buckle device for kids 22–44 pounds that creates a safe airplane seat for your child without the hassle of carrying a 20-pound car seat.

- ❑ **Toddler safety harness and leash.** You may have reservations about putting your toddler on a leash, until he dashes away from you in the security line or airport check-in. **Skip Hop** *($16)* and **BRICA** *($15)* make safety harness backpacks with a removable leash, while the **Eddie Bauer Harness Buddy** *($12)* is a softer stuffed animal backpack.
- ❑ **Child photo ID cards.** Child ID cards are a great way for parents, grandparents, nannies, and babysitters to always have a child's personal information on hand while traveling in case of emergency. These can be made at home or ordered online as plastic ID cards or as stickers for shoes, clothes, car seats, bags, etc.

Packing gear

- ❑ **Rick Steves' packing cubes** *($18)*. These see-through mesh packing cubes are terrific for carrying baby's clothing. Keep tiny socks together and organize your suitcase into separate compartments for quick, targeted access.
- ❑ **Ditty bags, or small nylon camping bags.** Control your own personal yard sale on the plane. These little bags are great for bundling up toys, washcloths, blankets, or any other items that you would like to keep handy in the seat with you. Ditty bags can be found with camping equipment or travel gear in most major stores.
- ❑ **The BityBean Ultra Compact Child Carrier** *($60)*. The eight ounce Bitybean looks like an Ergobaby carrier. Yet it is cleverly engineered to collapse to a size smaller than a water bottle, fitting into any purse, diaper bag, or backpack.

Sleeping on the go

- ❑ **Baby Bjorn Travel Crib Light** *($250)*. This travel crib weighs 13 pounds and folds out in one easy motion. Beware: pricing for this product varies by $70 on popular web sites, and it is priced high

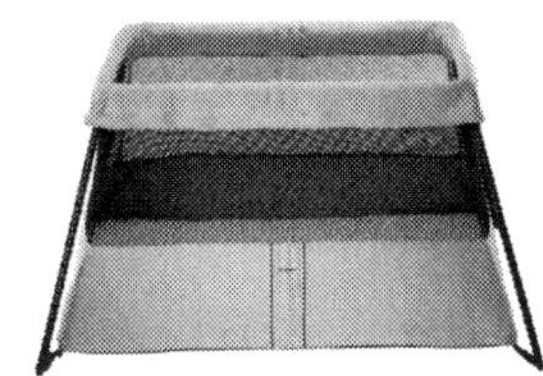

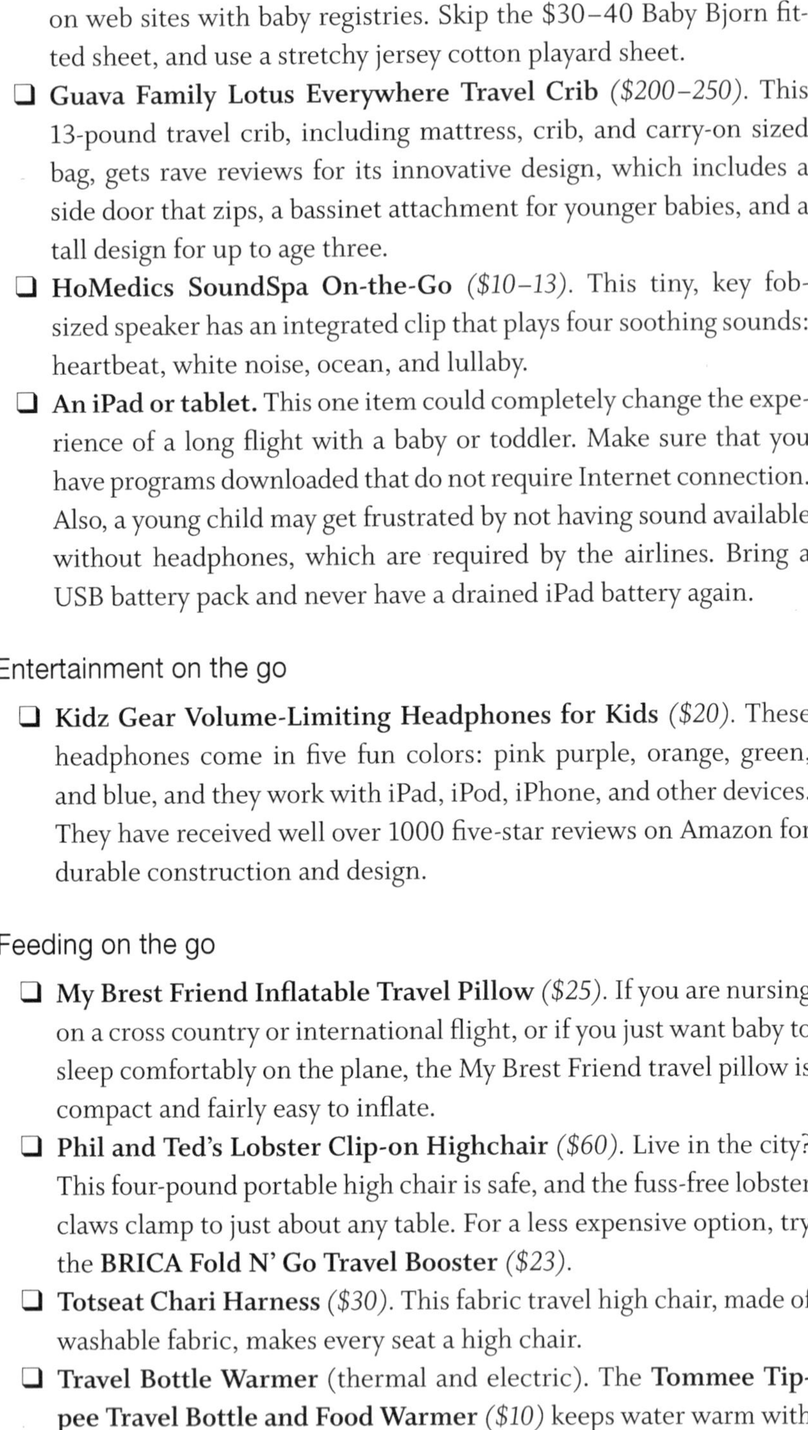

on web sites with baby registries. Skip the $30–40 Baby Bjorn fitted sheet, and use a stretchy jersey cotton playard sheet.

- ❑ **Guava Family Lotus Everywhere Travel Crib** *($200–250)*. This 13-pound travel crib, including mattress, crib, and carry-on sized bag, gets rave reviews for its innovative design, which includes a side door that zips, a bassinet attachment for younger babies, and a tall design for up to age three.
- ❑ **HoMedics SoundSpa On-the-Go** *($10–13)*. This tiny, key fob-sized speaker has an integrated clip that plays four soothing sounds: heartbeat, white noise, ocean, and lullaby.
- ❑ **An iPad or tablet.** This one item could completely change the experience of a long flight with a baby or toddler. Make sure that you have programs downloaded that do not require Internet connection. Also, a young child may get frustrated by not having sound available without headphones, which are required by the airlines. Bring a USB battery pack and never have a drained iPad battery again.

Entertainment on the go

- ❑ **Kidz Gear Volume-Limiting Headphones for Kids** *($20)*. These headphones come in five fun colors: pink purple, orange, green, and blue, and they work with iPad, iPod, iPhone, and other devices. They have received well over 1000 five-star reviews on Amazon for durable construction and design.

Feeding on the go

- ❑ **My Brest Friend Inflatable Travel Pillow** *($25)*. If you are nursing on a cross country or international flight, or if you just want baby to sleep comfortably on the plane, the My Brest Friend travel pillow is compact and fairly easy to inflate.
- ❑ **Phil and Ted's Lobster Clip-on Highchair** *($60)*. Live in the city? This four-pound portable high chair is safe, and the fuss-free lobster claws clamp to just about any table. For a less expensive option, try the **BRICA Fold N' Go Travel Booster** *($23)*.
- ❑ **Totseat Chari Harness** *($30)*. This fabric travel high chair, made of washable fabric, makes every seat a high chair.
- ❑ **Travel Bottle Warmer** (thermal and electric). The **Tommee Tippee Travel Bottle and Food Warmer** *($10)* keeps water warm with

no electricity needed. For car trips, try the **Munchkin Travel Bottle Warmer** *($23)*.

- ❑ **Summer Infant TinyDiner Placemat** *($14)*. For parents who like to eat out, I cannot say enough about this placemat. It folds up into a small cylinder shape, washes easily, catches stray food, suctions to any table, and provides a great eating surface for children.

- ❑ **Neat Solutions Neat-Ware Table Toppers** *($8–16)*. These disposable travel place mats come in 10- to 60-count bags.
- ❑ **BooginHead SippiGrip** *($8)*. This small Velcro strap ties around a sippy cup and attaches the cup to a stroller or high chair. No more games of pick up.

Baby equipment rental companies

For a directory of baby equipment rental companies by state and country, visit www.baby-equipment-rental.com. These companies rent strollers, car seats, swings, high chairs, security gates, and more.

- ❑ **Baby's Away.** This is the largest baby and child equipment rental company in the U.S. Enter your location to receive a product list with pricing.
- ❑ **Travel BaBees.** This national baby equipment rental company has franchises from coast to coast. Travel BaBees will drop-off and pickup all equipment. Check Yelp for the franchisee's local reputation, as quality varies region to region.

HEALTH, SAFETY, AND LIFESTYLE

Autism Awareness

The goal of this section is to address major topics that parents care deeply about but might not have time to research. Please note, many of these lists contain informational items to check off and put in your parenting tool box, but do not necessarily need to be added to any to-do list. Get ready! We're about to embark on a crash course of some of today's most complex and controversial parenting hot topics.

The exact number of children with autism is unknown. However, when I was born, autism affected 1 in 5000 children in the U.S. In 2014, that number surged to 1 in 68, a massive increase in one generation and a 30% rise from the official estimate just two years earlier.[62, 63]

What is autism?
What is autism spectrum disorder (ASD)?

Autism and Autism Spectrum Disorder (ASD) are general terms for a complex developmental disorder that affects the brain's social, behavioral, and communication skills. It is a physical condition linked to abnormal biology and brain chemistry, and it typically appears during the first three years of life. The characteristic traits of autism are repetitive behaviors and impaired social-emotional interaction. Each ASD case is different: 25% of people with ASD are nonverbal (learning to communicate in other ways), while roughly 40% have average to above-average intellectual abilities. Many people on the spectrum take pride in their "atypical" view of the world and some exhibit exceptional abilities in music, math, or academics.

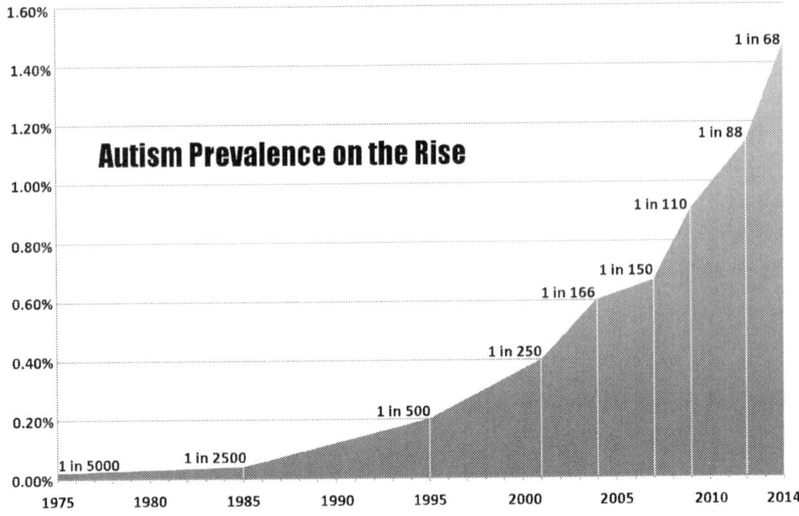

Source: Autism Speaks, CDC.

How common is autism?

In 2014, about 1 in 68 children were identified with autism spectrum disorder (1 in 42 boys and 1 in 189 girls). In 2012, 1 in 88 children were identified as on the spectrum—a tenfold increase over the last 40 years with boys nearly five times more likely to be diagnosed with ASD than girls. ASD is reported across all racial, ethnic, and socioeconomic groups.

Tracking autism over time has shown distinct challenges:

- The nature of the disorder is extremely complex.
- There are no specific biological markers for autism.
- Reporting and diagnostic tools for ASDs have changed over time.[62]

Signs of autism

Autism spectrum disorders (ASDs) can range in intensity from very mild to severe, affecting individuals in different ways. Some children with an ASD may show hints of future developmental delay within the first few months of life; however, the most obvious signs of autism tend to appear between 18 months and three years old. Most pediatricians will use a formal screening tool or checklist for autism when your child is 18 and 24 months old.[63, 64]

A child with an ASD might...

- ❑ Not respond to their name by 12 months
- ❑ Not point at objects to show interest (point at an airplane flying over) by 14 months
- ❑ Not play "pretend" games (pretend to feed a doll) by 18 months
- ❑ Avoid eye contact and want to be alone
- ❑ Not look at objects when another person points at them
- ❑ Have trouble understanding other people's feelings or talking about their own feelings
- ❑ Have delayed speech and language skills
- ❑ Prefer not to be held or cuddled or might cuddle only when they want
- ❑ Repeat words or phrases over and over (echolalia)
- ❑ Give unrelated answers to questions
- ❑ Get upset by minor changes
- ❑ Have trouble adapting when a routine changes
- ❑ Have obsessive interests in single subjects (like cars or trains)
- ❑ Flap their hands, rock their body, or spin in circles
- ❑ Have unusual reactions to the way things sound, smell, taste, look, or feel
- ❑ Lose skills they once had (for instance, stop saying words they were using previously)
- ❑ Have chronic bowel or gastrointestinal issues, such as diarrhea or chronic constipation. Up to 80% of children with ASDs have gastrointestinal (GI) abnormalities.

What if I think my child has an ASD?

- ❑ If you suspect a problem, talk with your child's doctor and ask for a developmental screening. Early detection is linked to better outcomes for children with an ASD. Your doctor may refer you to a multidisciplinary team for further evaluations. The following professionals can give a diagnosis of autism: developmental pediatrician, child psychiatrist, child psychologist, or pediatric neurologist.

- [ ] Contact your local Early Intervention (EI) agency for children under three years old, or public school system for children three years and older. Currently the main research-based treatment for an ASD is intensive structured teaching of skills, often called behavioral intervention or behavior analysis. It is important to begin this intervention as early as possible in order to help a child reach his or her full potential.

What causes autism?

Autism has no single cause. However, it is likely that both genetics and environmental factors play a role. Within the last five years, scientists have identified a number of gene mutations or irregular segments of genetic code linked to autism. Research indicates that the majority of genetic risk for autism comes from common gene variants rather than from spontaneous gene mutations (which make up a very small number of cases). Further understanding the genetic risk for autism can lead to a better understanding of the molecular roots of the disorder.[65]

Other studies of autism show abnormalities in the brain that likely occurred as a disruption during early fetal brain development, possibly due to environmental influences. The study of epigenetics describes how environmental factors affect certain genes, altering gene expression without changing the underlying DNA. Several studies on identical twins have supported that gene-environment mechanisms are likely at play, since identical twins sharing exact DNA show varying levels of ASD severity. To note, the term "environmental factors linked to autism" covers a multitude of influences outside of a child's inherited genes, ranging from chemical exposure to other factors, such as premature birth and low birth weight. Finally, while scientists do see commonalities among ASD cases, they do not yet fully understand how all of the pieces—genetic, immunologic, nutritional, and environmental—fit together in the autism puzzle.[66, 67]

Genetic vulnerability

No one gene causes autism, and many people with ASD have no reported family history of autism. However, twin and family studies suggest that most individuals have a genetic predisposition to autism.

- Identical twin studies show that if one twin is affected by autism, there is a 60% to 90% chance that the other twin will be affected.[63]
- Parents from families with autistic members are more likely to have autistic children, and families with one autistic child have a 3% to 14% greater chance of having another autistic child, a greater percentage chance than the population at large.
- The California Autism Twins Study (CATS), the largest study of twins with ASDs, found that when one identical twin develops autism, the chance of the other twin developing the disorder is 70%, while fraternal twins overlapped by a surprising 35% (significantly higher than the 3% to 14% for different age siblings). This provides evidence to support the claim that genes and certain environmental influences, especially those shared in the womb or shortly after birth, are likely at play.[68]
- Autism also tends to occur more frequently than expected among individuals who have certain medical conditions, including Fragile X syndrome, tuberous sclerosis, congenital rubella syndrome, and untreated phenylketonuria (PKU).

Environmental factors

The rapid rise in autism over the last twenty years cannot be linked solely to genetics. The human genome does not change that rapidly. Gene-environment interactions are likely happening:

- Some risk factors more closely associated with autism are:
  - ▸ Toxins ingested during early pregnancy
  - ▸ Infection during pregnancy
  - ▸ Maternal diabetes
  - ▸ Birth complications, especially those involving oxygen deprivation to the brain

- Other factors under investigation include:
  - Advanced parental age [69, 70]
  - Premature birth and low birth weight [71, 72]
  - Pesticide exposure during pregnancy [73]
  - Pharmaceuticals taken during pregnancy [74]
  - Proximity to a freeway [75]
  - Limited prenatal vitamin intake [76]
  - Radio waves from cell phones (low frequency cell phone signals are harmful to cell function allowing heavy metal toxins to build up)[77]
  - Increased surveillance and broadening of the ASD definition [78, 79]
- Scientists are looking closely at environmental exposures during pregnancy and shortly after birth. Children with autism may have particular vulnerabilities and metabolic impairment at this time that reduces the ability to process and rid the body of toxins.
- Some of the most powerful evidence for environmental factors causing autism is derived from studies of specific prenatal exposures: thalidomide, misoprostol, and valproic acid; maternal rubella infection; and the organophosphate insecticide chlorpyrifos.[74]
- In another study, analysis of brain tissue from ten out of eleven children, who died and also happened to have autism, found that ASD was likely to have originated before birth. This conclusion was based on a disruption of tissues in the cortex areas that likely occurred during early brain formation (from three to five weeks after conception to the second trimester) when brain cells specialize and move into their correct positions in the cerebral cortex.[80] These types of studies, including those with small sample sets, are particularly illuminating since scientists can look at the autistic brain on a cellular level.
- Finally, it is very possible there are undiscovered environmental causes of autism.

Toxins Suspected of Causing Autism, ADHD, and Other Neurodevelopment Disabilities (NDDs)

Autism, ADHD, and other neurodevelopment disabilities (NDDs) affect about 10% to 15% of births. It is estimated that one-third of those cases are attributed to genetics, while environmental factors, including toxic chemicals, are linked to the remaining 60% to 70%.[81] Although it is difficult to prove a cause-effect relationship between a single chemical and a disorder (since so many chemicals are used and ingested in combination with one another), experts have nailed down the major culprits.

However, before we proceed into another science-heavy discussion, I would like to help set the stage for this checklist. From the moment I started writing these books, I have struggled with how to present the material. My goal is not to dilute vital information, but with an estimated average 8th- to 9th- grade reading level for American adults, any discussion with fifteen letter words is going to make 99% of us tune out. I have been reading about these toxins for years, and nearly every chemical pamphlet and fact sheet is written over my head.

Yet this checklist ranks near the top of "all things modern parents should know," and the long names of these chemicals must be listed so that we know what to avoid. So please bear with me. I cannot change the fact that the elements of the periodic table were named after Russian scientists, Greek names for astronomical objects, and cities around the world, but I can help you cut down your chemical exposure by explaining where to find it and how to avoid it. Here are the top chemicals suspected

Keep It Simple

Environmental Toxins: The Worst Offenders

People often ask me, "What are the top three or four things causing autism in the environment?" To focus on the worst of the worst neurotoxins, avoid or minimize your exposure to:

- Lead
- Mercury
- Pesticides
- Endocrine-disrupting chemicals, such as BPA and phthalates

of causing autism, ADHD, and NDDs from the experts at The Mount Sinai Children's Environmental Health Center, with the support of the National Institute of Environmental Health Sciences and Autism Speaks. This list has been expanded to include action items, simpler language, and other supporting research.[82, 83]

❑ **Lead**

- ▸ *What is it?* Lead is a heavy metal and powerful neurotoxin that causes brain damage in developing babies.
- ▸ *Where do we find it?* Lead can be found in the paint in homes, buildings, and day care centers built before 1978 and in old plumbing. Lead dust is the number one cause of lead poisoning, and it is not always visible to the human eye. Babies and young children get exposed to lead when they put something with lead dust into their mouths.[84]
- ▸ *How do I avoid or minimize it?* Do not sand, paint, or renovate an old home while pregnant. Consider lead testing if your home was built before 1978. Do a thorough cleanup after all remodeling projects with wet mops, wet cloths, and

a HEPA vacuum (a high-efficiency air filter removes very fine particles from the air that pass through the filter.) Use a dust sampling kit to test for lead dust after the cleanup. Drink filtered water if you are concerned about lead leaching from older pipes. Limit shopping at bargain stores, such as a dollar-type store, for baby toys. Researchers note that bargain stores have the highest amounts of lead and arsenic in their toys and toy jewelry.[85]

❑ **Methylmercury**

- *What is it?* This organic compound is created by coal-powered industrial plants and ends up in our rivers, lakes, and oceans.
- *Where do we find it?* Methylmercury is found in fish and shellfish. A fetus is exposed to mercury in the womb, due to a mother's eating of fish. The developing fetal nervous system is significantly more sensitive to mercury, especially during early pregnancy. Impacts on cognitive thinking, memory, attention, language, and fine motor skills have been seen in children exposed to mercury in the womb.[86]
- *How do I avoid or minimize it?* Avoid seafood with the highest levels of mercury while pregnant and breastfeeding. Avoid handling mercury-containing products, such as thermometers, fluorescent light bulbs, and tilt-switches.

❑ **Polychlorinated biphenyls (PCBs)**

- *What is it?* PCBs are older industrial chemicals used in hundreds of products made before 1979, including electrical products, insulation, adhesives, caulking, paints, carbon copy paper, and engine coolant. The EPA classifies PCBs as probably causing cancer, and they are also linked to endocrine disruption, developmental disabilities, and decreased immune functions.

- *Where do we find it?* PCBs do not break down in the environment. Instead, they filter into the soil and water and slowly build up in animal fat and fish skins and ultimately in us.[87]
- *How do I avoid or minimize it?* PCBs collect in animal fat and fish skins, so trimming these can reduce exposure. Eat wild salmon. Studies show that PCBs can accumulate in farm-raised salmon, due to smaller feed fish full of chemicals. Steer clear of older fluorescent lights with PCBs. Keep young children from touching, peeling, and chewing older caulk in bathrooms and flooring.[88]

❑ **Organophosphate pesticides**

- *What is it?* Many of these pesticides were developed as chemical warfare agents during World War II, so it should be no surprise this group of pesticides is highly toxic. Organophosphate pesticides (OPs) cause a range of problems when children are exposed during pregnancy and in early childhood, such as reduced memory, mental and emotional problems, and higher risk for ADHD. OPs disrupt the nervous system by interfering with an enzyme that controls nerve impulses and acts as an important chemical regulator in the brain.
- *Where do we find it?* We find OPs, such as chlorpyrifos (pronounced klor-PEER-ih-fos), a widely used insecticide in the U.S., on conventional crops (especially cotton, almonds, oranges, and apples), feed crops (especially corn), and in other non-crop settings, such as golf courses, greenhouses, and buildings for structural pest control. OPs are specifically used to control cockroaches and pests in city apartments.
- *How do I avoid or minimize it?* Prioritize organic fruits and vegetables. Eat a variety of fruits and vegetables from different stores and sources. Wash fruits and vegetables under running water and peel away skins. Avoid fruit juice as a regular beverage for children. In homes with pests, clean up food crumbs and seal cracks and crevices as your first

defense before using insect sprays. Childproof all household pest sprays and lawn and garden products.

❑ **Organochlorine pesticides**

- *What is it?* Organochlorine pesticides (OCs) are some of the oldest and most toxic pesticides around. They were first made in the 1940s and 1950s and used widely in agriculture, forestry, and home pest control. Most OC solvents and spray fumigants, such as DDT and chlordane, have been banned in the U.S., due to health and safety concerns; yet they are widely used in developing countries, especially for fighting malaria. Because of their chemical makeup, OCs break down slowly and remain in soil, water, and the fatty tissues of our bodies. Organochlorine pesticides are linked to Parkinson's disease, neurological disorders, birth defects, and abnormal immune function.[89]
- *Where do we find it?* OC remnants can still be found in agricultural storage facilities and the environment. Endosulfan, a DDT-era insecticide banned in 2010 and phasing out until 2016, is one of the last OCs used on fruits and vegetables. The EPA classifies Endosulfan in its most extreme category (highly acutely toxic) because small amounts are lethal in lab studies.[*90]
- *How do I avoid or minimize it?* Prioritize organic fruits and vegetables. Eat a variety of fruits and vegetables. Wash fruits and vegetables under running water and peel away skins. Avoid fruit juice as a regular beverage for children. Do not treat head lice or scabies with lotions and shampoos containing Lindane.

---

* Endosulfan Group E phase out (use ends July 31, 2015): apple, blueberry, peppers, potatoes, pumpkins, sweet corn, tomato, winter squash

* Endosulfan Group F phase out (use ends July 31, 2016): livestock ear tags, pineapple, strawberry (perennial/biennial), vegetable crops for seed (alfalfa, broccoli, Brussels sprouts, cabbage, cauliflower, Chinese cabbage, collard greens, kale, kohlrabi, mustard greens, radish, rutabaga, turnip)

- ❑ **Endocrine disruptors (ECDs), such as phthalates and bisphenol A (BPA)**
  - ▸ *What is it?* ECDs are chemical toxins that act like hormones, tricking the body into over-responding, responding at the wrong time, or blocking natural reactions.
  - ▸ *Where do we find it?* ECDs are found in BPA (food and soda can linings, water bottles, and receipt paper), phthalates (pronounced THAL-ates, which are in plastics, cosmetics, vinyl tile, and air fresheners), and flame retardants (clothing, furniture coverings, computers, and mattresses).[91]
  - ▸ *How do I avoid or minimize it?* Limit the use of canned goods. Always reheat foods in glass, not plastic containers. Avoid plastics, but if you must use them, limit or lose the 3, 6, and 7 recycle symbols, and look for symbols 2, 4, and 5. Be wary of hand-me-down plastic toys, bottles, teethers, and feeding products made before 2009. Buy cosmetics and personal care products with safer ingredients. Avoid air fresheners and products with "fragrance" as an ingredient (phthalates are used to help to stabilize chemicals and make fragrance oils last longer.) Check for use of flame retardants on clothing, furniture, and baby products.

- ❑ **Automotive exhaust**
  - ▸ *What is it?* Vehicle emissions contain volatile organic compounds (VOCs), oxides of nitrogen, and carbon monoxide. While scientists are only beginning to understand the link between motor vehicle exhaust and brain cell development, evidence for a link between auto exhaust and brain disorders is growing.[75]

  - ▸ *Where do we find it?* Exhaust levels are highest next to busy highways or in densely populated areas.
  - ▸ *How do I avoid or minimize it?* Try to avoid living next to a busy highway. One study quantified that having a mother living within 1000 feet of a freeway while pregnant doubles the likelihood of having a child with autism.[75]

- [ ] **Polycyclic aromatic hydrocarbons (PAHs)**
  - *What is it?* PAHs are organic compounds that exist naturally in coal, crude oil, and gasoline. They are released into the air as carcinogens by the incomplete burning of fossil fuels.
  - *Where do we find it?* PAHs are present in fossil fuel products, and PAH levels may be 10 times greater in urban areas than rural areas. Around the home, PAHs are found in burned meat, anti-dandruff shampoos, cigarette smoke, mothballs, and coal-tar driveway sealants.
  - *How do I avoid or minimize it?* Eat less charbroiled meats, avoid cigarette smoke, and use nontoxic alternatives to mothballs, such as cedar chests, vacuuming often, and plant-based deterrents. Remove your shoes before entering your home, especially if you have contact with heavy oils, asphalt, or roofing tar.[92]

- [ ] **Brominated flame retardants (polybrominated diphenyl ethers or PBDEs)**
  - *What is it?* Thanks to heavy lobbying by the tobacco industry in the 1970s, these compounds work to inhibit combustible materials, such as sofas, from igniting. PBDEs are transmitted into our lungs through dust and into our blood through ingestion and skin contact. Mothers participating in research studies have been surprised to learn they had PBDEs in their breast milk. PBDEs are linked to cancer, autism, infertility, and other developmental problems.

  - *Where do we find it?* These chemicals are found in mattresses, furniture foam, motor vehicles, TVs and computers, and coatings on fabrics.[93] In 2011, a study of over 100 widely used baby products found that 80% of them contained flame retardants.[94] PBDE levels have doubled in people every three to five years for the past three decades.
  - *How do I avoid or minimize it?* Throw away ripped items with foam padding inside and watch for PBDE dust when pulling up old carpet. New foam items are not likely to contain

PBDEs; however, foam padding or furniture produced before 2005 should be inspected carefully. Use a vacuum fitted with a HEPA filter to reduce PBDE dust.

- ❑ **Perfluorinated compounds (PFCs)**
  - ▸ *What is it?* PFCs, or non-stick chemicals, are widely used to make products resistant to stains, grease, and water. Teflon and Scotchgard are two of the most recognized brand names of PFCs. PFCs break down very slowly in the environment and bind to organic tissue, including those that make up human blood and the brain. PFCs have been linked to several types of cancer.
  - ▸ *Where do we find it?* We find PFCs in stain-resistant carpets and furniture, grease-resistant food packaging (fast food containers, pizza boxes, and microwave popcorn), non-stick cookware, dental floss, clothing, and shampoo.
  - ▸ *How do I avoid or minimize it?* Check personal care labels for the words "fluoro" or "perfluoro" (dental floss, cosmetics, moisturizers, and eye makeup). When you start seeing scratches in your non-stick or Teflon-coated cookware, replace it with cast iron or untreated stainless steel. Choose clothing, carpeting, and furniture without stain-resistant treatments.[95]

Additional neurotoxins

Dr. Philip Landrigan of Mount Sinai School of Medicine in New York and his colleague, Dr. Philippe Grandjean of the Harvard School of Public Health, have studied industrial chemicals for over thirty years. In 2014, they sounded the alarms on environmental toxins and called for the urgent formation of an international clearinghouse for industrial chemicals to fight the "silent, global pandemic."[81] In their report, the list of ten suspected neurotoxins contributing to autism and ADHD was also updated to include:

- ❑ **Arsenic**
  - ▸ *What is it?* Arsenic occurs naturally in the environment (in rocks, air, soil, and water) and as a by-product of farming

and industrial activities. Arsenic is perhaps less known for its neurological nastiness than as one of the leading environmental causes of cancer deaths in the world. Arsenic has been linked to lung, skin, and bladder cancers, heart disease, stroke, and diabetes. However, it can also interfere with brain development and cause behavioral problems.

- *Where do we find it?* This odorless, tasteless potent poison is found in small amounts in our food and water.
- *How do I avoid or minimize it?* Widespread high concentrations of arsenic are found in the West, Midwest, parts of Texas, and the Northeast. Get your water tested if you drink from a well, especially in New England (Maine to Massachusetts) or the Midwest (Michigan and Minnesota), which are areas with high natural levels of arsenic in rock, or if you live in an area with mining or farming (central valley California, Western states), if you live near metal smelters where metal is made, or if you live near a garbage incinerator. Dr. Landrigan and other groups recommend assessing and limiting rice consumption, especially rice from Gulf Coast areas.[96]

❑ Toluene

- *What is it?* Toluene is a colorless, flammable liquid.
- *Where do we find it?* Toluene is added to gasoline to improve octane ratings. It is also used to produce benzene and other household products and solvents, such as paint, paint thinner, gasoline, rubber cement, nail polish, and detergents. Solvents with toluene attack the nervous system and have been linked to hyperactivity and aggressive behavior.

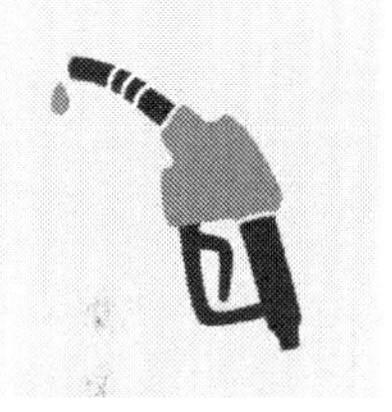

- *How do I avoid or minimize it?* If you smell fumes from these products, leave the room. Don't deliberately sniff it. Avoid exposure in the workplace, such as while printing or painting. Choose non-toxic nail polish.

❑ **Manganese**

- *What is it?* Manganese is a naturally occurring substance that can cause damage to the brain at high levels. Excessive manganese levels are linked with reduced intellectual function (ADHD and IQ reduction) and impaired motor skills (Parkinson's disease).[97, 98]
- *Where do we find it?* Manganese is a normal part of air, water, soil, and food. In small amounts, manganese is essential to keeping your organs, including the brain, healthy. However, high levels can be harmful. Young children are exposed to manganese through diet, including breast milk and formula, and through dust particles in the air and drinking water (soda cans also use manganese to stiffen the aluminum). Vegetarians who consume foods rich in manganese, such as grains, beans, and nuts, and heavy tea drinkers may have higher than normal manganese levels. Manganese inhalation can also be toxic.
- *How do I avoid or minimize it?* Check your well water for manganese levels, especially if you are pregnant. Filter your water. Avoid soy formulas with high manganese levels.[99] Do not feed baby soy or rice milk beverages as a substitute for infant formula.[100] Limit exposure to mining activities, automotive exhaust, and factories with welding or manganese products.

❑ **Fluoride**

- *What is it?* Fluoride compounds are salts that occur when the element fluorine combines with rocks or soil.
- *Where do we find it?* Fluoride is found in toothpaste and drinking water. Although helpful in small doses for dental health, too much fluoride can lead to tooth and bone lesions. An analysis of 27 studies on high levels of fluoride (mostly in China) concluded that high concentrations of fluoride can cause adverse effects on the brain.[101]

- *How do I avoid or minimize it?* Watch fluoride levels in your water. Keep young children from ingesting toothpaste by smearing small amounts on their toothbrush with your finger and keeping tubes out of reach.

❑ Tetrachloroethylene

- *What is it?* This is a chemical used for dry-cleaning and metal degreasing.

- *Where do we find it?* When you bring clothes home from the dry cleaners, tetrachloroethylene (perchloroethylene or PERC) is released in small amounts into the air. It can also be found in drinking water.[102]
- *How do I avoid or minimize it?* Dry-clean your clothes without the use of PERC. If you cannot find a PERC alternative, air out recently dry-cleaned clothes. Avoid living in an apartment directly above a dry-cleaning facility.

Vaccines

• • • • • • • • • •

The childhood vaccination debate exploded in 1998, when a respected global medical journal, *The Lancet*, presented evidence linking the measles, mumps, and rubella vaccine (MMR) to autism. The research, led by Dr. Andrew Wakefield, was based on a study of 12 children. In 2010, *The Lancet* retracted the story, and a multiple-year investigation by the British General Medical Council (the licensing agent of doctors in the UK) indicated that Wakefield manipulated data and provided false evidence while conducting the MMR-autism study. That same year, Wakefield was found guilty of charges of fraud and abuse by the council and was banned from practicing medicine.[103] However, these administrative actions mostly went unnoticed. Pandora's Box had been opened on vaccines.

Numerous studies following the Wakefield controversy concluded that it is unlikely that the MMR vaccine causes autism. During this time, some also suspected that a small amount of ethyl mercury called thimerosal, a common preservative in vaccines (including the flu vaccine), was causing autism and ADHD. Today, the vaccine debate won't go away, and stories linger about thimerosal and CDC data on the MMR vaccine. So what is a parent to do? While I cannot answer that question for individual families, I would like to help educate parents about vaccines.

- ❑ For a simplified explanation of vaccines and the vaccine schedule (See: Appendix D: Vaccines).
- ❑ Download the "CDC Vaccine Schedules" app free for iOS and Android.

Keep It Simple

Vaccine Safety

Most medical professionals believe that the benefits of childhood vaccines far outweigh the risks. I support this position, while remaining skeptical about the effects of vaccines on some children with certain vulnerabilities.

- ❑ Find easy-to-read and easy-to-print vaccine schedules online (e.g., pocket-size, Spanish version, catch-up schedules, etc.) Visit www.cdc.gov/vaccines/schedules/hcp/child-adolescent.html.

The Vaccine Debate

Why I support vaccines for the vast majority of children

- ❑ **Vaccines save lives.** It is estimated that three million children are saved worldwide by vaccinations, and two million die because they are not immunized.[104]
- ❑ **Parents do not understand the risks when they choose not to vaccinate.** Most parents today have never seen a child with paralysis by polio, brain damage caused by measles, or choking to death caused by diphtheria. However, an unvaccinated child who gets a vaccine-preventable disease runs all the risk of that disease, including death. An unimmunized child may also infect other vulnerable groups. If you are in doubt about these diseases and risks, talk to an elderly person who grew up with polio, measles, and other preventable diseases that adversely affected children in previous generations.
- ❑ **Parents do not understand community immunity or herd immunity.** Every disease is a plane ride away, and you cannot depend on others getting vaccinated to keep your unvaccinated child safe. If you choose not to vaccinate your child and your child gets sick,

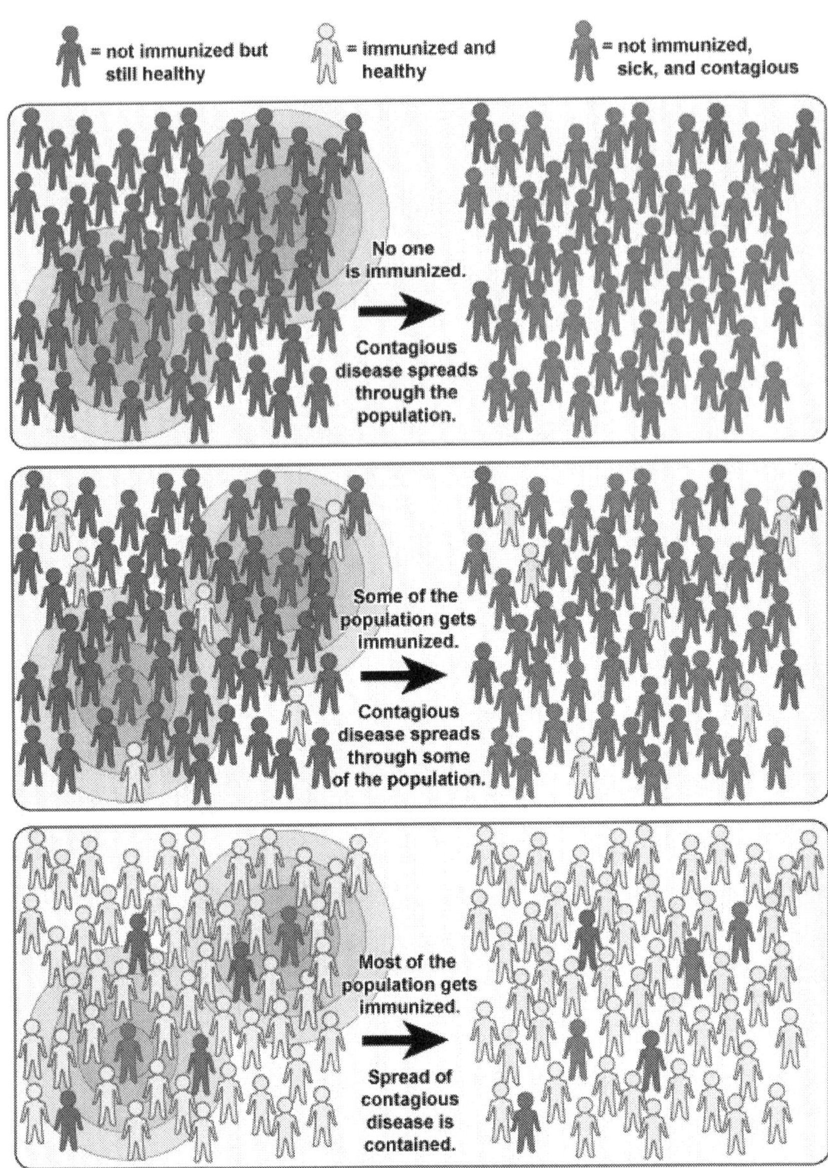

you could also put those who are unable to get vaccinated at risk, such as infants and toddlers who have not completed the vaccine schedule or children with other health issues. Today, certain areas of the country are getting into dangerously low vaccination rates. The state of Colorado has the lowest median vaccination rate at 82.9% of kindergarteners. In 2014, a public school in Malibu, CA, reported that only 58% of its kindergarteners were vaccinated, while in some California private schools, only 1 in 5 children are vaccinated. Consequently, the incidence of whooping cough and other 19th century diseases have risen sharply in those areas.

- ❑ **Autism rates have continued to rise, despite intense vaccine scrutiny.** After the Wakefield scare, Japan banned the MMR triple vaccine, yet autism rates continued to rise.[105] In 1999, thimerosal was removed or reduced to trace amounts from all vaccines given to children in the U.S. under six years old; however, autism rates continued to rise.[106] Questions about thimerosal and the MMR vaccine likely still remain to be answered. However, a large scale, national link between vaccines and autism is highly unlikely. Meanwhile, children are dying from diseases that were thought to be long gone decades ago.
- ❑ **The number of children in the U.S. dying or adversely affected by parents choosing not to vaccinate is undeniable.** One non-profit website, which calculates vaccine-related deaths and illnesses using CDC weekly reports, estimates that nearly 140,000 children were diagnosed with preventable diseases between 2007 and 2014. The number of vaccine preventable deaths of children during that time exceeded 6,200.[107]

Why I am skeptical about vaccines for a small number of children

- ❑ **No medical intervention comes without risk.** Medicines have risk. Care regimes from doctors have risk. Everything we put into our bodies comes with risk.
- ❑ **Inquiries about vaccines and neurological disorders in young children are completely reasonable.** This is a highly vulnerable group, especially children with certain immune, autoimmune, or inflammatory conditions. I do not doubt that a small subset of children has been adversely affected by vaccines and the mercury preservatives in vaccines.
- ❑ **The signs of autism develop at the same time that certain shots are administered.** This does not mean that one causes the other, but it does amplify the need for rigorous scientific study.

Reactions to vaccines

If you notice something unusual about your child's reaction following a vaccination, talk to your doctor immediately. If you believe that a vaccination caused an adverse reaction, a system is in place to hear your case. In 1988, the National Vaccine Injury Compensation Program (NVICP), or "vaccine court," was established to stabilize the vaccine industry and provide a forum for individuals found to be injured by vaccines. Monetary rewards are funded by a trust fund of excise taxes collected from vaccine makers. The vaccine court has rewarded large sums to individual cases since its inception, yet it has rejected claims linking thimerosal and the MMR vaccine to autism.

Alternative vaccine schedules

The regular vaccine schedule for children ages zero to six is approved by the American Academy of Pediatrics, the American Academy of Family Physicians, and the Centers for Disease Control. Alternative schedules or selective schedules, such as those published by Dr. Robert W. Sears in *The Vaccine Book: Making the Right Decisions for Your Child*, delaying shots or spacing them farther apart (to have no more than two given on one day) has not been studied. The AAP warns that altered approaches could leave too many kids unprotected for too long, while opponents argue that spreading out shots is better than no shots at all, especially for parents skeptical about the vaccine schedule.

Conclusions about vaccines

This is one of the most complex issues you will face as a parent. If you are the parent of an autistic child, you want answers. If you are the parent of a newborn baby, you don't want a vaccine or anything else to harm your child. If you are the CDC, you are trying to save lives and protect 75 million children and other vulnerable groups by squelching fear and an anti-vaccine movement.

Food Allergies

If you are new to the parenting scene, you might be wondering why so many children have food allergies today. If you take a child to any group function, allergy alert signs are posted everywhere, and entire schools are nut-free zones. When I was a child, peanut butter sandwiches were lunchbox staples. Today they are strictly banned, and the topic of food allergies is not one to be discussed lightly, especially if you are a parent with an allergic child.

Some allergic children respond to certain foods with itchy skin or a scratchy throat. Others are deathly allergic, meaning they can develop anaphylaxis (pronounced an-uh-fil-LAX-is), a medical emergency that requires treatment with an epinephrine (pronounced ep-in-EF-rin) injector, or EpiPen, and a trip to the emergency room for constriction of the throat, severe drop in blood pressure, and loss of consciousness.

Food allergy statistics

- Food allergy rates increased 18% between 1997 and 2007 for children under age 18.[108, 109]
- The largest study to ever track food allergies surveyed 38,000 children and concluded that food allergies are more prevalent and more dangerous than previously thought—8% of children under age 18 (about two kids per classroom) were found to be allergic to at least one food and 39% of the allergic children had severe reactions.[110]
- A nationwide telephone survey of 5,300 households (13,534 people total) showed the prevalence of self-reported peanut, tree nut, and

sesame allergies in children more than tripled between 1997 and 2008.[111]
- Children's food allergies cost an estimated $24.8 billion each year ($4,184 per year per child), and much of that cost is out of pocket in the form of co-pays, special foods, medications, and child care required to avoid allergens. Time missed from work and caregivers needing to leave or change jobs are also major issues, since many allergic children require weekly testing and shots.[112]

Nut-free schools (and day care centers)

Protecting children in schools is critical to the fight against food allergies.

- 25% of food-induced anaphylaxis reactions in schools occur among students *without* a previous food allergy diagnosis.[113]
- 16–18% of children with food allergies have experienced reactions to accidental ingestion of food allergens while in school.[114]

Understanding food allergies

A food allergy is when your body mistakes food as something harmful. When something harmful is identified inside your body, your immune system sends signals to your cells to release an antibody called immunoglobulin E (IgE) to neutralize the culprit. Eating the smallest amount of an allergenic food can trigger IgE antibodies, which release histamine into your bloodstream. Histamine, a chemical found in some of your body's cells, increases the production of mucus, affects nerve cells in the skin, and causes blood vessels to swell. Histamine and other immune-response chemicals are responsible for allergic reactions and symptoms, such as a rash, itchy throat, dripping nose, nausea, difficulty breathing, and anaphylactic shock.

What is causing the increase in food allergies?

There is no single cause for the rise in food allergies; however, there are various theories about what is likely contributing to the increase.

- **Hygiene theory.** This hypothesis asserts that we are "clean freaks." Clean water, antibiotics, and vaccines have eliminated challenges to our immune systems, which are designed to fight foreign things like parasites, viruses, and infection. When our immune system is less busy attacking germs, it goes after the next best thing: food proteins, such as eggs, wheat, and peanuts. The following list includes interesting research supporting the hygiene theory:
  - *Early exposure to bacteria:* Though inner city kids have higher allergy rates overall, a study of 516 children in Baltimore, Boston, New York, and St. Louis found that infants under age one with the highest exposure to specific cockroach, mouse, and cat allergens, as well as dust bacteria, were *less likely* to suffer from allergies, asthma, and wheezing.[115]
  - *Dirt doesn't hurt:* Children raised on farms have fewer allergies and less asthma.[116]
  - *Helpful bacteria in the gut:* In 2014, researchers found that mice raised in a sterile environment and given antibiotics early in life did *not* have common gut bacteria, Clostridia, which may prevent food allergies. Supplementing with probiotics containing Clostridia could reverse or lessen the allergy.[117]
- **Vaccine theory.** In the peanut allergy debate, some think the introduction of the Hib (Haemophilius influenze type B) vaccine in the early 1990s has contributed to a rise in peanut allergies. They note that in countries such as Indonesia and China, where large quantities of peanuts are eaten and the Hib vaccine is rarely given, peanut allergies barely exist. Others believe that yeast used in the Hib vaccine is causing asthma and breathing difficulties in some children.
- **GMO theory.** Food allergies shot upward in the late 1990s. Coincidentally, Genetically Modified Organisms (GMOs) were introduced into the food system in 1996, and some are concerned that transferring genes between all types of plants and foods can bring unintended consequences, including cross-pollination of allergenic proteins.[118]
- **Food additives theory:** Some doctors speculate that children may be having allergic reactions to food additives, rather than to specific foods themselves. For example, sulfites used to preserve wine, soft drinks, and dried fruit have been known to trigger asthma and

other allergic symptoms. Artificial food colorings and preservatives also show similar results.[119]

- **Limited diet theory.** Some suspect that limited, processed food choices of westerners may also be a culprit. Americans do not eat seasonally anymore. In fact, we eat about 20 of the same foods over and over in different combinations each day. Therefore, by focusing our diets, the immune system is less able to deal with the constant influx of the same foods. For example, nuts and nut byproducts are found in more foods and consumer goods than ever before, especially in processed foods and skincare products. Further supporting the limited diet or inundation theory, Asian scientists studied 25,692 school children in Singapore and the Philippines, and found that peanut and tree nut allergies are relatively low, while shellfish allergies predominate.[120]
- **Vitamin D theory**. This theory acknowledges that pregnant women and children receive less vitamin D from sunlight because they are indoors more often, and they use more sunscreen. Evidence shows that food allergies in children are higher in regions further from the equator. Vitamin D deficiencies can alter immune system responses.[121]
- **Detection bias theory.** Although most experts agree that a combination of factors is causing the increase, some believe that doctors are more aware of symptoms and are better able to diagnose food allergies than in the past.

These eight types of foods account for 90% of all allergic reactions in children:

- ❑ Eggs
- ❑ Cow's milk
- ❑ Peanuts
- ❑ Tree nuts (like walnuts, pecans, hazelnuts, almonds, cashews, and pistachios)
- ❑ Soy or soybeans (primarily in infants)
- ❑ Fish (like tuna, salmon, cod)
- ❑ Shellfish (shrimp, crab, lobster)
- ❑ Wheat

Note: The FDA estimates that 80% to 90% of children with allergies to milk, eggs, wheat, and soy should outgrow them by age five, while only 20% will outgrow a peanut allergy and 10% will outgrow tree nut allergies.

In adults, the most common foods that cause allergic reactions are:

- ❑ Shellfish, such as shrimp, crayfish, lobster, and crab
- ❑ Peanuts
- ❑ Tree nuts
- ❑ Fish

Symptoms of food allergies

A child can have an allergic reaction to a food within seconds, or a reaction may develop hours later. For example, an itchy mouth and throat might signal Oral Allergy Syndrome (OAS), which can occur as a child with hay fever eats fruits and vegetables that cross-react with pollen. However, an allergic reaction to foods like milk or soy may occur hours later. If you are uncertain about your child's reaction to a food, talk to your doctor. An allergist will be able to distinguish between symptoms of an immune reaction (food allergy) and an inability to digest a certain food (food intolerance).[108] Look for these signs and symptoms as you introduce allergenic foods to your baby:

- ❑ Swelling in the tongue and throat
- ❑ Tingling in the mouth
- ❑ Hives
- ❑ Eczema or an itchy rash
- ❑ Coughing or wheezing
- ❑ GI symptoms, such as abdominal pain, vomiting, or diarrhea
- ❑ Dizziness
- ❑ Loss of consciousness
- ❑ Anaphylaxis. This is a severe allergic reaction that can be fatal, due to its rapid onset.

Practical Tips from Real Parents

Food Allergies

Mild reactions (newborn to infant)

- Keep a careful food diary if you suspect that your baby may be having mild reactions, such as pink areas around the mouth, tummy discomfort, patches of hives or a rash, to certain foods.
- If your child has eczema or asthma as an infant, be on the lookout for food allergies later.
- If your child has eczema as a newborn, or if an older sibling has allergies, have the younger sibling's blood tested for allergies as a baby around 6–9 months. My third child tested negative to an allergy blood test as a baby and our allergist told me to introduce peanuts and eggs immediately. I did, and he has no allergies, unlike his older two siblings. I don't know if the early introduction is the reason he doesn't have food allergies or not, but the fact remains that he doesn't.

Food allergy concern or diagnosis

- Talk to your doctor about vaccinations. Certain vaccines have lactose, egg protein, or yeast protein added that is enough to cause an allergic reaction.
- Our child's food allergy diagnosis changed our life. If this happens to you, educate yourself as much as possible.
- Teach your family, nannies, babysitters, and anyone else caring for your child about his or her food allergy. Also, teach everyone how to use an epinephrine injector.
- Fill out an emergency plan with your allergist and share it with others.
- Visit your child's day care and talk about your allergy. Have a step-by-step plan in writing for any allergic reactions.
- Put reminders on your calendar for refilling your epi-pen prescription because they have an expiration date. Also, get extras. You will leave pens everywhere.

- Buy an ID bracelet for your child with your name, phone number, and their allergies.
- Expect to become a professional label reader. Check both the "Ingredients" labels and "Contains" labels.
- If your child is diagnosed with a food allergy, try shopping online at a food allergy-friendly website to save time painfully reading labels in the store. Amazon's VineMarket.com allows you to filter allergen-free products, such as peanut-free, dairy-free, soy-free, tree nut-free, gluten-free, and so forth.
- Don't think that lesser past reactions are an indicator of the future. Our son had several bad reactions to a certain food at age five that began with a mild reaction at age one.
- Children with food allergies are more likely to have environmental allergies. As babies and toddlers get older, food allergies typically improve but environmental allergies can get worse. Allergy shots have helped my son significantly.
- Be matter of fact when talking about your child's allergies. They are already scary for a child, especially when the throat constricts. A child needs to know they can trust you and that you have the tools (Benadryl and epi-pen) to keep them safe. They will follow your lead in how to respond.

Organic Foods

I understand that every family cannot make room in an already tight budget for organic food. However, I am overwhelmingly convinced that organic foods in key food groups are worth every penny, especially for pregnant women and children.

What is conventional food?

Conventional food production allows for the use of synthetic insecticides and pesticides, synthetic fertilizers, sewage sludge, antibiotics, growth hormones, chemical additives, and genetically modified organisms (GMOs) for two major reasons: to make food look appealing and to make it as cheaply as possible. Unfortunately, speeding up animal growth and producing aesthetically pleasing fruits and vegetables comes at the expense of our health.

What is organic food?

Organic food is required by the USDA to be produced without bioengineering or genetically modified organisms (GMOs), antibiotics, synthetic growth hormones, synthetic fertilizers, sewage sludge, ionizing radiation, and manmade pesticides.

Who should eat organic foods?

Pregnant women and young children are two vulnerable groups who could benefit the most from eating organic foods.[122]

- Children are not "little adults." Their body systems are not fully developed.
- Environmental chemicals can disrupt and alter the way genes work from the embryonic phase through early childhood, causing developmental defects.
- A baby's blood-brain barrier is leaky or more permeable than an adult's, allowing toxins to reach the nervous system more easily.
- A baby's blood does not contain certain components, such as serum proteins, that help prevent toxins from reaching susceptible organs.
- A baby's ability to metabolize, detoxify, and excrete toxins, especially in the first months of life, is different from an adult's (e.g., kidney and liver systems are not fully developed).
- Children eat fewer types of foods, making them more susceptible to certain crops (e.g., soy in formula, apples, potatoes, etc.).
- Pound for pound, children eat three to four times more food and drink 2.5 times more than adults.
- The EPA reports that known carcinogens average 10 times the potency for infants up to age two years, while other chemicals may be up to 65 times more powerful when ingested by a young child versus an adult.[123]

Testing of conventional foods

Results from the testing and monitoring of conventional foods are often controversial because it is nearly impossible to isolate chemicals in food production. With so many foods used and ingested in combination with another, the bar for banning a single pesticide or toxin is extremely high. Overwhelming evidence must be provided to spark action.

Media reporting on conventional foods is also tricky. There is incredible political and financial stake in the perceived safety of our food and the integrity of the agencies monitoring our food. Organic food is also more expensive than conventional food, making the issue politically charged.

What about reports that say organic foods are no better than conventional foods?

In September 2012, a Stanford University team conducted a meta-analysis of several decades' worth of previous research and concluded that organic foods are no more healthful or nutritious than conventionally grown foods, setting off a firestorm in the media. The study agreed that organic produce has lower levels of pesticides.

What does the American Academy of Pediatrics (AAP) say about organic foods?

The AAP weighed into the organic debate in October 2012, one month after the Stanford report, stating that organic foods have lower pesticide levels and may reduce diseases linked to antibiotic resistance. The AAP could offer no clinically relevant nutritional advantage of organic over conventional foods. The AAP urged that eating healthy food is more important than debating organic or conventional, but subtly agreed that organics are a better choice.

What is my conclusion about conventional vs. organic foods?

To borrow a line from Bill Clinton's 1992 presidential campaign, "It's not about nutrition, stupid." It's about the stuff sprayed on our food. It's about synthetic hormones used to plump up animals faster, causing early puberty in our daughters and cancer. It's about antibiotics in livestock production, creating a surge of antibiotic-resistant infections in hospitals. It's about GMO seeds creating unstable plant combinations that do not occur in nature and require more pesticides to be sprayed on our food. It's about chemically-treated sewage sludge (human and industrial waste) that is spread over conventional crops for fertilizer and dust control.

Is organic food perfect? No. Are all naturally-sourced pesticides harmless? No. Are organic farmers trying to cut costs and generate profits just like conventional farmers? Of course–and we must continue to monitor these companies by voting with our dollars. However, I am still convinced, beyond a shadow of a doubt, that organic foods are better for our long-term health than conventional foods, especially for pregnant women and children.

Differences between organic and conventional farming methods

Conventional Methods	Organic Methods
Applies synthetic fertilizers to unnaturally speed up plant growth	Uses natural fertilizers, such as manure and compost
Sprays plants with World War II-era insecticides and pesticides	Uses predator insects, physical planting controls, and naturally-sourced pesticides
Uses synthetic chemicals to manage weeds	Uses non-toxic products to manage weeds or rotates crops, mulches, and hand-weeds
Injects livestock with antibiotics and growth hormones to ward off disease and promote unnatural growth or milk production	Feeds livestock grass and organic feed while allowing animals at least some access to the outdoors

Why does organic food cost more?

Organic farms are typically smaller than conventional farms, and they do not benefit from economies of scale, as larger growers do. Smaller organic farms may not receive generous federal farm subsidies like larger, commodity-based farms. Growing organic food is also more labor-intensive. However, while conventional foods are less expensive up front, conventional farming does not account for costs "on the back side," such as environmental cleanup, potential health risks, and future health care costs. In general, organic prices reflect the price of growing food.

Which organic foods should I prioritize?

Prioritize animal and animal products first, due to the combined risks of antibiotics, growth hormones, and pesticide-tainted GMO feed. Animal products such as dairy, fish, poultry, and beef contain the most toxic pesticide residues because these animals eat large amounts of feed.

- ❑ Dairy (milk, yogurt, butter, cheese)
- ❑ Eggs
- ❑ Beef
- ❑ Chicken
- ❑ Pork
- ❑ Fish

Why animal products first?

To better understand this position, let's take a look at the conventional beef and dairy industries. Cows are made to eat grass. They have a highly specialized stomach, known as a rumen, filled with bacteria, which turns grass cellulose into protein. Yet today, as soon as a calf is weaned, it enters a world far from green pastures. At this point, a calf is typically shuttled to a feedlot, put in tight quarters with up to thousands of other cows, and fed small amounts of hay or straw, supplemented by corn, soy, grain, and other cost-cutting foods. Why feed cattle corn and soy instead of grass? It's plentiful, cheap, and subsidized by the U.S. government. Yet when droughts occur and prices for corn and soy go up, farmers have to get creative with their foods. Seafood byproducts, bulk candy and scrap chocolate (including the wrappers), rice, potatoes, sawdust, and poultry litter (chicken feces, bedding, and discarded bits of feed) become low-cost foods for beef cattle.[126]

In short, these fatty foods plump up the cows faster and shorten the maturity cycle until slaughter. While our great-grandparents ate cattle aged four to five years, farmers now target 14 months and strive for 11 months. So, how do you keep thousands of cows crammed into a small feedlot clean and sanitary? You don't. You load up their feed and drinking water with antibiotics to enhance growth and ward off disease, explaining why roughly 70% of the antibiotics in the U.S. are used for livestock production. Pharmaceutical and farm lobbies have successfully blocked legislative reform in this area for years, despite the growing threat of antibiotic-resistant infections.

In dairy cows, added hormones significantly boost milk production, yet the potential adverse effects on both cows and humans are numerous—clogged ducts and increased mastitis infection for the cows requiring more antibiotics, and dairy products linked to hormone-dependent cancers, such as testes, breast, and prostate cancers in humans.[127] In November 1993, the FDA approved Monsanto's New Animal Drug Application for Posilac, containing recombinant bovine growth hormone, or

Did You Know?

Global Agricultural Market Power (The OPEC of Food)

Many people are aware of the international cartel, OPEC (Organization of the Petroleum Exporting Countries), whose mission is to maintain steady income for the member states and to work together to influence world oil prices. The transformation of the global agricultural market is starting to look very similar.

- Two grain companies control 75% of the world's grain trade.[124]
- Ten companies control nearly 90% of the global agrochemical market and 67% of seed sales.
- The six largest producers of genetically engineered seeds (Monsanto, Syngenta, Dow Agrosciences, BASF, Bayer, and Pioneer/DuPont) are also the leading producers of insecticides and herbicides.

This type of market power enables a few giant companies to pay farmers low prices for crops, regardless of demand, and then charge the same farmers high prices for seeds, fertilizers, and pesticides. In the U.S., agro-business also benefits from generous government subsidies, overseas food aid programs, and public support for research. These transnational mega-companies like to argue their GMO crops help reduce world hunger, but I'm not buying it. Sure, overall crop yields increase and prices come down, but how did you get there? The current agricultural system favors only wealthy farmers, who can afford expensive inputs like seeds and fertilizers. These inputs increase food production beyond what we need, further driving prices down and pushing the smaller farmers out. Now we have a few protected wealthy individuals and thousands of landless peasants. Africa, a land of vast agricultural potential, was a net food exporter in the 1960s. Today, Africa imports 25% of its food and suffers from recurrent famines and food deprivation. Remind me how these companies are helping world hunger?[124, 125]

rBGH, for increasing production in lactating dairy cows. This may also be called recombinant bovine somatotrophin, or rBST. To note, Canada, Israel, Japan, Australia, New Zealand, and the twenty-eight countries of the European Union have banned the use of rBGH and rBST in dairy cows.

Antibiotics and added hormones to our foods have been linked to the following:

- **Early puberty in girls:** In 1900, the average age for menstrual period onset was age 14. In 2010, an article published in *Pediatrics* found a surprising rise in girls entering puberty between ages seven and eight. This study of 1,239 adolescents found that 10% of Caucasians and 23% of African Americans had begun puberty by age seven, twice the rate seen in a 1997 study. By age eight, 18% of Caucasian girls and 43% of African American girls had reached early puberty.[128] Early puberty is associated with increased breast cancer risk.[129]
- **Cancer:** Certain cancers, such as breast and uterine cancers, increase with longer exposure to estrogen and other hormones. Six different types of steroid hormones are currently approved for use in beef cattle and sheep by FDA: estradiol, progesterone, testosterone, zeranol, trenbolone acetate, and melengestrol acetate. Estradiol and progesterone are natural female sex hormones, testosterone is the natural male sex hormone, and the final three are synthetic chemicals that enhance animal growth. The hormone drugs are formulated as pellets and placed under the skin of the animal's ear.[130]
- **Antibiotic-resistant infections:** Superbugs are popping up in hospitals at an alarming rate, due to infections that are difficult to treat because of antibiotic resistance. The CDC issued a report in 2013 indicating that the U.S. could face "potentially catastrophic consequences" if it does not combat the issue. 23,000 people are dying per year as a direct result of antibiotic resistance, while 14,000 illnesses are linked to related infections, costing the U.S. $23 billion annually. Remember those back side costs of conventional foods? While it is unclear how much agriculture has contributed to the increase, livestock antibiotics (the primary suspect) are passed to humans in traces that have been linked to strains of extremely resistant bacteria.[131]

- **Foodborne illnesses:** Food-related illness linked to antibiotic-resistant bacteria has climbed noticeably in recent years. In 2011, there was a multi-state Salmonella Heidelberg outbreak from ground turkey. In 2012, Cargill Meat Solutions conducted a ground beef recall, and in 2013, there was a significant salmonella outbreak credited to Foster Farms tainted chicken. Would anyone like to join in on Meatless Mondays?

Pesticides and insecticides

Now that you have a better understanding of the perils of our meat and dairy industries, let's look at some considerations of pesticides and insecticides in other food crops, such as fruits and vegetables.

- **AAP statement on pesticides:** In a December 2012 report, the AAP made specific recommendations to reduce children's exposure to pesticides based on the premise that "prenatal and early childhood exposure to pesticides is associated with pediatric cancers, decreased cognitive function, and behavioral problems."[132]
- **Link to ADHD:** A 2010 study from Harvard University found that kids with above-average pesticide exposures are nearly two times as likely to have ADHD as children with undetectable levels.[133]
- **Link to lower IQ:** Several studies link prenatal pesticide exposures with decreased cognitive development on multi-ethnic populations. One study found a seven IQ point deficit in children whose mothers had the highest quintile levels of pesticides in their urine during pregnancy.[134]
- **Increased risk for children:** Children play on lawns and on floors, and they tend to put objects in their mouths, increasing exposure to pesticides used in the home and on yards. Home pesticide use overall has been linked to childhood cancers such as soft tissue sarcomas, leukemia, and cancer of the brain.[135]

If I am budget constrained, which fruits and vegetables are worth the organic cost?

The Environmental Working Group prioritizes twelve fruits and vegetables each year that are worth buying organic. This group estimates that you can reduce your pesticide exposure by 80% by choosing organic versions of these foods.[136]

The Dirty Dozen Plus

These are fruits and vegetables that are worth buying organic.

- ❑ Apples
- ❑ Strawberries
- ❑ Grapes
- ❑ Celery
- ❑ Peaches
- ❑ Spinach
- ❑ Sweet bell peppers
- ❑ Nectarines (imported)
- ❑ Cucumbers
- ❑ Cherry tomatoes
- ❑ Snap peas (imported)
- ❑ Potatoes
- ❑ Plus: Hot peppers and kale/collard greens for pesticides of special concern

The Clean Fifteen

If you are on a tight budget, don't waste your money buying these organic foods. The clean fifteen are the *least likely* to have pesticides detected on the parts you eat after typical washing.

- ❑ Avocados
- ❑ Sweet Corn
- ❑ Pineapples
- ❑ Cabbage
- ❑ Sweet Peas (frozen)
- ❑ Onions
- ❑ Asparagus
- ❑ Mangos
- ❑ Papayas
- ❑ Kiwi
- ❑ Eggplant
- ❑ Grapefruit
- ❑ Cantaloupe (domestic)
- ❑ Cauliflower
- ❑ Sweet Potatoes

Other organic priorities

Families may want to prioritize foods that are particularly popular with kids by putting these organic, non-GMO foods at the top of the grocery list.

- ❑ organic baby food
- ❑ organic peanut butter
- ❑ organic ketchup
- ❑ organic apples
- ❑ organic grapes
- ❑ organic potatoes
- ❑ organic dips and salad dressings (avoid cottonseed, corn, and soy-modified oils)
- ❑ 100% olive oil (70% of the worldwide extra virgin olive oil is estimated to be watered down with cheaper GMO oils).[137]

Genetically Modified Organisms (GMOs)

Did you know that 70–80% of the processed food in the supermarket is genetically engineered? GMOs are plants or animals that have been modified in a laboratory with DNA from bacteria, viruses, or other plants and animals. These combinations of genes do not occur in nature, and most GMOs used today either: 1) withstand the application of an herbicide, such as Monsanto's RoundUp Ready® crops, or they 2) produce an insecticide, such as Monsanto's Bt corn. Bt corn is genetically modified to have a natural bacterial toxin found in the soil inside the corn kernel. This toxin is in the seed to attack the crop's biggest predator, the corn rootworm. In the case of Bt corn, the corn itself is registered as an insecticide, and the USDA reports that 80% of the total planted acres of corn is Bt corn.[138] No one needs a degree in molecular biology to know that eating a registered insecticide is probably not good for pregnant women, infants, young children, or anyone.*

Other problems with these types of GMOs are: 1) they make crops even more resistant to herbicides, requiring farmers to spray more chemicals on the plants (good thing Monsanto owns the seeds and the

* Bt-corn receives its name from the donor organism, Bacillus thuringiensis, and HT-corn is herbicide-tolerant.

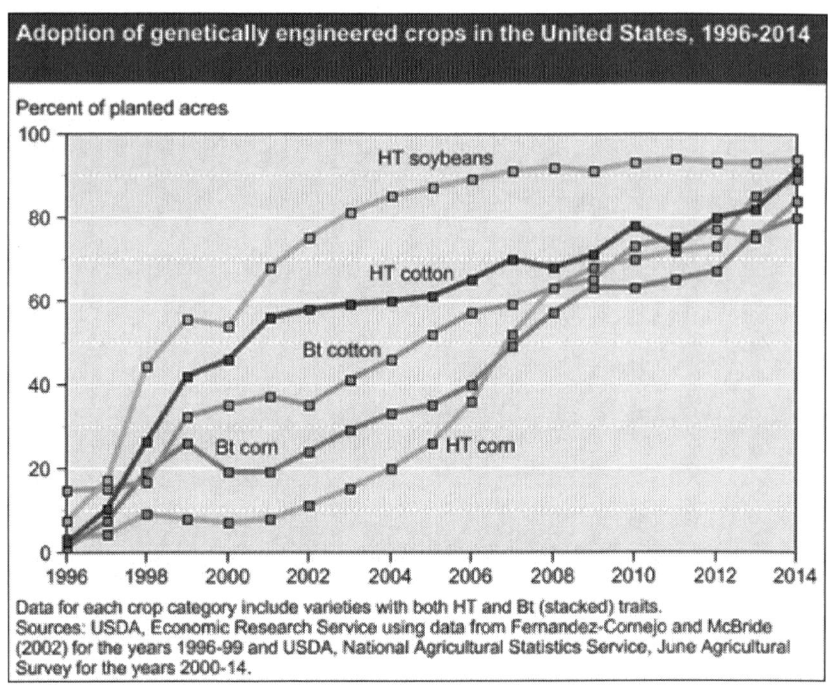

RoundUp), and 2) they create super pests. Rootworms immune to Bt corn are on the rise, causing soil-insecticide revenues at American Vanguard, FMC Corp., and Syngenta to climb sharply, due to "increased grower awareness" about rootworm resistance.

Finally, just how many of our crops are genetically engineered? In 2014, USDA analyzed the adoption of GE crops in the United States: [138]

- Cotton (cottonseed oil): 96% of total acreage is GE
- Soybeans: 94% of total acreage is GE
- Corn: 93% of total acreage is GE

Buying organic food on a budget

If you live in California, you are in luck, because organic and conventional foods are fairly close in price. However, buying organic food week after week for the rest of the country can be a real drag on your wallet. Here are some tips for organic shopping on a budget.

Did You Know?

Decoding the Stickers on Fruits and Vegetables

The stickers or labels attached to fruits and most vegetables in the supermarket have a function beyond helping to scan prices at the checkout counter. By reading the stickers or price look up (PLU) codes, you can tell whether your food is genetically modified (GMO), organically grown, or conventionally grown.

- *Four numbers:* If there are four numbers in the sticker code, this product is conventionally or traditionally grown using synthetic fertilizers, pesticides, and herbicides. The last four numbers of the PLU code represent the kind of vegetable or fruit. For example, all conventional bananas have a code of 4011.
- *Five numbers and the number starts with "8":* A five digit PLU code beginning with an "8" signifies that the fruit or vegetable is genetically modified (GMO).
- *Five numbers and the number starts with "9":* A five digit PLU code beginning with a "9" signifies that the fruit or vegetable is organically grown. Remember: eight I hate, but nine is fine.

- ❑ **Have a positive outlook about paying up for good food.** When you need a new car, you don't just go out and buy the cheapest car you can find. Pay up for what goes into your body and cut costs on what is just stuff.
- ❑ **Grow your own organic garden for the foods and herbs that you enjoy.**
- ❑ **Look beyond your local conventional supermarket for healthy food.**
- ❑ **Search LocalHarvest.org** to locate farms, farmer's markets, and Community-Supported Agriculture (CSA) programs in your area.
- ❑ **Shop at local farmer's markets** or local fruit and vegetable stands.

- ❑ **Buy a share in a Community-Supported Agricultural (CSA) program.** These programs typically cost $300 to $500 for a growing season (i.e., May through September), with cost depending on the number of family members to feed, such as one to three, three to six, etc. A growing season might typically extend from the summer months for most items and into the fall for other fruits and vegetables. Depending on your location, some offer weekly, monthly, or seasonal shares.
- ❑ **Join a co-op.** A food cooperative is a member-owned business that provides food and groceries at a discount. Search CooperativeGrocer.coop or OrganicConsumers.org for food co-ops in your area.
- ❑ **Buy organic fruits and vegetables in season.** Negotiate a discount at a local farmer's market for buying in bulk. Then freeze the leftovers.
- ❑ **Start a buying club with your friends.** Talk to a local co-op or meat farmer about buying a bulk order and splitting it with friends.
- ❑ **Take a trip through an area with family farms and stock up.** When our family lived in Washington DC, we used to take coolers and drive through the Shenandoah Valley countryside, collecting grass-fed beef and organic poultry, pork, and eggs with local prices solidly beating out urban farmer's market prices.

What if prices for organic fruits, vegetables, and meats are still out of my budget? How do I reduce toxin exposure with conventional foods?

Even if foods purchased are not organic, consumers should pay attention to how their food is sourced. For example, fresh produce from a roadside stand or produce labeled as "local" in the supermarket is probably a good option. Also, to help reduce repetitive exposure, shop at different stores and buy different varieties of foods. Place fruits and vegetables under running water and scrub them with a brush. For pregnant women and young children, cut out the cores and peel the skins from Dirty Dozen foods, and worry less about peeling away nutrients and more about reducing toxins.

- ❑ For apples and pears, cut out the fruit's core, top, and bottom.

- ❑ For strawberries, cut out the stalk and core (the white part).
- ❑ For peaches and nectarines, peel the skin.
- ❑ For grapes, avoid imported grapes during the winter months since international pesticide allowances are higher than domestic standards.
- ❑ For bell peppers, buy red, yellow, and orange varieties, which are typically grown in hothouses, rather than green peppers, which are grown in the outdoors.
- ❑ For leafy greens, remove the outer layers.
- ❑ For fish, beef, pork, and poultry, peel away the skins and extra fat, which typically have the highest concentrations of pesticides and environmental residues.

Understanding marketing terms

Expect that many of these labels will leave you scratching your head. For marketers, the key is to advertise at least one good health claim to distract you from other concerns.

- **100% Organic.** All ingredients must be certified organic.
- **Organic.** If you see the USDA Organic seal, this product has 95% or more organic content. USDA-certification for organic meat forbids the use of growth hormones, antibiotics, genetically modified feed, or animal by-products in raising the livestock. Beyond those practices, it does not address the treatment of the animals or the specific feed.
- **"Made With" Organic.** At least 70% of the product must be certified organic ingredients. These products cannot use the USDA Organic seal.
- **Grass Fed or 100% Grass Fed.** These terms imply that USDA grass-fed beef has only a grass diet and access to pasture year-round, while an organic pasture diet may be supplemented with grain. The grass-fed label does not limit the use of antibiotics, hormones, or pesticides.
- **Cage Free.** This term means that laying hens live outside of cages, typically in a barn, warehouse, or enclosed building. Cage-free does not mean that hens have access to the outdoors.

- **Free Range.** Producers must demonstrate to USDA that poultry has access to the outdoors. There are no USDA requirements for time granted outside or for the quality or size of the outdoor area.
- **Humane.** Many labeling programs make this claim; however, the USDA does not regulate this term or other similar labels such as "old fashioned," "pasture-raised," or "low stocking density."
- **Natural or All Natural.** For meat, poultry, and eggs, the USDA requires these products to be minimally processed; however, there are no specific guidelines. Therefore, "natural" and "all natural" are marketing label favorites because they imply everything and mean nothing.[139]

Green Cleaning

• • • • • • • • • • • • • • • • • •

In my former profession, you had to choose the right bomb for the right target. The same could be said for a sensible approach to household cleaning. Strive to reduce the "collateral damage" of using overly harsh chemicals on household surfaces, while still achieving overall cleanliness in the home. Blasting your bathroom with ammonia and bleach will certainly get the job done, although not without irritating your skin, eyes, airways, and with prolonged exposure, your nervous system.

Before children, you may have sprayed away at mildew and grime without ever considering the contents of your cleaning products. However, understanding a child's unique vulnerability to toxins changes everything, and over 150 chemicals found in the home have been linked to allergies, birth defects, cancer, and psychological abnormalities. Fortunately, there is hope. You do not have to give up your health for a clean home. A few non-toxic DIY mixes of common products can deliver more punch than you might expect for minimal cost.

Low cost green cleaning supplies

- ❑ **Plain liquid soap:** These gentle soaps, found at natural food stores such as Whole Foods or Trader Joe's, are made with natural oils, such as olive, palm, and coconut (e.g., castile soap), rather than petroleum or animal based products. *Suggestions for use:* Make a citrus scented, all-purpose scrubbing paste with a fresh lemon, baking soda, and a plant-based liquid soap.

- ❑ **Baking soda**: Use baking soda as a non-abrasive scrub or to absorb odors in trashcans and the fridge. Baking soda also combats oil and grease stains. *Suggestions for use:* Leave a box in your bathroom for impromptu cleanings of the tub, toilet, and sink. Use baking soda and a spray bottle of vinegar together to scrub away the ring around the tub. Sprinkle it in your kitchen sink and scrub.
- ❑ **Vinegar**: 100% distilled white vinegar is the strongest form of vinegar for your home. This all-natural cleaner tackles soap scum, dirt, mineral deposits, and creates an environment that inhibits mold, mildew, and bacteria. Buy cleaning vinegar in a gallon jug and make spray bottles of concentrated or diluted vinegar for everyday cleaning. *Suggestions for use:* Maintain a spray bottle of vinegar in the bathroom to keep your shower curtain free of mildew. Clean out your coffee maker with a solution of half water and half vinegar. For hardwood, vinyl, or tile floors: mix ¼ cup vinegar, 1-gallon warm water, and a few drops of essential oil, if desired. No need to rinse.
- ❑ **Lemon juice**: The acid in lemon juice removes dirt, grease, and rust stains. When mixed with salt or baking soda, it creates an all-natural scouring paste. *Suggestions for use:* Use four tablespoons of lemon juice with half a gallon of water instead of Windex on windows and mirrors (add vinegar or soap to remove tougher residues). Polish wood furniture with two parts olive oil and one part lemon juice for a fresh-smelling shine.

Green-washing of household cleaners

If you are not a home ingredient mixer, carefully select green cleaning products and beware of "green-washing." Green-washing is a form of marketing spin or green labeling that companies use to pad their profits and promote their public perception. In the world of household cleaners, the words "green" and "natural" are completely unregulated, and a product with a speck of an organic essential oil can label itself organic. Only foods are *certified* organic.

Making the cleaning situation even more perilous, current laws do not require household products to list ingredients. In 2012, the Environmental Working Group (EWG) found that only 7% of cleaning products adequately disclosed their contents, while 53% of the products under review had lung-damaging ingredients. Several products tested contained poisons and suspected carcinogens, such as formaldehyde (used as a preservative for some citrus, pine, and scented oils), chloroform (this toxic vapor escapes in the fumes of bleach products), and the chemical 1,4-dioxane (a common contaminant in detergents). If you want to check household cleaning ingredients, search more than 2000 products online on the EWG's Guide to Healthy Cleaning or the U.S. Department of HHS National Institutes of Health Household Products Database.

Cleaning products to avoid or restrict

Having a baby crawling on your floors, licking windows and mirrors, and pulling up on the rim of your toilet can change your perspective on cleaning products.

- ❑ Be aware of these particularly toxic types of cleaners: drain cleaner, acidic toilet cleaner, oven cleaner, furniture polish, silver and metal polisher, bleach, liquid cleaner with harsh chemicals, spot remover, and ammonia-based window cleaner.
- ❑ Don't buy products labeled "danger," "poison," or "fatal if swallowed," and if a product advertises that it "eats away something," know that your lungs could be included in that list.
- ❑ Avoid the EWG's Hall of Shame list of most toxic household cleaners, which basically includes all of the cleaning products that I used while growing up. Scratch these products from your shopping list: Simple Green All-Purpose Cleaner, Citra-Solv Cleaner and Degreaser, Scrubbing Bubbles Foamer, Mop and Glo Floor Cleaner, DampRid Mildew Stain Remover, Spic and Span Floor Cleaner, Easy-Off/Walmart/CVS Oven Cleaners, Drano Clog Remover, Glade Air Freshener Spray, Air Wick Automatic Air Fresheners, Febreeze Air Effects, Comet Powder, Old English Furniture Polish, Great Value Furniture Polish, Spot Shot Carpet Stain Remover, Static Guard spray, Target Up and Up Toilet Bowl Cleaner, and Lysol Toilet Bowl Cleaner with Lime and Rust Remover.

Going Green

. . . .

If you believe that small, incremental steps toward improving the quality of our environment can make a big difference, then try these tips for going green.

Before we get into a discussion about green living, let it be said: You do not have to grow your own food, wear organic free trade clothing, and drive a solar-powered scooter to be an environmentalist. Simply understanding a few concepts about being green and knowing what to prioritize can help transform how your family lives and contribute to a healthier planet.

Every time that I come to the dinner table with a new idea for greening our home or replacing certain products, my husband mockingly replies, "You have to be rich to be green." While he does have a point in some areas, especially with eco-friendly baby products, the truth is families can save a great deal of money *and* energy by making a concerted effort to go green.

Transportation

- ❑ **Buy a more fuel efficient car.** Upgrading from a 20mpg SUV to a 40mpg car can save 4,500 gallons of gasoline over the life of the car, adding up to a total savings of over $18,000. Compare different cars side-by-side or calculate ways to drive efficiently using tools and calculators on fueleconomy.gov.

Keep It Simple

Top Five Ways to Reduce Your Individual Carbon Footprint

The whole purpose of this book is to synthesize complex information down into bite-size pieces. So while you may not be able to put all of these green tips into practice, let's start with five priorities.

1. Green your commute.
2. Be more energy efficient at home.
3. Choose green electricity.
4. Eat less meat, especially red meat.
5. Buy less stuff.

- ❑ **Green your commute.** Try carpooling or use public transportation. Every gallon of gas burned in your car produces nineteen pounds of carbon dioxide.
- ❑ **Be mindful of high-polluting air travel, especially at work.** Take the train over a short flight, or skip unnecessary trips. Although, does it seem ironic that a person familiar with burning 2,000 pounds of jet fuel per minute (in afterburner) is suggesting that you limit air travel? Next tip.
- ❑ **Drive the speed limit.** Fuel efficiency for most cars decreases rapidly above 50 mph. For every five miles per hour that you drive over 50 mph, you are paying 23 more cents per gallon of gas in lost efficiency.[140]

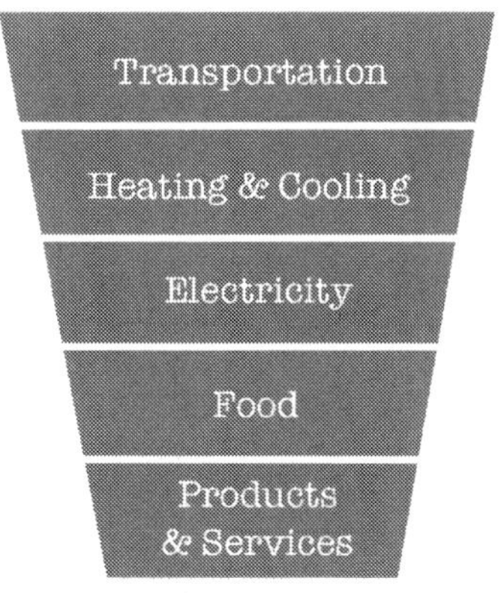

Household energy efficiency

- ❑ **Turn off lights, appliances, and computers when not in use.** Save an average of $90 per year.
- ❑ **Use a smart power strip.** Traditional power strips are an inexpensive way to increase the number of electrical outlets in your home; however, they also encourage users to leave appliances and computers plugged in 24/7. A smart strip will shut off products in standby mode. Energy experts estimate that standby power is 5–10% of total household energy consumption.
- ❑ **Replace older incandescent bulbs with compact fluorescent bulbs** (CFLs), **light emitting diodes** (LEDs), **and even halogens**. Save up to 75% on your lighting bill.
- ❑ **Replace aging appliances with new Energy Star appliances**. Save up to $75 per year.
- ❑ **Turn your thermostat down a few degrees in the winter and up in the summer**. 50% to 70% of a household's total energy budget is for heating and cooling.
- ❑ **Wash clothes in cold water**. 85% of the energy used in washing is from heating the water.
- ❑ **Wash your hands in cold water, and turn down your water heater.** Lowering the temperature from 140°F to 120°F can reduce costs by 6% to 10%. It prevents scalded hands for little ones, too. Consider a solar water heater.
- ❑ **Check your insulation, especially in homes more than 50 years old.** Insulation is important for heating and cooling. Focus on ceiling insulation.
- ❑ **Purchase green energy for your home.** Check Green-e.org for available green energy products in your area.

Eating smartly

- ❑ **Eat less meat, especially red meat.** Due to deforestation for pasture and feed crops, and high levels of methane, nitrous oxide, and ammonia emission, livestock production is responsible for 18% of greenhouse gases, a higher share than transport.[141] Replace a red meat meal each week with a plant-based protein and save $200–300

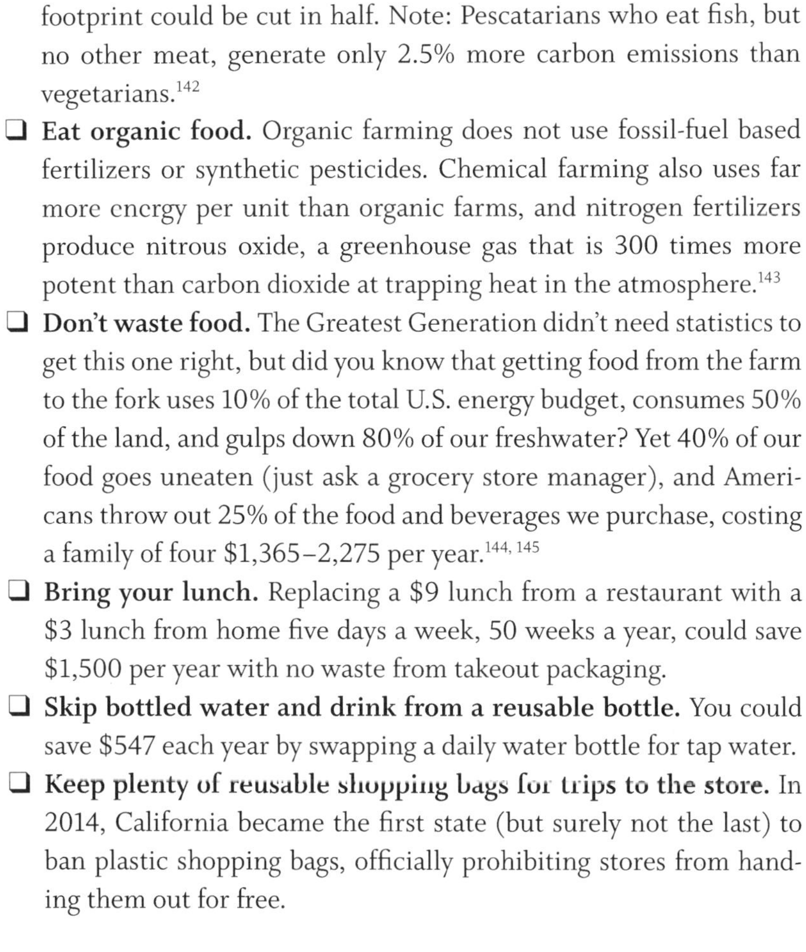

per year. Stop eating meat altogether and your food-related carbon footprint could be cut in half. Note: Pescatarians who eat fish, but no other meat, generate only 2.5% more carbon emissions than vegetarians.[142]

❑ **Eat organic food.** Organic farming does not use fossil-fuel based fertilizers or synthetic pesticides. Chemical farming also uses far more energy per unit than organic farms, and nitrogen fertilizers produce nitrous oxide, a greenhouse gas that is 300 times more potent than carbon dioxide at trapping heat in the atmosphere.[143]

❑ **Don't waste food.** The Greatest Generation didn't need statistics to get this one right, but did you know that getting food from the farm to the fork uses 10% of the total U.S. energy budget, consumes 50% of the land, and gulps down 80% of our freshwater? Yet 40% of our food goes uneaten (just ask a grocery store manager), and Americans throw out 25% of the food and beverages we purchase, costing a family of four $1,365–2,275 per year.[144, 145]

❑ **Bring your lunch.** Replacing a $9 lunch from a restaurant with a $3 lunch from home five days a week, 50 weeks a year, could save $1,500 per year with no waste from takeout packaging.

❑ **Skip bottled water and drink from a reusable bottle.** You could save $547 each year by swapping a daily water bottle for tap water.

❑ **Keep plenty of reusable shopping bags for trips to the store.** In 2014, California became the first state (but surely not the last) to ban plastic shopping bags, officially prohibiting stores from handing them out for free.

Reduce, reuse, and recycle

❑ **Think before you buy new and save big bucks.** Source reduction and reuse of products has a far greater impact on the environment than recycling. As for saving money, let's use baby products as an example. When we had our first child, we found our stroller, bouncer seat, Jumperoo, activity mat, and front carrier all on Craigslist. Numerous other items, such as an infant tub, changing pads, books, toys, and riding vehicles were all found at consignment and yard sales, including our child's bedroom set, which made its way from a random parking lot in downtown Washington DC to our

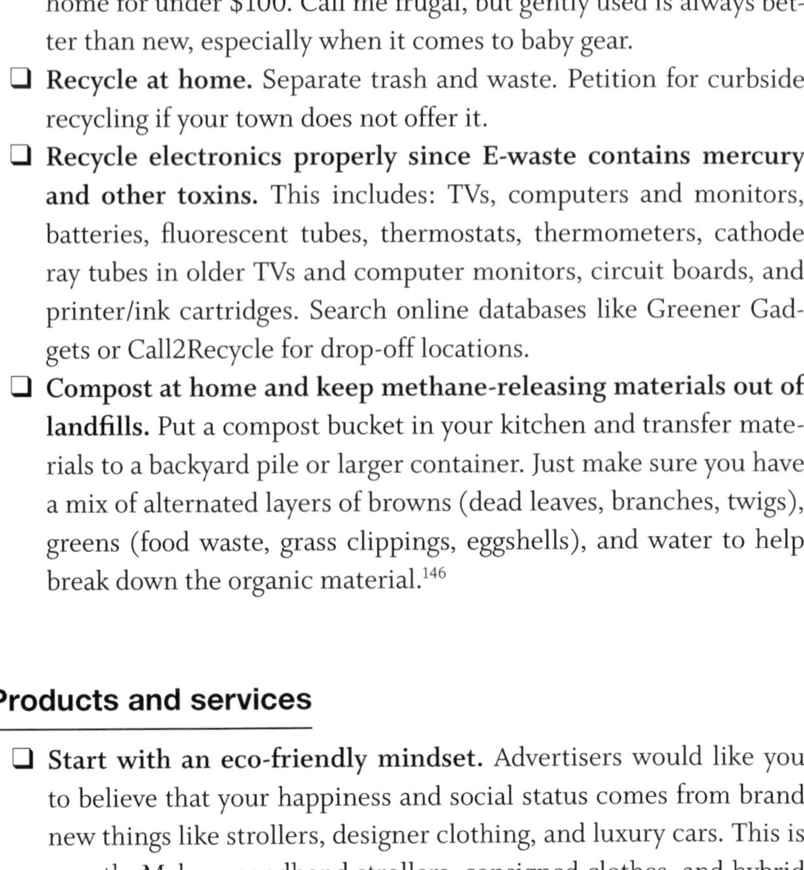

home for under $100. Call me frugal, but gently used is always better than new, especially when it comes to baby gear.

- ❑ **Recycle at home.** Separate trash and waste. Petition for curbside recycling if your town does not offer it.
- ❑ **Recycle electronics properly since E-waste contains mercury and other toxins.** This includes: TVs, computers and monitors, batteries, fluorescent tubes, thermostats, thermometers, cathode ray tubes in older TVs and computer monitors, circuit boards, and printer/ink cartridges. Search online databases like Greener Gadgets or Call2Recycle for drop-off locations.
- ❑ **Compost at home and keep methane-releasing materials out of landfills.** Put a compost bucket in your kitchen and transfer materials to a backyard pile or larger container. Just make sure you have a mix of alternated layers of browns (dead leaves, branches, twigs), greens (food waste, grass clippings, eggshells), and water to help break down the organic material.[146]

Products and services

- ❑ **Start with an eco-friendly mindset.** Advertisers would like you to believe that your happiness and social status comes from brand new things like strollers, designer clothing, and luxury cars. This is a myth. Make secondhand strollers, consigned clothes, and hybrid cars cool in your neighborhood.
- ❑ **Buy products that are locally made and support local businesses.**
- ❑ **Visit your public library to borrow books and movies.** Download a media console for Android or iOS, such as Overdrive, and listen to audio books rented from the library.
- ❑ **Visit favorite green web sites for current news and information**. These include sites such as **Treehugger** (providing up to thirty fresh posts per day), **Grist** (touting sharp yet snarky policy wonks—*Newsweek* calls it "*The Daily Show* of the environment"), and **WorldChanging** (featuring some of the smartest minds covering environmental issues and solutions).
- ❑ **Have fun being green with innovative apps**:
  - ▸ **GoodGuide:** barcode scanning app used to find safe, green, and ethical products

- **greenMeter:** calculates real time fuel usage using iOS's built-in accelerometer
- **GasHog:** calculates the fuel economy of your last tank, as well as historical averages
- **HootRoot:** gets you from point A to point B with the lowest carbon emission
- **CarbonCalc:** find your carbon footprint and compare it to the average American and E.U. citizen; buy carbon offsets via PayPal (carbon offsets fund projects that reduce the emissions of greenhouse gases, such as renewable energy)
- **Carbon Tracker:** uses GPS to track your carbon footprint based on your travel
- **Meter Readings:** monitor your household utility meters
- **Control4 MyHome:** control the power in your home with one device. Turn on/off your thermostat, lights, television, and more to save money while you are away.
- **iRecycle:** finds the closest recycling centers for all types of materials
- **What's Fresh:** tells you what fresh foods are in season in your area
- **LocaVore:** finds restaurants and markets with locally grown foods
- **Gorgeously Green Survival Guide:** fun app that tells you what's in your makeup and sunscreen before you buy it
- **Get Green:** provides a tip of the day on how to be green

Financial Tips for Baby's First Year

This may seem random to have financial information in a baby book. However, I'm not trying to win awards for maintaining the status quo. I spent years studying and working in an industry that makes ridiculous amounts of money because the people in control of the system have all the information and the people who depend on the system have little to none. So let's get smarter on a few things financial for baby's first year.

- [ ] **Set aside at least three months' living expenses for emergencies** and then add three months more, if you can.
- [ ] **Create a budget using software or an online tool.** For a free, web-based personal financial tool that plugs into all of your banks, credit cards, investments, and retirement accounts, showing you where your money goes with cool charts and graphs, try Mint.com or the Mint Mobile app.
- [ ] **Purchase life insurance for you and your spouse or increase current coverage.** Consider purchasing a term insurance policy, which is cheaper than permanent insurance and has a death benefit without an investment account attached. A twenty or thirty-year premium term policy, which is convertible to permanent insurance in the future, is adequate. With a routine physical and a medical questionnaire, you can lock in rates for the next twenty to thirty years.
- [ ] **Consider disability insurance.** While supporting your child, you will need to guarantee income if you can't work.
- [ ] **Make a will.** Half of all Americans and 70% of adults under age thirty-four do not have a will.[147] If you and your spouse die without a will, the state will choose a guardian for your child and decide how

your property is to be divided and distributed. If you have family assets that you would like to be passed directly to a child, and not your spouse, a trust must be established.

- ❑ **Do your banking at a credit union, if possible**. Credit unions are nonprofit cooperatives that are owned by their members. The revenue generated by credit unions is used to cover operating costs, but they do not have shareholders and a main goal of maximizing profits beyond costs like a bank. In general, credit unions have higher returns for deposits, lower rates on loans, and fewer fees. Find a credit union near you at MyCreditUnion.gov.
- ❑ **If you are buying a new home to make space for baby, consider these tips.** I purchased my first home as a single, clueless twenty-something and gave up thousands of dollars, due to my lack of negotiation skills and limited knowledge about compound interest, mortgage rates, and credit scores. Educate yourself and save big bucks.
  - ▸ **Maximize your credit score before applying for a mortgage or loan.**
  - ▸ **Never buy a mortgage from your bank**. A default move might be to walk into Wells Fargo, Chase, or your local Bank of America to finance your new home, but don't do it. These retail rates are probably higher than you can get elsewhere.
  - ▸ **Look up wholesale mortgage rates online and compare rates** from a number of banks, lenders, and mortgage brokers.
  - ▸ **Beware of the "bait and switch" tactic.** Don't select a mortgage provider based on quotes offered online or over the telephone. Loan providers can't legally be held to price quotes until you "lock in" your interest rate since the market is constantly changing. Many will offer low-ball, phony rates to rope you in as a client. Shortly before signing the dotted line, the lender will present new loan terms. By this time, borrowers feel they have too much invested to back out.
  - ▸ **Beware of "house flipping" scams.** If the home you are considering was recently a foreclosure or bargain snag fixed up by an investor, beware of inflated real estate appraisals. Values of these types of homes tend to get over-inflated so that everyone (investor, appraiser, and local closing agent) gets a piece of the pricey pie.

- ❑ **Check your credit score regularly, especially before applying for a mortgage or loan.** CreditKarma.com and Credit Karma Mobile provide free credit scores and free credit monitoring. To bump up your credit score, try these tips.
  - ▸ **Dispute all errors.**
  - ▸ **Negotiate past late payments** (i.e., write a letter to Visa, explain any hardship or mistake, and offer payment of your balance for "erasing" a blemish on your credit).
  - ▸ **Ask to increase any available credit limits on existing accounts**, as long as it will not encourage you to spend more.
  - ▸ **Do not close any credit card accounts.** If you opened a card for a specific reward, such as bonus points or airline miles, but then must pay an annual fee later, call and negotiate dropping the fee, or downgrade the card (i.e., "I would like to downgrade my platinum card with the $50 fee to a gold card with no fee.")
  - ▸ **Pay your bills on time.** This makes up 35% of your credit score. Now that you are a parent, expect to be more absent-minded than ever before. Set up auto-payments.
  - ▸ **Pay off any credit card balances before applying for a loan**, even if you typically pay the balance month to month.
- ❑ **Take advantage of child tax deductions, credits, and savings programs.** Talk to an attorney for tax advice. Looking into these types of tax savings programs could save you thousands of dollars.*
  - ▸ **Dependent exemption.** When you add a child to your family, you can add one more tax exemption called a "dependent exemption" to your personal exemption, or exemptions if you are filing jointly. The dependent exemption reduces your taxable income, and the amount you save depends on your tax bracket—the higher your bracket, the more you save up to a phase-out income.
  - ▸ **Child Tax Credit.** The popular $1,000-per-child tax credit, provided your income is below a certain threshold ($55,000 married filing separately, $75,000 single, or $110,000 for married filing jointly) is complex but worth checking out. The child tax credit was enacted in 2013 as part of the "fiscal

* See http://www.irs.gov/Individuals/Parents for current information.

cliff" bill and offers parents a reduction of their tax bill dollar for dollar, if they qualify.

- **The Child and Dependent Care Tax Credit.** This offering provides a 20% to 35% credit for the first $3,000 of child care expenses, or a $6,000 limit with two or more qualifying children, including day care centers, nannies, and even day camps during the summer break.
- **Dependent Care Flexible Spending Account (FSA).** Check to see if your employer offers a Dependent Care FSA, which lets you set aside a portion of your paycheck tax free to pay for child care expenses. This also lowers your taxable income. There are typically limits to the amounts contributed.
- **Medical Flexible Spending Account (FSA).** This FSA lets you set aside a portion of your wages tax free for out-of-pocket medical expenses, such as co-payments, deductibles, some drugs, and other qualifying expenses. FSAs are available through many employer-based health plans; however, the major disadvantage is that you must spend what you put into the account.
- **Affordable Care Act Tax Provisions for Individuals and Families.** If you get coverage through the health insurance marketplace, you and your family may be eligible for the Premium Tax Credit (PTC).

- [ ] **Get started on college savings**. Set up a fund that you, grandparents, and relatives can contribute to early on, if budget allows. For a baby born in 2015, a college cost calculator from Collegesavings.org estimates that in 18 years, the cost of tuition, fees, room, and board for four years of private college will add up to $657,011 (using a 7% cost inflation rate). The cost of out-of-state public college will amount to $509,029. In-state public college will cost $295,308, and four years of in-state community college, $172,293.* Just for fun, I tried another cost calculator on Finaid.org and estimated what sending a baby born in 2015 to Duke University might cost seventeen years later (based on current tuition). The answer: $891,006.

---

* Note: The national average tuition cost has inflated 6-7% each year for the past 30 years. Total cost estimates based on national averages are calculated by the College Board's Trends in Pricing.

Saving Money on Baby Costs

If you add up the average cost for baby's first year, using moderately-priced baby registry items and day care, you can expect to exceed $10,000. If you hire a full-time nanny and select top-of-the-line baby gear and eco-friendly products, you can expect to top $20,000 per year. With USDA estimates projecting middle class parents to spend $245,340 for child expenses up to age 18, some of these cost-cutting measures for baby might be looking pretty good.*

- ❑ **Don't rush into upgrading your home.** This is probably the thing that you can do to save the most money on baby costs. Infants do not take up that much space.
- ❑ **Embrace hand-me-downs.** Children outgrow clothes, toys, and gear quickly. Start a baby-gear swap among friends with children of different ages, sharing high chairs, baby food blenders, bouncers, jumpers, and age-specific toys. Once baby is on the go, many of these expensive items will become unnecessary.
- ❑ **Breastfeed your baby.** The cost of formula and supplies can be $1,500 per year, or more, if you plan to buy premium equipment and organic formula.
- ❑ **Make homemade baby food.** An organic baby food pouch that costs $1.80 has about $0.30 of the same fresh food ingredients.
- ❑ **Buy generic store-brand formula and disposable diapers.** The FDA regulates a minimum standard for nutrients in infant formula,

* Costs by location are lower in the urban South ($230,610) and rural ($193,590) regions of the country. Families in the urban Northeast had the highest costs to raise a child ($282,480).

and private label diapers are typically older brand name diapers in a different package.

- ❑ **Use coupons for diapers and formula.** Once your baby settles on a diaper brand, register on the brand's web site for coupons and free samples. Do the same for infant formula. You may not be a coupon clipper for the rest of your shopping list, but diapers and formula are products that you will buy consistently. Keep coupons in your wallet.
- ❑ **Shop at warehouse stores, such as Costco, Sam's Club, or BJs, for diapers, wipes, and formula.** Look for monthly coupons in store booklets. When the coupons apply, stock up. If you live in the city, try the Boxed mobile app for warehouse-sized purchases and prices without the drive to the suburbs.
- ❑ **Use cloth diapers and wash them yourself.** Expect to save money over disposables, especially if the same diapers and inserts are used with multiple children.
- ❑ **Buy baby products online.** Look for free shipping. Always use a promo code. Take advantage of tax-free purchases in a few remaining states. In general, don't buy everyday items at stores with a baby registry.
- ❑ **Research prices online before making purchases in a brick and mortar store**. Bring coupons from competitors. Ask retailers for discounts, such as discounts for multiples, or coupons that can be accessed via text or email.
- ❑ **Use deal sites to snag bargains and money-saving tips**, such as Groupon, Living Social, babycheapskate.com, livingonthecheap.com, and freecycle.com.
- ❑ **Try a nanny share or sitter swap** with trusted neighbors and friends.
- ❑ **Use your family for free babysitting**, and offer acts of kindness in return (e.g., help set up a new router or printer for your parents, help your younger sister organize her apartment, etc.).
- ❑ **Buy white or unisex-colored clothing** that can be used for a boy or girl. White onesies can be used as undershirts for both genders in winter. Buy all wearable blankets, pacifiers, toys and gear in gender-neutral colors.
- ❑ **Buy kids' clothing the next size up or two at the end of the season**. Stock up at closeout prices, especially mid-summer and at the end of the year.

Did you Know?

Online Dynamic Pricing

Online dynamic pricing or price customization is fully legal, which means that different people pay different prices for all types of things online. This means that purchases of luxury goods or pricey hotels will likely make your toys and baby food pouches more expensive. Before buying anything online, follow these guidelines:

- Before all purchases, clear your browser data and cookies and log out of your account.
- Do not let retail or service websites, such as travel sites, store your personal information. This connects your IP address to your physical address. It may be inconvenient to type in your shipping and personal information each time, but it could also save you money in the long run.
- Let items linger in your cart. Online retailers see this and will often give a little push, such as a coupon or free shipping, to complete the transaction.
- Don't rush through to the payment page. If pricing software senses that you are clicking quickly toward the payment page, those who seem too eager will receive higher prices (and no special offers).
- Before making a sizable purchase online, have a friend or family member price check it for you, in case you were unable to clear your history completely.
- Do not make large purchases or shop for travel with a Mac, if possible. Mac users are notoriously big spenders. For example, they spend up to 30% more a night on hotels, and companies know they have a significantly higher average income.[148] Sort product lists by price knowing that Mac users will receive higher-priced products on the first page of offerings.
- Try to avoid putting in your zip code before a purchase, or try different zip codes and see if the price changes.
- Never make purchases by clicking links in the "Customers Who Purchased This Also Bought..." section. Log out and revisit the site without your customer name on the page.
- Download a good spyware program if you want to clear spyware (or your paper trail) off the computer.

- ❑ **Turn everyday items into toys,** such as spatulas, pots, pans, measuring spoons, cups, etc.
- ❑ **Try not to load up on toys from dollar-type stores or the entry section at Target, etc.** These toys typically break within minutes, or they are thrown away days after purchase.
- ❑ **Use your local library for free story time and parks for playtime.** Visit a recreation center for mommy-and-me-type classes.
- ❑ **Send "wish lists" with practical items to gift givers and family for holidays and birthdays.** This can help with your budget for shoes, clothing, and essential items.
- ❑ **Avoid purchasing food and baby supplies while on the go.** Put a small bag in your car with emergency diapers and wipes, pack snacks, and fill bottles and sippy cups ahead of time to avoid expensive meals and a la carte supplies. Eat at restaurants with a salad bar to feed babies and toddlers healthy foods from your plate.

Choosing a Child Care Center

If you work outside the home, your choice of child care may be one of the most important decisions that you make for your child. Child care should be thought of as a fluid situation that may change depending on your circumstances. For example, if your baby was born prematurely or has health issues, you may want to wait a few months to introduce baby to a larger child care center, especially during cold and flu season. As your child gets older, you may be able to transition more easily from a nanny or babysitter to a child care center. Here are some considerations for child care.

Comparison of child care options

Child care center (day care center)

Pros: state regulated; possibly accredited beyond state requirements (such as National Association for the Education of Young Children or NAEYC); extra resources for toys and supplies; other children to play with; accountability; additional safety; higher supervision of caregivers

Cons: a strict schedule requires precise drop-off and pickup times (with fees incurred for every minute late); potential overstimulation; lack of peaceful sleeping options; more germs than care at home; other children may adversely affect your child

Average Cost: $380 to $1,564 a month for babies and toddlers*

Home day care

Pros: usually less expensive than other options; home environment; smaller group than a day care center; other children to play with; usually more flexibility with drop-off and pickup times

Cons: no backup if the care provider gets sick; less stringent accountability and licensing; safety standards may be lower; more germs than care at home; closed during holidays and vacation time; TV may be used excessively for younger children who can't tattle

Average Cost: $300 to $1,000 a month for babies and toddlers

Nanny

Pros: more convenient than day care; flexibility in scheduling; peaceful sleep in familiar surroundings; consistency with one caregiver; one-on-one attention (interactive conversation with an adult); a nanny may care for a sick child when a day care center would require backup

Cons: nanny supervision is low; a baby or toddler cannot communicate indiscretions; dependence on one person; need for backup care; the extra expense and paperwork of being an employer (nanny taxes, paying for sick time and vacation time, etc.)

Average Cost: $2,167 to $3,033 a month for babies and toddlers

Let's proceed with how to choose a child care center (the Hiring a Nanny or Babysitter checklist is coming up next).

---

* Source for child care costs: National Association of Child Care Resource and Referral Agencies (NACCRRA)

Did You Know?

Scheduling Technology, Low-Income Working Parents, and Child Care

Did you know that sophisticated workplace technology is doing battle with modern families, especially lower income parents? According to the Bureau of Labor Statistics, nearly half of part-time workers ages 26 to 32 receive their schedules with less than a week's notice, and hours can vary dramatically. Nearly every major restaurant and retail store in the U.S. uses data software that schedules workers based on the smallest details, such as weather changing, trucks arriving, and events shifting. When sales are up, workers are called in at the last minute; when sales are slowing, workers are sent home. This is not helpful to employees trying to establish a consistent routine for child care. In fact, these policies are terrible for children and their families. A single mom can hardly decide whether to use a day care center or babysitter when she doesn't even know when she will need them. With such an erratic schedule, how can she commit to classes to further her own education, or commit to pick up and drop off times for a child's early education? Spread the word and perhaps our nations' largest employers, such as Wal-Mart, McDonalds, and Target will be forced to think more about their people than their bottom lines.

Start early

- ❑ Start researching child care as early as possible. This process may take time.

Assess child care in your area

- ❑ Begin your search by talking to friends and co-workers in the area.
- ❑ Call local experts, such as a local Child Care Resource and Referral (CCR and R) agency, if desired.[149]

- ❑ Search "day care" or "child care" and your city online to find day care centers, or register for an online child care service such as Care.com or Sittercity.com. Narrow your choices with filters for geography, cost, facilities, nanny experience, languages spoken, reviews from parents, etc.
- ❑ Assess whether your family qualifies for any child care financial assistance.
- ❑ Obtain information about complaints and licensing violations.

When your base narrows, assess your child care options with the following questions:

Child-to-staff ratio and group size

- ❑ How many children are being cared for in the child care program for your age group? Double-check real vs. aspirational numbers. Visit during working hours to crosscheck.
- ❑ How many teachers or caregivers are present? State minimums exist for each age group (e.g., one home caregiver is limited to caring for two infants.)
- ❑ What is the turnover rate for teachers/staff?

Supervision and security

- ❑ Are children supervised at all times?
- ❑ Is supervision consistent during meal time and nap time?
- ❑ How do the caregivers discipline children?
- ❑ If the center is a home day care, are children taken out of the home? Does the provider walk or drive?
- ❑ Are there security cameras at the front desk to monitor visitors coming in and out?
- ❑ What is the pick-up and drop-off policy?

Director qualifications

- ❑ Does the director of a child care center have at least a bachelor's degree in a child-related field?
- ❑ How long has the director worked in child care? (At least two years of experience is preferable.)
- ❑ Does the director understand children well?
- ❑ Is this someone whom you would like to work with on a regular basis?

Lead teacher qualifications

- ❑ Does the lead teacher in a child care center have a bachelor's degree in a child-related field?
- ❑ Has the teacher worked in child care for at least two years?
- ❑ What is the level of interaction between teachers and parents?
- ❑ Is there any form of regular communication between teachers and parents?

Hand-washing and diapering

- ❑ Do all caregivers and children wash their hands often? (e.g., when children walk into the classroom, before eating, and after using the bathroom or changing diapers?)
- ❑ Is hand-washing consistent for older children who may be around your baby?
- ❑ Is the place where diapers are changed clean?
- ❑ Do caregivers always keep a hand on the child while changing his diaper?

Eating and sleeping

- ❑ What is the feeding schedule and meal policy?
- ❑ Is the program willing to use and warm breast milk?
- ❑ Does the center or home day care provide snacks and meals? At what age? What is the cost?

- ❑ If food is brought from home, is the center willing to heat it?
- ❑ Is each child able to sleep according to his own rhythms, or is a schedule set by the center?
- ❑ Where will my child sleep?

Immunizations

- ❑ Is your child up-to-date on all of the required immunizations?
- ❑ Does your state have a standard medical entry form for child care centers? What other information do you need to gather from your child's pediatrician for entry?
- ❑ Does the child care program have records proving that the other children in care are up-to-date on all required immunizations? Ask about the number of exemptions.

Hazardous or toxic substances

- ❑ Are hazardous or toxic substances kept away from children? (e.g. cleaning supplies, rodent traps, pest sprays, gardening supplies)
- ❑ Has the building been checked for dangerous substances like radon, lead (lead dust from paint), carbon monoxide, and asbestos?
- ❑ Is poison control information posted? Are teachers trained for poison incidences?

Emergency plan

- ❑ Does the child care program have an emergency plan if a child is injured, sick, or lost?
- ❑ Does the child care program have a food allergy plan?
- ❑ Does the child care program have a standard process about who to contact in an emergency?
- ❑ Consider leaving your cell number on your child's check-in sheet each day, in addition to forms filled out for day care entry.

Fire/emergency drills

- ❑ Does the child care program have a plan in case of a disaster like a fire, tornado, flood, blizzard, or earthquake? National emergencies?
- ❑ Does the child care program do practice drills once every month?

Child abuse and accountability

- ❑ Have all caregivers had background checks?
- ❑ Can caregivers be seen by others at all times, so a child is never alone with one caregiver?

Medications

- ❑ Does the child care program keep medication out of reach from children?
- ❑ What is the medicine policy? What is the policy for applying diaper cream and sunscreen?
- ❑ Are the caregivers trained and the medications labeled to make sure the right child gets the right amount of the right medication at the right time?

Staff training and first aid

- ❑ Have caregivers been trained to keep children healthy and safe from injury and illness?
- ❑ Does the staff know how to do basic first aid and CPR?
- ❑ Has the staff been trained to understand and meet the needs of children of different ages?
- ❑ Are all child care staff, volunteers, and substitutes trained on and implementing infant back sleeping and safe sleep policies to reduce the risk of SIDS (sudden infant death syndrome)?
- ❑ When infants are sleeping, are they on their backs with no pillows, quilts, stuffed toys, or other soft bedding in the crib with them?

Playgrounds

- ❑ Is the playground regularly inspected for safety?
- ❑ Does a fence surround the playground?
- ❑ Are the soil and playground surfaces checked often for dangerous substances and hazards?
- ❑ How old is the equipment?
- ❑ Is the equipment the right size and type for the age of children who use it?

Cost benefit analysis

- ❑ If a child care center is significantly more or less expensive than its competitors, why?
- ❑ Do you have a back-up plan if your child is sick? How much will that cost per hour?
- ❑ Do you have a list of priorities for your child care needs?
- ❑ Is it worth paying more to have your child at home with a nanny, or do you prefer the accountability and structure of a day care center?
- ❑ Is home day care a better option to balance cost and size of the day care center?

Other considerations

- ❑ How is TV used in the day care?
- ❑ What is a typical day in the day care center?
- ❑ Are you allowed to observe the prospective day care center, or home day care, during working hours? Assess overall impression, happiness of the children, and level of speaking engagement with the children.
- ❑ Have you talked with other parents with children currently attending the prospective child care center?
- ❑ Do caregivers respect the culture, languages, and values of the families in the center?[150]

Practical Tips from Real Parents

Day Care and Child Care Centers

- If possible, choose a day care center near your work. Late fees can add up if you have to commute through traffic, or if you are habitually late.
- Make sure that you read the fine print with late fees for pickup. One day care we considered was $5 per minute late (after a five minute grace period). This seemed excessive at first, but now I understand why. The parents, including myself, were always running late.
- Home day care can be good or bad for baby's first year. In an environment with just a few children, your baby will probably get more attention and more sleep than in a commercial day care center. However, you have to constantly assess how other children coming into the home are affecting your child.
- With home day care, be mindful of males living in and passing through the home. No one wants to think about this stuff, but child sexual abuse offenders are 90% to 95% male.
- Expect lots of colds the first year in day care. Babies put everything into their mouths, and it is impossible for workers to keep your child from getting sick.
- If your baby has a perpetual diaper rash, put together a rash kit and provide explicit instructions for baby's diaper care.
- If your child seems unusually unhappy at drop-off or pickup, don't discount this reaction. There may be a problem.
- Don't be afraid to speak up or change your child care center if you think something is wrong.

Hiring a Nanny or Babysitter

A few years ago, a friend and his expecting wife shared how thrilled they were to have selected a nanny for their unborn child who would teach their baby three different languages. Seriously, whose child isn't trilingual these days? I withheld any sarcastic comments. However, it really bothered me–this intelligent, well-meaning couple may have unknowingly selected the wrong caretaker for their child. Above all other qualifications, a good nanny or babysitter should have:

- Knowledge of child development
- Self-control
- Emotional maturity

She should understand why children behave the way they do, and she must be able to calm and soothe an upset child. She should understand that safety comes first and be familiar with the repetitive, unpredictable nature of child care. Languages spoken, academic degrees, and other societal measures of achievement are not at the core of what it takes to love and nurture a child. Moreover, children need consistency. If a nanny is only able to work a few months while taking classes for a short time, she may not be a good fit for a long-term job.

Getting started

- ❑ **Start early.** The process of hiring a nanny requires time and effort. It may take two to three months to conduct a search without an agency.

- ❑ **Do not rush the process.** Anyone can call himself or herself a nanny. There is no regulating agency that licenses or monitors nannies; therefore, your effort in screening individuals is key to discerning caretakers that can be trusted with your child.
- ❑ **Assess your budget for a nanny agency.** Agency fees can range from $1200–5000. Some busy, working parents find this service to be worth the money, while others find the fee prohibitively expensive.
- ❑ **If you decide to use an agency, call several different ones and ask to speak with the director**. Read the small print before you sign any contract.
- ❑ **For self-searchers, get organized**. Label all emails and forms with a "Nanny Search" header or filter. Keep a notebook to log phone calls and notes.
- ❑ **If you are using an online service, such as 4nannies.com, Care.com, or Sittercity.com, search for online promotion codes and reduced or free first month rates.** Care.com is my favorite online service.

Self-search: advertising the position

- ❑ **Post your job with an online service and browse candidates in your area**. Contact anyone who fits your profile, even if the availability does not match up completely.
- ❑ **Ensure that your job posting establishes clear expectations.** This should help filter candidates. Consider the following questions:
  - ▸ How many days per week? Hours?
  - ▸ Will you request occasional overtime or overnights for work travel?
  - ▸ How many years of experience are required?
  - ▸ Is proximity to your home required?
  - ▸ Does your candidate have reliable transportation?
  - ▸ What specific duties are expected, especially if housekeeping is included? Cooking, cleaning, laundry?
  - ▸ Are driving duties expected? Do you require a clean driving record?
  - ▸ Is health insurance provided?

- ▸ How much paid vacation time is provided?

- ❑ **If you are uncomfortable with an online search, post ads at a local college, church or synagogue, or on a local moms group list-serve.**
- ❑ **Protect your personal information** by not including your home phone or address until you have narrowed candidates. Establish a separate email address for your search, if desired.
- ❑ **Request that candidates leave their name, phone number, years of experience, and other qualifications on your cell phone or email.**
- ❑ **Conduct a quick Internet search to assess each candidate.** Eliminate those with unsavory Facebook profiles, photos, tweets, etc.
- ❑ **Call your list of candidates with a standard set of questions.**
- ❑ **Set up interviews only with those who answer the questions to your satisfaction.** Verify the hours and days required and a short job description before confirming an in-person interview.

Self-search: conducting background checks

- ❑ **Collect identification information for each applicant.** Remember, this is standard procedure for any job application, and a full-time nanny is going to be with your child daily. You do not need to collect this information for a simple babysitting job.
  - ▸ Birth certificate or Social Security Card
  - ▸ Valid driver's license
  - ▸ Home phone, address, and cell number
  - ▸ Character references (no family members)
  - ▸ Work references (addresses and phone numbers, no friends or family)
  - ▸ CPR certificate, if required
  - ▸ Proof of a physical exam from the last two years, if required
  - ▸ Resume and cover letter
- ❑ **Make copies of IDs and crosscheck references.**
- ❑ **Consider visiting the home of references to ensure that kids are present.**
- ❑ **Conduct a criminal background check.** Check for aliases and numerous addresses in a short period of time. Conduct background

checks with a healthy dose of skepticism. Many candidates will provide misleading information, overestimate qualifications, and supply friends and family as references.

Interviewing

- ❑ **Make a list of your priorities**, such as years of experience, experience with infants, clean driving record, irons, cooks, cleans, etc. Seek the best candidate for your priorities.

Interview questions: personality assessment

Applies to both nannies and babysitters

- ❑ Can you tell me about your childhood?
- ❑ Tell me about your past experience nannying or babysitting. What were the ages of the children?
- ❑ Do you enjoy working with children?
- ❑ What do you find most challenging about nannying?
- ❑ Please explain any gaps in work history.
- ❑ What is your child-rearing philosophy?
- ❑ What is your view on disciplining children as a nanny?
- ❑ How would you handle the following situations:
  - ▸ What if our infant has a high fever?
  - ▸ What if our infant has colic and will not stop crying?
  - ▸ What if our daughter swallowed a coin and was choking?
  - ▸ What if our son fell down the stairs?
  - ▸ What if our toddler son bites, or hits, the baby?
- ❑ Are you flexible and able to roll with it, or do you prefer structure and planning ahead?

Interview questions: job assessment

- ❑ Are you willing to do light housework?
- ❑ Are you willing to iron? Fold clothing?

- ❑ Are you willing to cook? Take care of our pet?
- ❑ Are there household activities that you will not do?
- ❑ Are you willing to take our baby on walks outside regularly?
- ❑ How many children are you comfortable supervising?
- ❑ How flexible is your schedule if we need to leave early, get home late, or travel overnight?
- ❑ What is your driving record?
- ❑ Are you willing to abide by household rules for TV watching and media use while on the job?

Finalizing details

- ❑ Consider a trial period, observing your prospective nanny and evaluating whether you are ready to enter into a contract together.

When your nanny or babysitter arrives at your home

- ❑ Make sure that you have your nanny's personal information on file: address, cell phone number, and email.
- ❑ Post information for all members of your family.
- ❑ Post your home address and phone number, in case of emergency.
- ❑ Determine the best way to reach each other during the day, or in the case of an emergency.
- ❑ Post numbers for the pediatrician/pediatrician's office, schools, and a close friend, family member, or neighbor that could assist in case of emergency.
- ❑ Ensure that both you and your nanny have a signed work agreement, including agreed-upon pay, work hours, and expected duties.

Nanny Taxes

Here's the scoop on nanny taxes. You will have some friends who choose to pay their nannies in the clear (filing taxes), and you will have some friends who choose to pay their nannies under the table (paying cash). Be assured this topic will never be discussed at playgroups or dinner parties. Moreover, some expecting parents may not understand that workers must prove eligibility to work in the U.S. before filing taxes (employees affirm this by filling out a form called an I-9.) So to help you navigate this tricky topic, especially for full-time nanny positions, let's discuss nanny taxes.

Pros: By paying taxes, you will not have to worry about the IRS or legal troubles, especially if you are an aspiring CEO or public official. Paying employer taxes allows your nanny to receive benefits that other professional workers enjoy, such as Social Security income, Medicare, disability, and unemployment benefits.

Cons: Your nanny will make roughly 15% less than her hourly rate, and you will pay 10% more for taxes and other costs. The paperwork is complicated, necessitating regular filings to your employee, the IRS, and state government. Note: You can hire companies, such as HomePay or HomeWork Solutions to do the hard work for you, or use DIY online subscription services, such as QuickBooks or NannyPay.

Practical Tips from Real Parents

Hiring a Nanny or Babysitter

- Your baby is hard-wired to want and need you, and he is going to cry for you. Loudly. This is the toughest part about leaving a child with someone else.
- If you are a working mother without family in the area, know that you will be delicately handling a nanny relationship for years to come, and it's not easy.
- There is no perfect nanny. No one can be expected to take care of your child exactly as you do.
- Micro-managing your nanny can have horrible consequences. Pick your battles.
- Treat your nanny well. This is a business relationship, but it is also a personal relationship that you do not want to jeopardize.
- Do not undercut your nanny's pay, vacation time, or talk down to her. Treat her professionally, and invest in her as part of your family.
- Be careful with hiring nannies for children between ages zero and three. When children are older, they can tell you what they did all day. Trust your child, regardless of age, if he or she is consistently fussy with a nanny.
- Nanny cams are legal in all fifty states, even without consent, as long as they are not in a bathroom or a private place, such as an au pair's bedroom. However, we found that we didn't have time to watch our nanny cam footage (to actually catch something), and if you don't trust your nanny, then you probably shouldn't hire her anyway. Note: Some states protect against using audio in recordings.
- Be sure to explicitly state rules about phone use at home, while driving, and at the park, especially once baby is mobile. Set hard and fast rules about TV and screen time, and don't keep convenient junk food around the house, or else that is what your nanny will feed your child.
- If your child is consistently dirty and unclean, talk to your nanny or babysitter. This can be a bad sign of other areas neglected. Safety and sanitation should be non-negotiable.

- If your nanny has other children, your relationship may be in constant conflict, especially when you are late, because she has to make provisions for her own children.
- A nanny with her own children will be out of work more often, requiring back-up care. On the other hand, someone who is significantly older may not have the energy to chase an energetic toddler, and teenagers are on their phones constantly. Take your pick.
- Many nannies will want to care for your child along with their own child or children. Just know that a nanny's own active toddler may consistently wake your newborn, while a nanny's newborn may keep your older baby or toddler from going outside, to the park, etc. due to their nap schedule. Make sure that you receive a discount for this inconvenience.
- If you live in an urban area, you will notice that nanny pricing is all over the map. Super affluent households throw normal wages through the roof in certain cities.
- Set your rules and schedule very clearly up front to avoid seeming like a micro-manager later, such as rules for healthy foods, diapering, TV, cell phone use, tummy time, learning activities, outside time, discipline, safety, etc.

Childproofing and Child Safety

You may not need to reference this checklist until baby is on the move. However, when that time comes, I want to help you think of all types of safety considerations. Children are infinitely curious, and parents and caretakers have lots of competing distractions.

Kitchen

Critical "must-do" safety checks

- ❑ Does the cabinet under the sink contain cleaning supplies, bug sprays, dishwasher detergent, and dishwashing liquids? Is it locked with a childproof latch?
- ❑ Are knives, forks, scissors, and other sharp tools in a drawer with a childproof latch?
- ❑ Are glass dishes and appliances with sharp blades stored out of reach?
- ❑ Are matches and lighters stored in a locked or out of reach drawer?
- ❑ Are bottles containing alcohol stored out of reach?
- ❑ Are plastic garbage bags and small grocery bags out of reach?
- ❑ Are refrigerator magnets and other small choking hazards out of reach?
- ❑ Are vitamin or medicine bottles stored out of reach?
- ❑ Is your fire extinguisher out of reach?
- ❑ Does the child's highchair have a safety belt with a strap between the legs? Do you *always* use this belt?

Important safety considerations
(varies child to child, depending on level of curiosity)

- ❑ Have you considered knob protectors on the stove knobs?
- ❑ Have you considered a dishwasher lock so kids can't reach breakable dishes, knives, and other dangerous objects?
- ❑ When cooking, are all pot handles on the stove turned inward or placed on back burners where your child can't reach them?
- ❑ Are appliances unplugged when not in use, with cords out of reach?
- ❑ Are childproof latches installed on cabinet doors?
- ❑ If your child is particularly curious, have you considered a refrigerator lock?

Child's room/bedroom

Critical "must-do" safety checks

- ❑ Is your baby's crib a hand-me-down? If so, is it a "drop side" crib? These cribs are illegal for sale in the U.S. If it is, do you have a repair kit installed to bolster the drop side? Are your crib screws tight?
- ❑ Are crib slats less than $^2/_8$ to $^3/_8$ inches or six centimeters apart?
- ❑ Is the crib mattress firm and flat? Does it fit snugly in the crib (no more than two finger widths between the mattress and slats)?
- ❑ Is the crib free of soft pillows, large stuffed animals, and soft bedding?
- ❑ Are window blind and curtain cords tied with clothespins, or cord clips? Are they kept well out of reach and away from cribs?
- ❑ Does your baby's changing table have a safety belt?
- ❑ Are nightlights in the nursery not touching any fabric, such as bedskirts or curtains?
- ❑ Are bookshelves and other furniture secured with wall brackets so they can't be tipped over?

Adult's bedroom, office, living, and dining rooms

- ❑ Are medication bottles, coins, scissors, and other small or sharp objects out of reach?

- ❑ Are window blind and curtain cords tied with clothespins or cord clips?
- ❑ Are there protective pads on the corners of coffee tables, furniture, fireplaces, and countertops that have sharp edges? Did you know that you can match colors of padding to your furniture (white corner pads for white furniture)?
- ❑ Are doorknob covers in place to secure off-limits rooms, such as the office, garage, or utility room?
- ❑ Are trash cans regularly changed? Dumpster diving is a favorite pastime for babies and toddlers.

Bathroom

- ❑ Is the thermostat on the hot water heater set below 120° F (49° C) for preventing burns?
- ❑ Are razor blades, scissors, and clippers stored out of reach (including Mom's razor on the side of the tub)?
- ❑ Are all prescription and nonprescription medications, cosmetics, and cleaners stored in a locked cabinet? Are childproof caps on all medications?
- ❑ Do the outlets have ground fault circuit interrupters, which protect against electrocution if an electrical appliance gets wet? If you live in an older home that may not be "up to code," have an electrician inspect your circuit breaker panel.
- ❑ Are toilets always left closed?
- ❑ Are all hair dryers, curling irons, and electric razors unplugged when not in use? When Mom finishes with the flat iron or curling iron, does she have a safe place to let it cool (including the cord)?

Garage and laundry area

- ❑ Are tools and supplies used for gardening, automotive, and lawn care stored safely away from children?
- ❑ Are hazardous chemicals for the car, pool, and gardening in a locked area?

- ❑ Are recycling containers storing glass and metal out of reach? Are garbage cans covered?
- ❑ Are bleaches, detergents, and all other cleaning products out of reach?
- ❑ Are apartment or high rise laundry chutes locked with childproof locks?

Walls and floors

- ❑ Are walls in good condition, with no peeling or cracking paint (especially in homes built before 1978)?
- ❑ Are rugs fitted with no-slip pads underneath?
- ❑ Have you purchased a handy sweeper to keep floors free of old food and dirt from shoes?
- ❑ Have you swept your floor for random screws, nails, hooks, coins, push pins, and old Christmas tree hangers (getting down on hands and knees with eyes at floor level)?
- ❑ Have you considered a "no shoes inside" rule for your household?

Doors and windows

- ❑ Have you considered doorknob covers so that your child cannot leave the house? Have you considered a door alarm, if you live in a high traffic area?
- ❑ Are there safety bars or window guards installed on upper-story windows left open for fresh air? Note: A Naval Academy classmate and friend lost his four-year-old child from a fall through a second story window screen.
- ❑ Are window blind cords tied with clothespins or cord clips?

Stairways

- ❑ Are there hardware-mounted safety gates at the top and bottom of every stairway? The top of the stairs gate should be secured with screws into the wall or banister railing.

- ❑ Are you considering skipping a safety gate because you have a toddler sibling or an elderly family member who cannot pass the stairs freely? Don't do it. Baby potentially falling far outweighs the inconvenience of the gate.
- ❑ Are stairways clear of tripping hazards, such as clothing or toys?
- ❑ Are railings and banisters secured?
- ❑ Is the door to the basement steps kept locked? Is there a safety gate behind the door? Don't rely on memory to close the basement door. Look for inexpensive extra gates at yard sales.

Electrical

- ❑ Are unused outlets covered with safety plugs?
- ❑ Are major electrical appliances grounded?
- ❑ Have cord holders been used to keep longer cords fastened against walls?
- ❑ Are televisions, computers, and stereo equipment securely positioned against walls?

Heating and cooling elements

- ❑ Are baseboard heaters covered with childproof screens if necessary?
- ❑ Have gas fireplaces been secured with a valve cover or key?
- ❑ Do all working fireplaces have a screen and other barriers in place when in use?
- ❑ Have your chimneys been cleaned recently?
- ❑ Are all electric space heaters at least three feet (91 centimeters) from beds, curtains, or anything flammable?
- ❑ Are window A/C units away from baby's bedding?

If you own firearms

- ❑ Are firearms stored in a securely locked case out of kids' reach? All firearms should be stored unloaded and in un-cocked position.
- ❑ Is ammunition stored in a separate place and in a securely locked container out of kids' reach?

- ❑ Are keys kept where children cannot find them?

Outdoors (backyard and pool)

- ❑ Are sidewalks and outdoor stairways clear of concrete cracks or missing pieces?
- ❑ Are swing set parts free from rust, splinters, and sharp edges?
- ❑ Are parts on swing sets or other outdoor equipment securely fastened?
- ❑ Is there climb-proof fencing, at least four feet (1.2 meters) high, on all sides of the pool?
- ❑ Does the fence have a self-closing gate with a childproof lock?

Emergency equipment and numbers

- ❑ Have you placed a list of emergency phone numbers in your home for caretakers?
- ❑ Are there fire extinguishers installed near the dryer and in the kitchen?
- ❑ Are there smoke detectors on each floor of your home? In each bedroom?
- ❑ Have you tested smoke detectors within the last month?
- ❑ Have you changed the batteries in the smoke detectors within the past six months?
- ❑ If you cook with or heat your home with natural gas or have an attached garage, have you considered installing a carbon monoxide detector in your home?
- ❑ If you live in a high crime or high traffic area, have you considered a home security system to protect your children and family members?

Prioritizing child safety

To help prioritize child safety, here are the five leading causes and total number of unintentional injury deaths among children by age group (the percentages for each age group are listed in parentheses).

Rank	Age <1	Ages 1–4	Ages 5–9	Ages 10–14
1	Suffocation 907 (77%)	Drowning 450 (31%)	Motor Vehicle Traffic 378 (49%)	Motor Vehicle Traffic 491 (68%)
2	Motor Vehicle Traffic 91 (8%)	Motor Vehicle Traffic 363 (25%)	Drowning 119 (15%)	Transportation other 117 (15%)
3	Drowning 45 (4%)	Fire/Burns 169 (12%)	Fire/Burns 88 (11%)	Drowning 90 (10%)
4	Fire/Burns 25 (2%)	Transportation other 147 (10%)	Transportation other 68 (9%)	Fire/Burns 53 (6%)
5	Poisoning 22 (2%)	Suffocation 125 (9%)	Suffocation 26 (3%)	Suffocation 41 (5%)

Source: National Center for Health Statistics, Centers for Disease Control and Prevention

Cold and Flu Season

You will be amazed how often a baby or small child can be sick, and there is not enough soap or hand sanitizer in the world to prevent every occurrence. Truthfully, the immune system needs exposure to bacteria, viruses, and other germs to work as designed. However, here are some tips for hopefully preventing a few sleepless nights and days of missed work with a sick child.

For newborns

- ❑ Do not allow people to hold or touch your baby until they have washed their hands.
- ❑ Avoid kissing baby on the face, especially if you have a cold.
- ❑ Keep a newborn baby away from crowds, especially indoors.
- ❑ Don't let anyone smoke around baby.
- ❑ Limit the time that preterm and high risk babies spend in a day care center, especially late fall to early spring when respiratory syncytial virus (RSV) – a highly contagious virus that infects the respiratory tract – and other illnesses are most prevalent.

For older babies

- ❑ Teach your child and all caregivers to wash their hands frequently with soap and water for twenty seconds. Sing the Happy Birthday or ABC song if you are having difficulties reaching twenty seconds.

- ❑ Wash your child's hands before eating and after trips to public places, despite protests and squirming. Roll up sleeves to the elbows to prevent unintended clothes changes.
- ❑ During peak cold and flu season, "detox" after day care. Wash baby's hands, take off her shoes, and remove all clothing when you get home.
- ❑ Use hand sanitizer, if soap and water are unavailable, but don't substitute triclosan-containing products for regular hand washings.
- ❑ In cold weather, bundle up the kids and go outside instead of hanging out in densely populated indoor areas such as malls, play gyms, and indoor playgrounds. Remember, germs are not just spread through direct contact. The flu virus spreads easily when respiratory droplets from an infected person's cough or sneeze move through the air to the mouth or nose of others in close proximity.
- ❑ Teach your kids to sneeze into their elbow if they don't have a tissue handy.
- ❑ If you know someone is sick, politely skip your visit or play date, especially if he or she has a fever.
- ❑ Clean and disinfect highly used surfaces. Studies have shown that the cold virus can survive up to two days on household surfaces:
  - ▶ Telephones and cell phones
  - ▶ Keyboards (including iPads and your mouse)
  - ▶ Doorknobs and cabinets
  - ▶ Refrigerator and microwave door handles
  - ▶ Light switches
  - ▶ Remote controls
  - ▶ Bathroom and kitchen faucets
  - ▶ Dishwasher handles
  - ▶ Sponges
  - ▶ Salt and pepper shakers
  - ▶ Toothbrushes
- ❑ If baby has a cold, wash plastic toys in soap and hot water. Put cloth books and plush toys in the laundry. Wrap stuffed animals in a pillowcase for protection.
- ❑ Do your best to keep siblings' toothbrushes separate, since as many as 10 million germs and bacteria can be found on a single toothbrush. The American Dental Association recommends replacing toothbrushes every three to four months.

- ❑ Keep a sick child at home until at least twenty-four hours after a fever has subsided, and he/she has no yellow or green mucus in the nose.
- ❑ Try a smart combination of remedies to treat minor illnesses at home:
  - ▸ Plenty of fluids: soak baby's nose with saline drops and suction out mucus before feedings
  - ▸ Plenty of rest
  - ▸ Plenty of love and attention
  - ▸ A warm bath: the steam from the warm water should help clear congestion
  - ▸ A vaporizer or humidifier: a vaporizer heats water until it turns to steam and a humidifier creates a cool mist (either one should help baby breathe easier as long as it is kept clean, though warm-air vaporizers do carry the risk of scalding)
- ❑ Be judicious when caring for your baby's first illnesses, but be aware of first time parent "fever phobia." The American Academy of Pediatrics (AAP) notes that fever is not an illness, but rather a physiologic response that is beneficial for fighting infection. Fever in and of itself it not known to endanger a generally healthy child; rather, fever may be beneficial.[151]
- ❑ Talk to your doctor about accurate medicine dosing and careful use of infant pain relievers. The AAP has recommended a milliliter-only standard to reduce the high incidence of parent medication errors.[152]
  - ▸ Always use the medicine dispenser that came with your medicine.
  - ▸ Double check all labels and measurements.
  - ▸ Never use a kitchen utensil to dispense medicine to your child.
  - ▸ Follow through with all prescriptions. If you receive an antibiotic for your child, give it to her in full. Don't stop it when your child is feeling better or she could get ill again.
  - ▸ Never give a child expired or unused medications.
  - ▸ Note your child's weight, since dosages for most nonprescription drugs are based on weight, not age.
  - ▸ Do not give any type of medicine to a child under age 3 months.
  - ▸ Do not give ibuprofen, such as Advil or Motrin, to a child less than 6 months old.

Practical Tips from Real Parents

Washing Hands and Preventing Illness

- ❏ Repetition, repetition, repetition. Make family hand-washing rules and routines, such as everyone must wash their hands before they eat and once they enter the home, especially after work or day care.
- ❏ Keep washcloths everywhere. Soap them up and wash away.
- ❏ Buy some fun soap or an automatic soap dispenser. This will get your kids wanting to wash their hands fast.
- ❏ If your little one is protesting hand-washing, try washing her favorite bath toy.
- ❏ If you have backaches from holding your heavier baby, wash his hands in the bathtub. Sit on the side while holding him. By the time he is standing, the tub will be at the perfect height.
- ❏ Worry less about baby crawling on dirty floors and more about baby in a close group setting with other potentially sick children.
- ❏ Talk to your doctor about when you should call him or her *before* your child gets sick.
- ❏ Adjust your context for fevers. For small children, a fever below 102 is generally considered low, 102 to 104 is moderate, and 104 and above is high. (Note: Call your child's doctor for any fever in an infant under age three months.)
- ❏ Boost baby's immunity with good nutrition. If your baby is old enough, give her a treat of 100% fruit or vegetable juice in the heart of cold and flu season.
- ❏ Slow down your schedule, if baby is getting sick again and again. Stress, lack of rest, and lack of a consistent routine can make it harder to fight off illness.
- ❏ Don't over-use acetaminophen and ibuprofen. I see many parents depending on these pain relievers to help their children sleep at night, especially in the winter or following illness, but they do not understand the risk of adverse drug effects and cumulative toxicity.

Raising a Smart Baby

Seeing the world through a child's eyes is one of life's most precious joys, and it is my hope that by the end of this list, you will see that raising a smart child is not about preparing him for the Ivy League. It's about instilling a wonder of the world, a curiosity, and a love of learning that will last a lifetime.

The following list is full of rich and meaningful learning tips. Entire books have been condensed into single bullet points; however, this is not to promote short attention spans. Rather, I want to expose parents to all types of research and literature to broaden their own libraries and scope for child development. For a deeper look at specific topics, please reference the "Notes" section in the back of the book.

- ❑ **Start with the idea of "It's never too early."** Learning begins the day your child is born, and a child who is nurtured with love and attention at a very early age will develop more readily in later years.
- ❑ **Do not hesitate to take your child to events and places that will broaden her mind**, such as museums, concerts, shows, and other events. Admission is likely to be free for children age two and under. Try not to underestimate your child's ability to grow from an experience but also have an exit plan in case the stimulation is too much.
- ❑ **Enjoy every day experiences.** Every outing doesn't have to be extraordinary. Any old place is new and interesting to a baby. A trip to the grocery store or a walk to the park is novel and exciting for baby.
- ❑ **Bond with baby. Hold baby often. Make her feel loved and protected.** The human brain is wired for survival first. If it doesn't feel

safe and secure, it can't learn. Studies on education gaps for children in poverty have shown this for decades. Prolonged, severe, or unpredictable stress in early childhood alters brain structures, impacting a child's social, emotional, cognitive, and physical growth for life. Bonding activities, such as skin-to-skin contact, holding baby, reading to baby, wearing baby, and learning to regulate negative emotions in the presence of baby build up a sense of safety and security.[153]

- ❑ **Try not to share your stress with baby.** Anxiety is contagious, and baby strongly depends upon emotional cues from his parents. The part of the brain most affected by stress early in life is the undeveloped prefrontal cortex, which is critical in self-regulating activities. This area of the brain is directly tied to executive function, including the abilities to make complex decisions, manage time and attention, plan and organize, and regulate inappropriate speech or behavior.
- ❑ **Breastfeed your baby.** Whether it is increased mother-baby bonding, natural DHA-ARA intake, or both, research is adding up to support breastfeeding and higher IQ.
  - ▸ In two studies involving more than 3,000 breast fed infants in United Kingdom and New Zealand, breastfeeding raised intelligence an average of nearly seven IQ points if the children had a particular version of a gene called FADS2 (about 90% of the population carries the FADS2 gene variant).[*] [154]
  - ▸ In 2013, another large study found that breastfeeding longer can make children smarter. Researchers at Boston Children's Hospital followed 1,312 babies and mothers from 1999 to 2010 and concluded that babies who were breastfed longer had better cognitive development later in life (controlling for mother's IQ and child's upbringing). A full year of breastfeeding could boost a child's IQ by four points over that of a child who did not breastfeed.[155]
- ❑ **Make learning fun.** In the 1980s, psychologist Benjamin Bloom conducted a groundbreaking study of world-class scientists, athletes,

---

* To scale seven points, IQ tests typically use a standardized scale with 100 as the median score. A score between 90 and 110, or the median plus or minus 10 indicates average intelligence. A score above 130 indicates exceptional intelligence, and a score below 70 may indicate mental retardation.

and musicians. In the study, Bloom's team interviewed 21 concert pianists, who were renowned for winning prestigious international competitions. What Bloom's team uncovered was somewhat unexpected. There was a remarkable absence of raw talent or genius during the pianists' early years. As it turned out, the members of this group were hardly Beethoven virtuosos. Most of them didn't stand out on national, regional, or even local levels. The common thread among this talented group was simple—they all described a "warm, loving, and supportive environment" for learning during their first experiences with music.[156]

- ❑ **Move over Tiger Mom. Bring in Dolphin Dad.** Happiness researcher and quick-witted TED talker Shawn Achor asserts that instead of tiger parenting, parents might consider dolphin parenting.[157] Dolphins are "playful, social, and intelligent." Parents should smile more and encourage their children, not by being delusional, but striving to be "rationally optimistic." Children raised by authoritarian or tiger parents may struggle with depressive symptoms, anxiety, and a feeling of alienation from others.[158]
- ❑ **Nurture the whole child.** Being smart goes beyond IQ. Raising a smart child includes teaching cognitive skills (ABCs and 123s), social-emotional cues (good behaviors and self-control), and non-cognitive skills or character traits (setting rules, emphasizing effort over results, asking questions rather than telling answers, and teaching perseverance by allowing your child to fail). The best predictor for academic success is not IQ. It's self-control.[153, 159]
- ❑ **Praise your child's effort rather than his personal qualities.** Researchers have found that toddlers ages one to three years who receive praise for their efforts (e.g., "You worked really hard on that") rather than praise based on personal characteristics (e.g., "You're a good girl" or "You're really smart") are more likely to prefer challenging tasks later and believe that future performance can be improved through hard work.[160]
- ❑ **Be a good role model for your child's development.** Children mimic their parents' behavior. If you react dramatically to small events, expect overreactions from your child. If you hit or yell when frustrated, expect your child to hit and yell. If you complain about

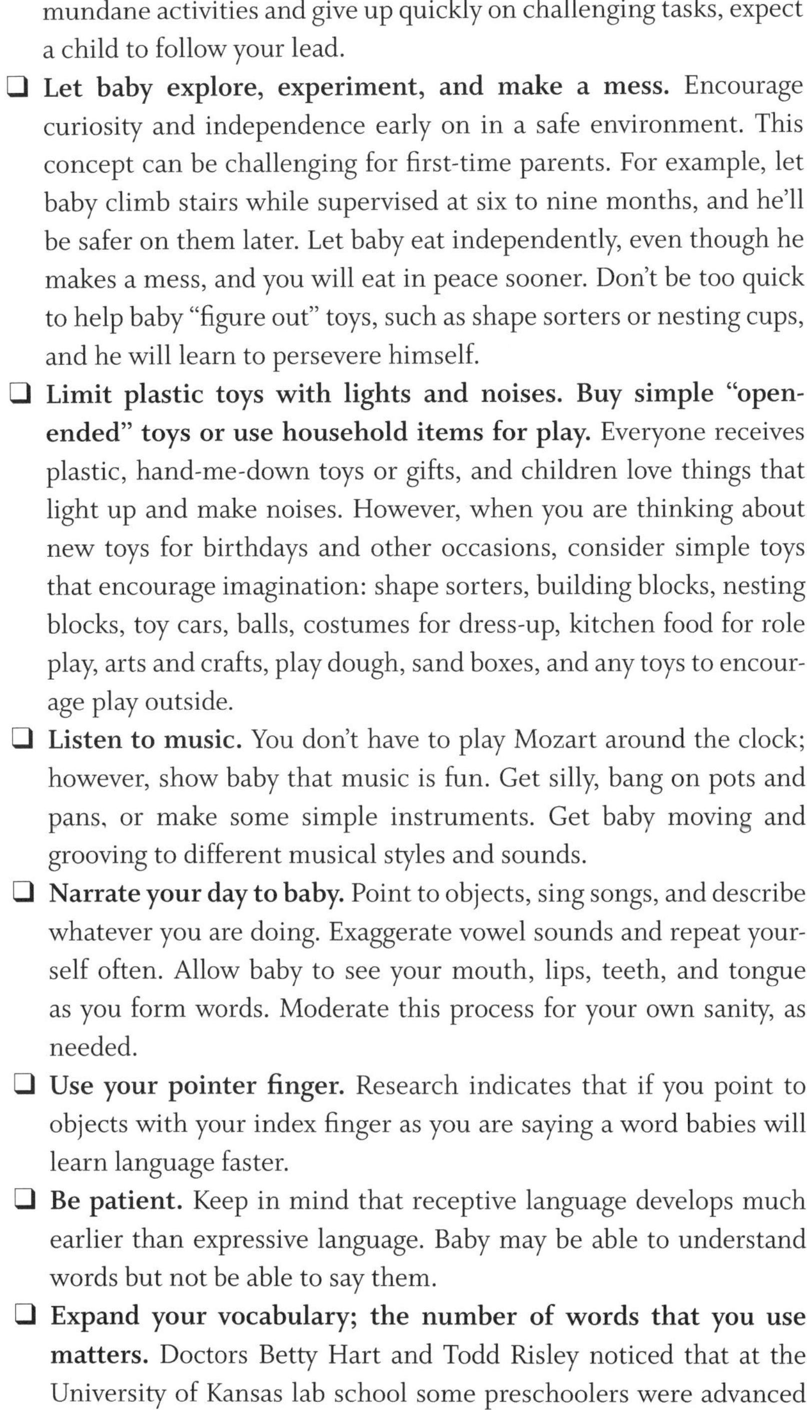

mundane activities and give up quickly on challenging tasks, expect a child to follow your lead.

❑ **Let baby explore, experiment, and make a mess.** Encourage curiosity and independence early on in a safe environment. This concept can be challenging for first-time parents. For example, let baby climb stairs while supervised at six to nine months, and he'll be safer on them later. Let baby eat independently, even though he makes a mess, and you will eat in peace sooner. Don't be too quick to help baby "figure out" toys, such as shape sorters or nesting cups, and he will learn to persevere himself.

❑ **Limit plastic toys with lights and noises. Buy simple "open-ended" toys or use household items for play.** Everyone receives plastic, hand-me-down toys or gifts, and children love things that light up and make noises. However, when you are thinking about new toys for birthdays and other occasions, consider simple toys that encourage imagination: shape sorters, building blocks, nesting blocks, toy cars, balls, costumes for dress-up, kitchen food for role play, arts and crafts, play dough, sand boxes, and any toys to encourage play outside.

❑ **Listen to music.** You don't have to play Mozart around the clock; however, show baby that music is fun. Get silly, bang on pots and pans, or make some simple instruments. Get baby moving and grooving to different musical styles and sounds.

❑ **Narrate your day to baby.** Point to objects, sing songs, and describe whatever you are doing. Exaggerate vowel sounds and repeat yourself often. Allow baby to see your mouth, lips, teeth, and tongue as you form words. Moderate this process for your own sanity, as needed.

❑ **Use your pointer finger.** Research indicates that if you point to objects with your index finger as you are saying a word babies will learn language faster.

❑ **Be patient.** Keep in mind that receptive language develops much earlier than expressive language. Baby may be able to understand words but not be able to say them.

❑ **Expand your vocabulary; the number of words that you use matters.** Doctors Betty Hart and Todd Risley noticed that at the University of Kansas lab school some preschoolers were advanced and some were far behind in their testing. What was causing these differences so early? After analyzing 23 million bytes of data collected from 1,300 hours of visits with 42 families, the researchers discovered that while child care routines were similar across socioeconomic groups, the number of words introduced to the children varied significantly. Researchers grouped the families into three socioeconomic categories based on the parents' occupations and income.[161]

- ▸ *Professional family*: This child will have heard 45 million words before kindergarten.
- ▸ *Working-class family*: This child will have heard 26 million words before kindergarten.
- ▸ *Welfare family*: This child will have heard only 13 million words before kindergarten.
  - All three children will show up for kindergarten on the same day, but one child will have heard 32 million fewer words.
  - To get this child caught up, a teacher would have to speak 10 words per second for 900 hours to reach the 32 million mark by year's end.
  - Further testing of the same children supported that academic success at ages nine and 10 was attributable to the amount of talk heard from birth to age three years.
  - This study is often criticized because it contains a small sample set and does not show correlation to language use or parental interest.
  - Other similar research indicates that access to high-quality early education programs largely explains early reading discrepancies.[162]

❑ **Read aloud to your baby.** Jim Trelease, author of *The Read Aloud Handbook*, says there is perhaps no single act that a parent can do for a child's education that is more effective than reading.[163]

- ▸ Reading aloud to children promotes language development, forges a bond between parent and child, encourages longer attention spans, and provides a head start in the foundation of all knowledge: reading. Math requires reading. Science requires reading. Writing requires reading.

- Fill your child's bookcase with used books and take her to the library often. Let your child know that when she comes to you with a book, you pay attention.
- Make reading fun. The sillier, the better. There is a good reason why *Green Eggs and Ham, Everyone Poops, Cloudy with a Chance of Meatballs, Pinkalicious, Moo Baa La La La,* and *Chicka Chicka Boom Boom* are some of the best children's books out there: they're fun! So don't be quick to discount *Captain Underpants* and *Fancy Nancy* as frivolous when they get your child away from the TV and excited about reading.
- Still not convinced? When asked to explain how he went from a poor, fatherless, inner-city home led by a mother with a third-grade education to being a world-famous brain surgeon, Dr. Ben Carson points to two factors: his mother's religion and "the pivotal moment when she limited [my] TV viewing and ordered [me] to start reading."[164]

❑ **Introduce a foreign language.** The brains of young children are hard-wired to learn language. Experts estimate that we begin to lose the ability to hear and say new sounds by ages eight to 12 years. So why not take advantage of this window of opportunity? You don't even have to speak a second language yourself. Learn with your child using apps, audio files, or language videos, and keep it light and fun. Children who learn a second language:

- Do significantly better at tasks requiring divergent thinking, problem solving, and creativity[165]
- Score higher on standardized tests in language arts, reading, and math than students not enrolled in foreign language programs[166]
- Display more openness to cultural diversity[167]

❑ **Seek culturally diverse books and children's media, and be aware of what your child is picking up from home**. Shankar Vedantam, author of *The Hidden Brain*, notes that for every fifty mentions of the word "tolerance" by a teacher or parent, there are several hundred implicit messages of racial bias that children absorb through culture, including books, television, and attitudes of those around them.[168, 169]

- ❑ **Think about how you introduce stereotypes in your home.** Research on negative stereotypes leading to adverse outcomes for women and minorities is plentiful. Social psychologist Claude Steele, best known for his work on "stereotype threat," discovered that the mere knowledge of stereotypes can be enough to negatively affect performance. For example, if you remind an Asian female that she is female before a math test, expect her to do worse. Remind her that she is Asian and expect her to do better.[168, 170, 171]
- ❑ **Use repetition to baby's advantage.** Japanese violinist Shin'ichi Suzuki observed that children across the globe learn their native tongue with ease because of one simple concept: repetition. Whatever is important to your family can be cemented with daily repetition at dinnertime or bedtime or anytime, whether it is reciting prayers, saying poems in a parent's native language, or telling stories about cultural or religious traditions. Children love hearing familiar stories over and over, and they will learn what matters to your family through repetition.[172]

Finally, on the subject of modern parenting and child development, my math-minded husband likes to humorously point out that one half of the population is below average, including children. This is particularly interesting in light of numerous playground conversations we have had with parents who think their child is advanced, gifted, or at least above average for any type of feat (*Look! He's pouring sand into a bucket at seven months—he's a genius!*) In social psychology, this is called illusory superiority, a cognitive bias that causes people to overestimate their positive qualities and underestimate their negative ones. So be prepared when a well-meaning mom or dad tries to "one-up" you at the sandbox, but know the occurrence is not exclusive to parents. College professors, financial markets traders, engineers, and drivers young and old all suffer from the same delusions—they are nearly all above average.[173-176]

Practical Tips from Real Parents

Early Education for Babies and Toddlers

- Put baby on a schedule. This will help him know what is coming up next.
- Try not to compare your baby to others. It's nearly impossible to avoid this temptation; however, kids develop at their own pace. Some are faster and some slower. Keep in mind that "developmental ages" are just a guideline. Note: This input is from a mother of five children.
- Don't pay any attention to comparisons about whose baby crawled when or whose baby walked early. Rolling over, crawling, and walking are not steadfast markers for intellectual development.
- Read aloud to your baby at least once per day, in addition to bedtime stories. Make reading part of baby's everyday life. Start a library. Show picture books to distract baby during tummy time.
- Use sign language early and often. Learn simple sign language from YouTube videos, apps, and resources online.
- Count blueberries and Cheerios for early math recognition.
- Point to body parts while bathing or during diaper changes.
- Visit your local parks and playgrounds often. Kids learn quickly from watching other kids.
- Pretend to be animals. It is fun, and you can teach them facts about the animal while you are growling and mooing at one another.
- If you must choose between going to a farm and heading into the city with a baby, go to the farm. Babies love animals, and their first words after mom and dad are animal noises.
- Try to link book concepts with hands-on learning. Read about animals and then go to the zoo. Point to foods in a picture book, then visit the grocery store.

- Don't be so obsessed with colors, shapes, and ABCs-123s that you forget to teach your child to use his imagination. Talk to your child about how many things a cardboard box can be: a racecar, a rocket ship, a boat, a bed, etc. Play construction site in the sand and dirt, stock a box of dress-up costumes, have picnics and tea parties, make soldiers' forts out of pillows, or build a train with chairs.
- Talk about your child's feelings and your reactions to good and bad behaviors as they occur. Good behavior must be taught.
- Consider purchasing an activity book for toddlers around baby's first birthday to inspire inexpensive activities that will stimulate brain development. Recommendations include: Slow and Steady Get Me Ready, Gymboree Baby and Toddler Play books, and The Toddler's Busy Book.
- Understand that ages recommended on toys are often listed more as legal and liability disclaimers rather than actual developmental recommendations. Most toys are age appropriate before the age listed.
- Play child-friendly music in the house and car. Do not think that your children are oblivious to explicit lyrics and bad language on the radio. They are little sponges.
- Play "brain games" in the car such as I Spy, the rhyme game, or counting games, or simply ask your child questions while driving, even if they do not respond.
- Keep track of your baby's milestones and developing personality traits by emailing yourself a real-time running commentary about your child. Maintain a unique and consistent subject line so that you can find these emails easily and record them in your child's baby book. Siblings will have a blast comparing what they were like as babies later.

Raising Baby in a Digital Age

Here's some food for thought: In densely populated areas across the country, parents compete fiercely for slots at certain nursery schools and public charter schools. They ask highly detailed questions about child development, teacher training, and the educational philosophies behind these schools and care centers. Yet would these same parents want to leave their child in an environment that stifles creativity, encourages inactivity, and leads to increased aggression and higher risk for attention problems? Many children today spend hours with just this type of babysitter: the TV.

The AAP states that television and entertainment media should be avoided for infants and children under two. Many parents choose to overlook this recommendation, and adding siblings to a family makes the zero-TV rule even harder to follow. However, parents may not understand that an infant's brain is developing rapidly at this time–so rapidly, in fact, that watching television can literally rewire the brain.

- ❑ **Limit screen time to as close to zero as possible and choose play instead.** When a baby plays with a toy, he picks it up, pokes it, tastes it, throws it, and moves it through space. He develops useful skills and a competence for handling objects. A baby sitting in front of the TV does not have the same sensorial experience.
- ❑ **Screen time rewires the brain.** TV moves at an unnatural and unrealistic pace, over-stimulating the developing brain. Rapidly shifting scenes from video can cause permanent changes to neural pathways, reducing attention spans and creating a new normal for how the pace of life unfolds. The constant noise from televisions

left on during household activities may also interfere with how baby develops his inner speech, as he learns to think through problems.[177, 178] Finally, heavy media use in the home interferes with a child's development simply because parents are likely to be spending less time interacting with and talking to their child.[26]

- ❑ **If you turn on the TV, select high quality programs.** Avoiding screens is easier with an infant. However, when a mobile child starts finding danger, making messes, and generally tearing your house apart, turning on the TV can be an appealing option for any frazzled parent. If you must turn on a screen, strive for limited viewing, and know that all programming is not equal. You can meet the AAP's high quality standard by cherry-picking educational DVDs or shows with a finite ending, rather than turning on the TV into infinity.
- ❑ **Throw out the garbage.** I think that most cable TV shows for kids are junk. Sit down and watch one for yourself. You can barely process the frenetic pace, rapid scene changes, random noises like beeps and squeaks, and illogical scenarios. Researchers agree. Fast-paced cartoons, such as SpongeBob SquarePants, are linked to lower attention spans, reduced impulse control, and slower thinking in children.[179]
- ❑ **Compile a list of educational programming.** Nearly every parent, even those who restrict media use, will be tempted to park his or her child in front of a screen at some point, whether it be for air travel, illness, moments of desperation, or simply to cook dinner in peace. Here are some of my favorite DVD/TV recommendations for younger children:
  - ▸ **Best overall program:** *Sesame Street*: this is probably the most thoroughly researched and tested show ever produced, and it has won more Emmy awards than any other show in television history. Sesame Street's promotion of early education, social awareness, and diversity are unsurpassed, and the lovable characters will be some of your child's first friends.
  - ▸ **Best TV channel (PBS Kids):** *Curious George* (problem solving), *Daniel Tiger's Neighborhood* (social-emotional and life skills), *Super Why* (reading), *Dinosaur Train* (science), and *The Cat in the Hat* (exploring and curiosity)
  - ▸ **Best for sign language:** *Baby Signing Time* series

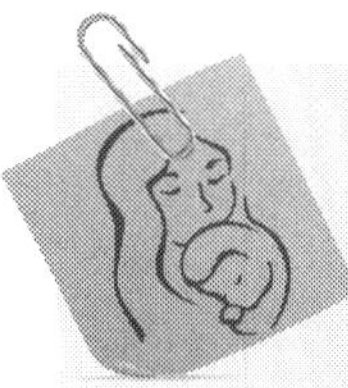

Going Deeper

Gender and Racial Bias in the Media

Okay, I am back on the subject of negative stereotypes again; but please hear me out, especially if you have a child who is female or a member of a minority group. Have you ever thought about why women and minorities might be underrepresented in children's TV and media? Well, for starters, the animation industry has been dominated historically by white males, such as Disney's "nine old men" group of core animators. The Director's Guild of America also reports that Caucasian males directed 72% of TV programming in 2012–2013. Is it really any wonder that our media lens is skewed? Who wouldn't write from their own perspective? Perhaps this also explains why our most iconic cartoon characters—Mickey Mouse, Popeye, Fred Flintstone, George Jetson, Scooby Doo, Thomas the Train, Tom and Jerry, Winnie the Pooh, Charlie Brown, Bart and Homer Simpson, SpongeBob, and all of the Smurfs except one represent white males. I am not advocating TV or media that is feminizing to little boys, but a 2011 study of 400 white and minority children found that TV watching lowered self-esteem for all groups tested, except white males. This result is just a warm-up for outcomes with adolescents and video games.[181]

So what is a concerned parent to do? Parents of girls and minorities should carefully assess their child's TV programming: Is a minority or female the lead character? Are at least two minorities or females part of the core cast? Does the show embrace diversity and promote a positive message? If not, try to find encouraging programing with minority leads and a diverse set of characters. Cultural messaging matters for boys and girls of all ethnic backgrounds.

- **Best for learning ABCs and 123s:** *Leap Frog: Letter Factory* (the best video of the series), *Word Factory, Phonics Farm, and Numberland*
- **Best for problem solving:** *Blues Clues*: this show is touted for its educational "stickiness factor" in *The Tipping Point* by Malcolm Gladwell.[180]

- **Best for diversity:** *Doc McStuffins, Sid the Science Kid, Handy Manny, Dora the Explorer, Maya and Miguel,* and *Ni-Hao Kai-lan*
- **Best for introducing the arts:** *Classical Baby: Music, Art, and Dance,* which introduces classical music, dance, and fine art
- **Best foreign language:** *Little Pim* or *Muzzy* from Early Advantage
- **Best moral and faith-based videos:** *Berenstain Bears, Veggie Tales, Little Bear, Jellytelly.com (Christian), EWTN Kids (Catholic), Torahtreasure.com or Jewishkids.org (Jewish), or a website for your faith*
- **Best short children's videos:** *Wonderopolis.org, National Geographic Little Kids, NGA Kids (National Gallery of Art)*, and *YouTube videos* on any interesting subject, such as ballet, trains, airplanes, musical instruments, etc.

Tips for Living Healthier as a New Parent

If I have one grand tip for living healthier as a new parent, it is this: sacrificing your marriage, your fitness, or your well-being for your child is not necessary. Life can get out of balance when you go gangbusters on raising children and leave everything else behind. When you give up doing the things that are life-giving to you, resentment and bitterness can creep in and adversely affect your life and relationships. For example, when you and your partner stop exercising, everybody gets grumpy. When the family's schedule revolves around baby's naps and routine, you become disconnected from others. When you and your partner adjourn to separate screens at night, you may be numbing your anxiety and stress with social media and TV, but you're also numbing your joy.[182]

So how do we live healthier lives and fuel ourselves as new parents? How do we model the behaviors and choices we desire for our children without exhausting ourselves? Striving to live healthier doesn't mean that you have to run marathons or have it all together. We can all set goals for ourselves and our families, even lofty ones, and still fall short, but at least we're trying.[182]

Physical health and exercise

Parenting young children is likely to deplete your physical care and exercise routine without intervention. For starters, you are tired and have less time for you. For women, your fitness level is likely to be less than

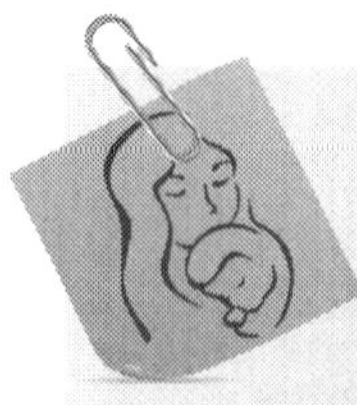

Going Deeper

The HIP Way to Raise Children: High Investment Parenting

I have made many mistakes as a parent of young children. Perhaps my most critical error has been thinking that I could just squelch my own needs and desires for a few hard years and approach parenting like a start-up business. I thought, "If I just work like a dog in this new mom role, and we put in all the right ingredients like breast milk and books and two parents, we are going to pop out an intelligent, well-adjusted child, right?" Well, not exactly. Young children have their own set of rules and trying to parent them using HIP processes learned in business or academia is a surefire way to lose yourself and your sanity.

what you had before pregnancy, especially in the abdominal region. Here are a few tips for kick-starting an exercise program and improving your overall physical health.

- ❑ **Take care of your body in big ways**: eat healthy foods, exercise, and don't skip visits to the doctor and dentist. You may need a checkup more now than ever. For example, having gestational diabetes during pregnancy increases your future chances of developing diabetes by 35% to 60%.[*183]
- ❑ **Take care of your body in small ways:** shower regularly, floss your teeth, shave your legs, and treat that nagging injury. It sounds simple; however, many new parents neglect smaller things that can add up to bigger issues later, such as anxiety and depression.
- ❑ **Get moving. Sitting is the new smoking.** A 20-year study of 32,000 participants in Australia concluded that lack of exercise poses a greater risk for heart disease in women over 30 than smoking or obesity.[184]

---

* If you had gestational diabetes during your pregnancy, it is important to get tested for diabetes six to 12 weeks after birth and every three years afterward.

- ❑ **Start slowly.** Walking is a great way to get exercise back into your life because baby can come along. The American College of Obstetricians and Gynecologists (ACOG) says that you can start exercising when you feel up to it; however, talk to your doctor first, especially if you had a complicated pregnancy, C-section, or difficult birth.
- ❑ **Get over the exercise hump.** An object at rest will remain at rest, and an object in motion stays in motion. Once you get going, it will get easier.
- ❑ **Trick yourself.** Actress Jennifer Garner, my favorite celebrity mom, once said that in order to lose her baby weight, she had to make a pact with herself that she would get on a treadmill for just ten minutes per day. Who doesn't have ten minutes? Once she was there, she almost always went past her goal. Getting there was the real battle.
- ❑ **If you are staying at home, or working from home, buy some exercise DVDs and make space for a mat and small weights.** Popular DVD selections include: *The Tracy Anderson Method: Post Pregnancy Workout; Lindsay Brin's Postnatal Boot Camp*; *Shiva Rea Mama and Baby Yoga; Element: Prenatal and Postnatal Yoga; Jillian Michael's 30 Day Shred*; *Zumba Fitness*; *Women's Health: Total Workout in Ten;* and *P90X: Tony Horton's 90-Day Workout* for hard-core moms and dads.
- ❑ **Join a gym with quality child care.** Ask for a free trial session to assess the staff. If you are uncomfortable leaving a younger baby, consider this option when baby is older.
- ❑ **Join a Stroller Strides** (now called Fit4Mom.com), **Stroller Fit, or Baby Bootcamp class in your area for physical, social, and emotional benefits**. Do dips, lunges, and squats surrounded by the comfort of women who understand your sleep-deprived schedule and new body limitations.
- ❑ **Exercise during your lunch break at work**. Bring your tennis shoes and ask a co-worker to join you for a walk if a full workout is not feasible.
- ❑ **Cultivate social support for exercise**. Schedule workouts with a friend. Invite your partner to do a DVD program with you, or alternate gym time at night.

- [ ] **Try a jogging stroller**. Baby's neck muscles may be strong enough for a slow jog on smooth terrain at six months old. For jogging on rough or uneven terrain, you should probably wait until closer to one year.
- [ ] **Try a yoga class.** Yoga is gaining popularity in the U.S., and it can be an excellent way to counteract stress and anxiety, in addition to helping your posture. Mayo Clinic and the National Institutes of Health support yoga as a top integrative therapy for anxiety, depression, back pain, heart disease, and high blood pressure.[185]
- [ ] **Download some fitness apps to help you get motivated**. Just remember that the apps which require location services and push notifications can be a massive battery drain.
  - Best for daily activity tracking: Fitbit or Argus
  - Best for runners: Map My Run
  - Best gradual approach: Couch-to-5K
  - Best for yogis: Yoga Studio
  - Best for dieters and calorie counters: Calorie Counter or Weight Watchers Mobile
  - Best for toning a flabby body: Nike Training Club
  - Best for busy parents: Hot5 (free 5-minute video workouts) or Johnson and Johnson 7 Minute Workout
  - Best for distracting non-exercisers: Zombies, Run! Part interactive fitness trainer and part horror flick, this app guides you through interval training while fleeing from zombies.
- [ ] **Take care of your neck and back. Avoid a constant forward head position**. More than 50% of office workers have experienced neck and back pain while hunching over a computer. Now add holding, feeding, and constantly looking down at a child to office neck, text neck, and driving neck. The average human head weighs ten pounds in an upright position. For every inch that your head is tilted forward, the weight on the spine increases an additional ten pounds. That means if your head is tilted forward one to two inches, your neck is strained as if it were supporting a twenty or thirty-pound head!

Eating healthy

As you know, I have a few hot buttons, which if pressed at the right moment can send me into a filibuster-style rant. The food industry is one of those. Harry Truman once said, "If you can't convince them, confuse them." Perhaps this is why food companies spend billions of dollars each year advertising unhealthy foods: to confuse us about what is really healthy. Minimally processed foods, such as fresh fruits and vegetables, are not big moneymakers, which is why you don't see Kate Upton seductively promoting broccoli or red peppers in Super Bowl commercials. The real money comes from turning government-subsidized commodities, such as corn, wheat, and soybeans, into processed foods.

Another problem with how food is sold to us as Americans is that we approach our diets one nutrient at a time. Corporations market and label foods with health claims based on one vitamin, one mineral, or one type of fat, and we take individual supplements for the nutrient of the day, whether it is probiotics, omega-3 fatty acids, vitamin D, calcium, etc. While there is no problem with better understanding the nutrients that our bodies need, this narrow view of nutrition does not solve our problems with weight and obesity. How food interacts with our body systems is a complex subject that requires broader thinking. No one has summarized a high level approach to food better than Michael Pollan, who simply states: "Eat food, not too much, mostly plants."

Dietary advice and diet fatigue

In just a few short years, we've gone from Atkins to South Beach to the Paleo diet. A decade ago, corn was the enemy; today the nemesis is wheat. Nuts and seeds were once too fatty, and now they're healthy. Eggs and cholesterol used to be bad, but now they're good, making vitamin D and brain cells. Talk about diet fatigue.

What is clear about media reporting on diet and nutrition is that we should treat this type of information with a healthy dose of skepticism. First of all, to create a bestselling book, one must present a radical and novel idea about diet, which is often more about marketing and less about science. Secondly, dietary advice often leads to certain "unintended consequences." Decades ago, when the government urged Americans to reduce dietary fat, the intent was likely not to create a deluge of low-fat, high-starch, high-sugar junk foods. The goal was to prioritize other nutritional sources, such as fruits and vegetables, beans/legumes, and lean proteins, over higher fat meats. It was the food industry, not government nutritionists, that capitalized on the low fat message by marketing bags of baked Cheetos as health food.

Today, we might be observing a different type of "unintended consequences" with the Paleo diet and other gluten-free regimes. Everyone can agree, these diets get one thing right–cutting down on processed foods. However, many dieters have not considered the consequences of eating too much protein while cutting out foods with essential nutrients, especially plant-based foods. Also problematic is not understanding the proportions and types of foods that our ancestors ate. Hunting and gathering did not mean having beautifully packaged meats available around the clock. Today, plant-based foods often get pushed aside because they require more time to prep, while the plump animals bred to create convenient meat products, such as packaged ham and turkey, are scarfed down as "diet food." These meats are hardly the wild game that cavemen hunted. This brings me to another key concept: hunting. Who chased down these animals to the point of exhaustion?

With that understanding, let's proceed with a few tips for eating healthier:

- ❑ **To lose weight, you have to burn more calories than you eat.** Weight loss programs that rely on gimmicks and diet aids such as prepackaged foods, drinks, or pills typically do not work in the long term.
- ❑ **Shop around the edges of the supermarket.** Food in these areas is more likely to be in its original state and not genetically engineered. If you do eat processed foods, look for the "Non-GMO Project Verified" label.

- ❑ **Ditch processed foods for fresh, whole foods.** Instead of applesauce, eat an apple. Instead of a raspberry breakfast bar, eat fresh raspberries with oatmeal. Instead of snacks with 20+ ingredients, eat fruits, vegetables, nuts, seeds, and popcorn.

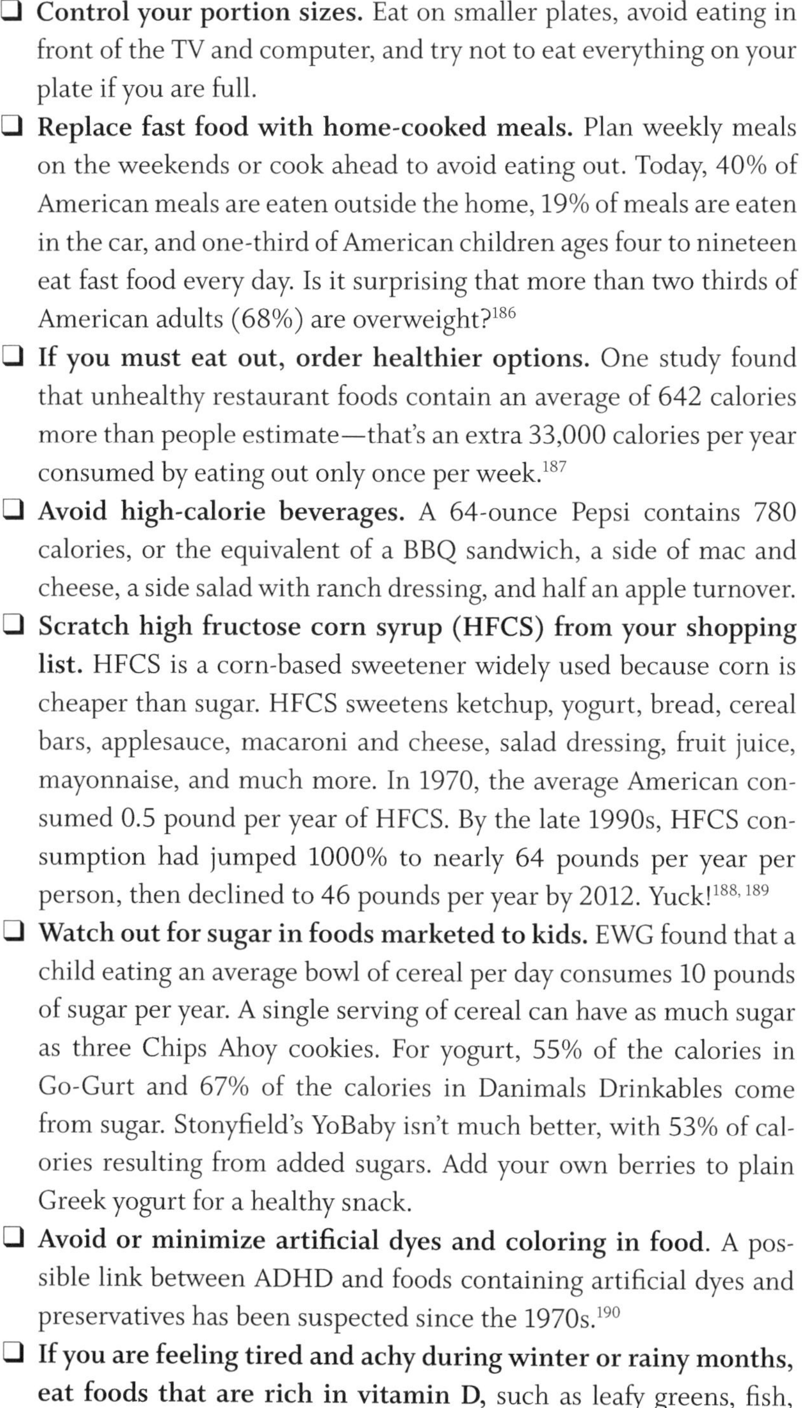

- [ ] **Control your portion sizes.** Eat on smaller plates, avoid eating in front of the TV and computer, and try not to eat everything on your plate if you are full.
- [ ] **Replace fast food with home-cooked meals.** Plan weekly meals on the weekends or cook ahead to avoid eating out. Today, 40% of American meals are eaten outside the home, 19% of meals are eaten in the car, and one-third of American children ages four to nineteen eat fast food every day. Is it surprising that more than two thirds of American adults (68%) are overweight?[186]
- [ ] **If you must eat out, order healthier options.** One study found that unhealthy restaurant foods contain an average of 642 calories more than people estimate—that's an extra 33,000 calories per year consumed by eating out only once per week.[187]
- [ ] **Avoid high-calorie beverages.** A 64-ounce Pepsi contains 780 calories, or the equivalent of a BBQ sandwich, a side of mac and cheese, a side salad with ranch dressing, and half an apple turnover.
- [ ] **Scratch high fructose corn syrup (HFCS) from your shopping list.** HFCS is a corn-based sweetener widely used because corn is cheaper than sugar. HFCS sweetens ketchup, yogurt, bread, cereal bars, applesauce, macaroni and cheese, salad dressing, fruit juice, mayonnaise, and much more. In 1970, the average American consumed 0.5 pound per year of HFCS. By the late 1990s, HFCS consumption had jumped 1000% to nearly 64 pounds per year per person, then declined to 46 pounds per year by 2012. Yuck![188, 189]
- [ ] **Watch out for sugar in foods marketed to kids.** EWG found that a child eating an average bowl of cereal per day consumes 10 pounds of sugar per year. A single serving of cereal can have as much sugar as three Chips Ahoy cookies. For yogurt, 55% of the calories in Go-Gurt and 67% of the calories in Danimals Drinkables come from sugar. Stonyfield's YoBaby isn't much better, with 53% of calories resulting from added sugars. Add your own berries to plain Greek yogurt for a healthy snack.
- [ ] **Avoid or minimize artificial dyes and coloring in food**. A possible link between ADHD and foods containing artificial dyes and preservatives has been suspected since the 1970s.[190]
- [ ] **If you are feeling tired and achy during winter or rainy months, eat foods that are rich in vitamin D,** such as leafy greens, fish,

Did You Know?

The Gluten-Free Craze

Several medical journal articles and two *New York Times* best sellers, *Wheat Belly* by cardiologist William Davis and *Grain Brain: The Surprising Truth about Wheat, Carbs, and Sugar – Your Brain's Silent Killers* by neurologist David Perlmutter, have spearheaded a mainstream gluten-free movement. In *Wheat Belly*, Davis contends that the genetically modified wheat of today, which he calls "frankenwheat," is nothing like the wheat that our parents consumed. He argues that wheat is the single largest contributor to obesity. In *Grain Brain*, Perlmutter maintains that our digestive systems and our brains are highly sensitive to what we eat. In his book, Perlmutter explains that dietary carbohydrates, both refined and healthy whole grains, cause high blood sugar and inflammation of the brain that leads to an array of neurological diseases, such as Alzheimer's, Parkinson's, ADHD, anxiety, and depression. He calls gluten "a silent germ" and believes that Alzheimer's is a preventable disease.

sun-dried tomatoes, egg yolks, cheese, fortified cereal, and milk. You may be vitamin D deficient. Take a walk or sit outside. The body makes vitamin D when it is directly exposed to sunlight. Exposure to the sun shining through a window will not produce vitamin D.[191]

- ❑ **Establish a "gluten aware" diet, but don't go overboard.** Gluten is a protein compound found in wheat and similar grains that makes dough rise, keeping it firm and chewy. This protein is known to cause health problems in people with gluten sensitivities, such as celiac disease, which affects about 1% of the population. Some doctors believe that gluten overload is affecting everyone else, too, especially with processed foods. Yet going gluten-free "just because" can waste your money and deplete B vitamins, calcium, zinc, iron, and magnesium, while many gluten-free foods have extra calories and sugar to make up for expected tastes and textures. Also, don't confuse "gluten-free" with "low carb." Some gluten-free products like pasta are actually higher in carbs than regular pasta.

- ❑ **Establish a "Paleo aware" diet, but don't go overboard.** If you follow the Paleolithic Diet, you cannot have grains, dairy, legumes, sugar, and salt. Our ancestors ate seasonal foods, high in fat, with very few carbohydrates, mostly from fruits in the late summer. However, cutting out dairy altogether can reduce your calcium and vitamin D, while eliminating healthy carbs can deplete B vitamins, iron, magnesium, and fiber. This is especially important for women of childbearing age, who need vitamin B_9 or folate to prevent birth defects.
- ❑ **Talk with your pediatrician before putting your child on any type of specialized diet.** Well-meaning parents can create nutritional deficiencies with popular diets and misinformation about certain foods.

Environmental Health

- ❑ **Use hands-free technology and limit distractions while driving.** You have precious cargo on board.
- ❑ **Open doors and windows for fresh air**. Americans spend 90% of their time indoors, and the EPA ranks indoor air quality as one of the top five environmental risks to public health.[192]
- ❑ **Consider using plants in your home to reduce indoor air pollution.** Kamal Meattle, an entrepreneur and environmental activist in India, discovered that three common houseplants may help reduce pollutants in the air: Areca palm, Mother-in-Law's tongue, and Lunaria (money plant).[193] Another NASA study recommends the following plants for removing formaldehyde, benzene, and carbon monoxide: Bamboo palm, Chinese evergreen, Gerbera daisy, and Dracaena (Janet Craig).[194]
- ❑ **When it comes to child safety, try not to worry about the wrong things.** The media is full of horrible stories about school shootings, kidnappings, and rare health scares. Yet the chances of these events affecting your child are highly unlikely. Focus on preventing things that are more likely to happen, such as car accidents, abuse (usually committed by a person who knows the child), drowning, and household safety (guns, fire/burns, household chemicals, and sleeping arrangements). Install safety gates for pools and stairs, always

wear seat belts and helmets, and childproof your home to significantly reduce risks.

Mental Health

Sometimes books offering helpful advice are written by astute humblebraggers. These people write about vulnerabilities while running marathons, earning millions of dollars, balancing crazy schedules, and basically being superhuman. Let me assure you this is not the case with this guide. To the contrary, my unanticipated fragility, lack of joy in accomplishing daily tasks as a stay-at-home mom, and conflicted feelings about everything have fueled me to further explore these issues. I'm not writing about a healthy, balanced life because I have one. I'm writing about it because I want one.

Balancing your own needs with a new baby's needs can be quite challenging, especially in light of today's work demands. As a new parent, you will constantly assess the balance between yourself and your work and child. What is work-life balance anyway, and how is it defined for you? For a stay-at-home parent, will there ever be peace and contentment if household responsibilities are endless and your child is infinitely needy? Or if you work outside the home, how can you establish balance if executives creating company policies have the *least* amount of work-life conflict in your firm? Is working part-time worth the cut in pay and reputation when the hours reduced aren't proportional? Can a person be a great employee and a great parent? I don't know the answers to these questions. What I do know is that these issues can wreak havoc on your mental health.

Moreover, decisions that you make as a parent, such as deciding how long to breastfeed, or whether to stay at home with your child, or whether to work in a demanding job, may never find resolution. In certain situations, there may be no good answer, only hard choices. What is ideal for you may be wearing on your child, and what is best for your child may be draining you. Whether you are a new mother or father who works inside or outside the home, you are likely to have a more delicate state of mental health after becoming a parent. Finding others who understand and support you in this role is critical to surviving this transition.

- ❑ **Invest time and energy in relationships and organizations that support you as a parent.** Make sure this inner circle allows you to be your imperfect self.
- ❑ **Take care of your basic needs and hygiene for better mental health.** Just ask any new mom or dad what it feels like to get to the end of the day without a shower. There are direct links between physical care and mental health.
- ❑ **Schedule time for yourself.** You never had to do this before. However, plan parts of your days and weekends in advance so that everyone gets alone time.
- ❑ **Let your child open doors and deepen relationships within your own family.** Children are wonderful ambassadors at the park, the coffee shop, and even in your own family. You may not have a great relationship with your mother, but that door might reopen via a grandchild.
- ❑ **If you are overwhelmed by a struggle for work-life balance, take action.**
  - ▶ *Reduce or alter your working hours:* Seek to reduce work hours or request a more flexible schedule. Leave the office earlier and finish up work after baby's bedtime.
  - ▶ *Be more efficient:* Delicately explain to co-workers that you can no longer take two-hour lunches or spend evenings chatting at your desk.
- ❑ **If you are overwhelmed with new dad duties, talk about it.** For men, navigating an upended schedule and a greater workload at home without the "cultural pass" that many women enjoy after childbirth can be overwhelming. Try not to stick your head in the sand and stew. Talk to your partner.
- ❑ **Try your best to minimize mommy guilt, mental health enemy number one for women with children.** Sociologists call discretionary free time spent worrying "contaminated time."
- ❑ **Stop worrying about what others think.** When you find yourself constantly comparing yourself to others, author and researcher, Brene Brown, says to stop the broken record in your head and tell yourself, "I am enough."[182]
- ❑ Organize your life in small ways for big improvements to your well-being.

Keep It Simple

Apps that Make Life Better

Too much technology can add unnecessary noise to our lives; but keeping it simple with just a few "must have" apps can help us streamline tasks and add fun, inspiration, and innovation to our daily lives. Here are my favorites:

- Personal finance: Mint
- Credit score and credit monitoring: Credit Karma
- Scanning tool (for receipts and documents): Turboscan
- Password manager: Last Pass (configures with fingerprint ID)
- Podcast downloader: Downcast
- E-books and audiobooks (from the public library): OverDrive
- Music (never buy a song again): Spotify
- Note taking: Evernote
- Shopping (nutrition): Shopwell
- Shopping (green product ratings): GoodGuide
- Maps: Google Maps
- Weather: Yahoo Weather

- ▸ Use Sunday evenings to plan your week, pre-cook meals, and coordinate schedules.
- ▸ Pack baby's day care bag and supplies at night, when you are less stressed.
- ▸ Pack your own bags and lunches when you are less stressed.
- ▸ Listen to an inspiring audio book, podcast, or TED talk while you are doing dishes or household work.
- ▸ Budget TV time with no commercials and combine it with necessary tasks (e.g., watch a favorite show on Netflix while folding baby's laundry).

- ▶ Check your calendar each night at the same time to ensure that you don't miss pediatric appointments, meetings, calls, etc.
- ▶ Organize your electronic life. This includes deleting photos regularly, clearing out your inbox, and using apps and tools to increase productivity, not waste your time.

- ❑ **Tune out Facebook, social media, and celebrity websites, especially if you are having a bad day.** Remember that everyone presents their unrealistic "best self" with social media. And research shows that spending too much time on celebrity websites, such as TMZ and Us Weekly, yearning for a body and lifestyle out of reach, can fuel feelings of isolation and inadequacy. Celebrities don't have completely different genes from the rest of us; they have plastic surgery.[195]
- ❑ **Play more.** Researcher and psychiatrist Stuart Brown contends that "The opposite of play is not work, it is depression." Play is not silly, undignified, or purposeless; rather, play helps promote creativity, efficiency, and productivity. Do something fun and active. Spend time with others who are playful. Take a break and play with your child.[196]
- ❑ **Know that happiness alone does not give life meaning.** Psychologist and author Martin Seligman, an authority on learned helplessness and positive psychology, suggests these keys to the good life:
  - ▶ **Positive emotion:** experiencing peace, gratitude, pleasure, curiosity, and optimism, practiced by writing down things that go well and why
  - ▶ **Engagement:** discovering and using your greatest strengths to perform tasks will help you experience a state of flow and presence in the moment with your work
  - ▶ **Relationships:** having meaningful, positive relationships is core to our well-being
  - ▶ **Meaning:** belonging to and serving something bigger than oneself
  - ▶ **Achievement:** striving to better ourselves, knowing that determination will contribute more than raw talent or IQ[197]

Spiritual Health

I am sensitive to the fact that many readers may not be religious at all. In fact, it is estimated that religious "nones," or individuals selecting no religious affiliation are on the rise, representing one-third of Americans under age thirty. However, spiritual considerations as a young adult can look very different from those as a parent. Many new parents find themselves thinking profoundly about their spiritual beliefs after baby arrives. Some may desire to reconnect with cultural and faith traditions from childhood, while others are seeking deeper meaning for life and a support network for their family. We all long for purpose, perspective, and authentic community. So don't be surprised if you find yourself in the midst of a spiritual awakening after having children.[198]

Relational Health

Among all the things that we pursue today—money, career, fame, reputation, vanity—the strongest predictor of happiness, by far, is social relationships. Time spent with family and friends is the best investment that we can make for our own well-being. On the contrary, our most challenging days are not simply when bad circumstances happen, but when we feel disconnected from others.

- ❑ **Make a goal of connecting with at least one friend or family member per day.** Reaching out to others can be difficult when baby is pulling you inward; however, try to balance that with your own need for connection.
- ❑ **Get out of the house**. If you are at home with a newborn feeling lonely and depressed, get out of the house. Going to the post office counts as an outing.
- ❑ **If you are a single parent, seek support and know that you are not alone.** Sometimes it may feel as if everyone around you is coupled up like the "smug marrieds" in Bridget Jones' Diary. However, according to the 2010 census, 67% of men and 57% of women between the ages 20 and 34, the prime childbearing years, have never been married.

- [ ] **Check in with your spouse or partner regularly, focusing on the topics that matter most.** One study concluded that the following attributes and behaviors correlate highly with strong marriages:[199]
    - Open communication
    - Marital generosity (serving or sacrificing for your spouse)
    - Financial thrift
    - Shared housework
    - Time set aside for marriage
    - Religious faith
    - Good sex
- [ ] **If you are experiencing sexual difficulties after baby, talk about it, identify the issues, and work together to make it better.**
    - *Loss of libido for Mom:* A decreased sex drive after baby is completely normal. Factor in the fatigue, healing from labor and delivery, and the simple worry of getting pregnant again too soon, and you have a recipe for sexual aversion.
    - *Make it all about Mom:* Try a small, discrete vibrator to use with your partner that looks like an egg or a space pen. This should help spice things up without worrying about your child finding an interesting new toy by your bedside.
    - *Body sensitivities:* Set rules about breasts, for example, if you are sore or touched out from breastfeeding.
    - *Emotional disconnection:* Spend a few evenings together and schedule time for intimacy. A study of 16,000 adults estimated that increasing sex from once per month to once per week increases happiness by the same amount as a $50,000 per year pay increase.[200]
- [ ] **Spend money on experiences, not just stuff.** Researchers have known for years that spending money on things does not boost our mood or make us happy, but spending money on experiences does. Why? Because they happen in relationship with others.
- [ ] **Define your family values and goals.** Companies, military units, non-profit groups, and nearly every organization on the planet goes through this exercise. Why wouldn't we do the same for our most important team—our family? It doesn't have to be formal or fancy; it's just a loose mission statement that defines who you are and what you stand for as a family. Discuss how you would like to interact

with one another and how you would like to prioritize your time. For example, "We want to be a family who loves one another, communicates well, does not fight all the time, and spends weekends together outdoors." When the details of life start to take over, you can always go back to the basics of what your family values.

Parenting Perspective: Enjoy every second

Congratulations! We have come to the end of our checklists. I hope that you feel better equipped to tackle the first year of parenting. When life gets hectic, don't forget to embrace the everyday moments with your child: the cuddles, the hugs, and the laughs when baby dumps a bowl of blueberry puree on his head. Life is a beautiful mess. Be assured that letting go and keeping it simple will help you enjoy the ride that much more. Here's to finding much joy in parenting!

Appendix A: Abbreviated Checklists

Baby Care

Basic Baby Care

Breastfeeding basics

- ❑ Know that newborns nurse every 1½ to 3 hours or 8 to 12 times per day for several months
- ❑ Breastfeed within an hour after birth, if possible
- ❑ Hold baby skin-to-skin
- ❑ Gently wake sleeping baby at the breast
- ❑ Feed for 15–20 minutes per breast
- ❑ For tight ducts, alternate feeding positions
- ❑ For clogged ducts, place warm washcloth on sore area before feeding
- ❑ Wash breasts with water only; no soap
- ❑ Wear a supportive bra that doesn't restrict milk flow
- ❑ Take 500 mcg of folic acid per day while breastfeeding
- ❑ Wait 3 hours to feed again after consuming alcohol, or "pump and dump"

The first week: breastfeeding is going well if...

- ❑ Baby breastfeeds 8 times per day
- ❑ Baby has 3–4 bowel movements per 24 hours by day 4
- ❑ Baby audibly gulps at feedings
- ❑ Your nipples do not hurt when baby nurses
- ❑ Baby is gaining weight within 10–14 days
- ❑ You are making 19–30 ounces of milk each day by end of week 1

Pumping and collecting breast milk

- ❑ Wash hands thoroughly
- ❑ Wash all pump parts and accessories, or use steaming bags
- ❑ Wait 3–4 weeks before introducing bottles
- ❑ If returning to work, store pumped milk 1–2 weeks ahead
- ❑ Aim to pump 3 times during 8-hour day

Storing breast milk

- ❑ Swirl warmed milk to mix cream and liquid
- ❑ Avoid adding warm milk to already cooled milk
- ❑ Freeze milk in 2–5 oz. feeding portions
- ❑ Label bags with the date stored, leaving room for expansion
- ❑ Lay bags flat to freeze
- ❑ Use oldest milk first

Storage guidelines for breast milk (for healthy full-term babies)

- ❑ Room temperature: 4–6 hours at 66–78°F (19–26°C)
- ❑ Cooler with 3 Ice Packs: 24 hours at 59°F (15°C)
- ❑ Refrigerator: 3–8 days at 39°F or lower (4°C)
- ❑ Freezer: 6–12 months at 0–4°F (18–20°C)
- ❑ Thawed breast milk: use within 24 hours

Bottle-feeding basics

- ❑ Know that whole milk is not a substitute for formula
- ❑ Sterilize new bottles in boiling water before first use
- ❑ For well and non-chlorinated water, boil water for formula for first six months
- ❑ Avoid bottled water; Mix formula with filtered tap water
- ❑ Wash hands thoroughly before mixing
- ❑ Mix formula exactly as recommended by manufacturer
- ❑ Do not buy outdated or expired formula

- ❑ Do not leave formula unrefrigerated for over 4 hours
- ❑ Do not freeze formula
- ❑ Feed formula immediately, or refrigerate and use within 24 hours
- ❑ Make several bottles ahead of time, refrigerate, and use throughout the day
- ❑ Do not mix breast milk with formula
- ❑ Do not warm formula in the microwave
- ❑ Never put baby to bed with a "propped" bottle
- ❑ Accustom baby to room-temperature formula as soon as possible
- ❑ Talk to pediatrician before switching to expensive, sensitive formulas
- ❑ Choose organic formula, if possible

The first week: formula feeding is going well if...

- ❑ Your baby is drinking 1.5 to 3 oz. every 2–3 hours
- ❑ You are changing 5–6 wet and 3–4 poopy diapers per day
- ❑ Your baby's stool is yellow to green by the end of week one
- ❑ Your baby is satisfied after feedings
- ❑ Your baby is gaining 4–7 ounces per week

Burping

- ❑ Pat baby on the back at regular intervals
    - ▸ Breastfeeding: every 5 minutes in first few weeks (increase interval as baby matures)
    - ▸ Bottle feeding: every ½ ounce in first few weeks (every 2 ounces as baby matures)
    - ▸ Burp any time baby is fussy while feeding
    - ▸ Burp at the end of every feeding
- ❑ Try multiple burping positions
    - ▸ Baby sits upright over your shoulder
    - ▸ Baby sits on your lap
    - ▸ Baby lies across your knees
- ❑ Always have a burp cloth ready

Diapering

- ❑ Expect baby's first stool to be odorless, thick, and tarry
- ❑ Know that by day 3–4, bowel movements should be brown, yellow, or green
- ❑ Always place a clean diaper beneath baby before removing dirty one
- ❑ For girls, wipe front to back
- ❑ For boys, have a cloth handy in case of spraying

Diaper rash

- ❑ To minimize diaper rash, change diapers frequently
- ❑ If disposable wipes are too harsh, use alternatives:
  - ▸ A soft cloth with warm water after pee diapers
  - ▸ Warm water with sensitive soap after poop diapers
- ❑ If a rash develops, clean baby's bottom in sink or tub after all bowel movements

Yeast rash vs. regular diaper rash

- ❑ Know that yeast rash is a red, bumpy rash that lasts over 2–3 days and doesn't respond to rash treatments
- ❑ After a doctor confirms yeast rash, apply topical anti-yeast or anti-fungal cream

Bathing

- ❑ Give sponge baths only until umbilical cord falls off (14 days)
- ❑ After cord falls off, give 1–2 baths per week for 10 minutes or less
- ❑ Between baths, spot clean the neck, skin folds and bottom areas
- ❑ Use pH balanced bath products made only for baby's skin
- ❑ Before baby's first bath, lay out necessary supplies
- ❑ Wash baby gently but assertively
- ❑ Never use a Q-tip in baby's ear

- ❑ Use a folded towel or baby bath cushion to catch baby on the kitchen or bath counter for drying
- ❑ Apply baby lotion to moisturize slightly damp skin

Umbilical cord care

- ❑ Keep umbilical cord clean and dry
- ❑ Do not clean with alcohol
- ❑ Expect cord to turn from bluish to yellowish green to brown to black
- ❑ Expect cord to fall off about two weeks from birth
- ❑ Fold baby's diaper beneath the umbilical cord

Circumcised males

- ❑ Keep area clean by bathing in warm water with a baby cleanser
- ❑ Any swelling, redness, or slight yellow discharge should cease after 7–10 days
- ❑ Doctor may advise applying ointment to tip to prevent it from sticking to diaper

Uncircumcised males

- ❑ Keep area clean with warm water and gentle baby cleanser
- ❑ Never force the foreskin back to clean the tip of the penis
- ❑ Gently tense the foreskin against the tip and wash with care

Care of the vagina

- ❑ Gently clean genital area from front to back with a soft cloth, using only water
- ❑ Bloody vaginal discharge may appear during the first few weeks

Nail filing and clipping

- ❑ Clip and file baby's nails after a bath, while baby is feeding
- ❑ Expect baby to fuss during nail clippings, but push through it

Reduce risk of sudden infant death syndrome (SIDS)

- ❑ Put baby to sleep on her back on a firm mattress
- ❑ Remove all blankets, sleep positioners, bumper pads, and pillows
- ❑ Put baby within arm's reach at night in a co-sleeper; avoid bed sharing

Pacifier use

- ❑ Offer a pacifier at sleep and nap times
- ❑ Do not force a pacifier into the mouth
- ❑ Do not coat a pacifier with any sweet substance
- ❑ Do not reinsert a pacifier after baby falls asleep
- ❑ If a baby refuses a pacifier do not force him or her to take it
- ❑ If nipple confusion is a concern, wait 3–4 weeks after breastfeeding is established to introduce pacifier
- ❑ Do not use pacifiers to replace or delay meals; offer it only when you are sure baby is not hungry

Crying and Colic

Why do babies cry?

- ❑ They are hungry
- ❑ They are tired
- ❑ They have a dirty diaper, or a diaper rash
- ❑ They are too hot, or too cold
- ❑ They have gas, reflux, or other tummy issues
- ❑ They want to be held
- ❑ They want less stimulation
- ❑ They want more stimulation

- ❑ They are sick
- ❑ They are teething
- ❑ They are picking up your anxious or depressed mood
- ❑ They are responding to a random irritant: this tag on my shirt is scratchy, someone's hair is wrapped tightly around my finger or penis (this is common), or something is pinching me

Colic triggers you can control

- ❑ Mom's diet. The worst colic trigger foods are:
  - ▶ dairy products
  - ▶ coffee/tea/soda
  - ▶ soy products
  - ▶ peanuts
  - ▶ shellfish
  - ▶ chocolate
  - ▶ gas-producing vegetables (peppers, onions, broccoli, cabbage, and cauliflower)
  - ▶ acidic foods (tomatoes, citrus, berries)
  - ▶ spices (garlic, chili pepper, curry)
- ❑ Infant formula. Talk to pediatrician about switching formulas
- ❑ Over-feeding with a bottle: feedings should be 2 to 2.5 hours apart
- ❑ Too much foremilk: let baby finish one breast before offering the second
- ❑ Medicine (that Mom is taking)
- ❑ Hypersensitivity to bright lights or loud, abrupt sounds

Colic triggers you cannot control

- ❑ An intense temperament
- ❑ An immature nervous system
- ❑ An immature digestive system
- ❑ Acid reflux
- ❑ Increased hormone levels that make people fussy
- ❑ Embryonic and post-natal experiences that altered the enteric nervous system, or the "second brain" in the gut

If your baby won't stop crying, what can you do?

- ❑ Take a few deep breaths and calm yourself first
- ❑ Take baby outside
- ❑ Hold and cuddle your baby in an upright position
- ❑ Rock your baby
- ❑ Sing lullabies, or make calm "shushing" noises
- ❑ Give baby a massage with lotion
- ❑ Bicycle baby's legs to potentially release gas
- ❑ Offer baby a pacifier or your pinkie finger for sucking
- ❑ Swaddle baby in a thin blanket; make her feel secure and warm
- ❑ Put baby on her side to move the gas around, then put her on her back to sleep
- ❑ Try a "colic hold:" hold out your arm in front of you, palm facing up, and place baby stomach-down on your forearm, with your hand cupping the upper chest; walk baby around the house flying him like Superbaby
- ❑ Put baby on his stomach across your knees while rubbing or patting his back
- ❑ Wear baby in a sling or front carrier
- ❑ Take baby for a car ride
- ❑ Turn on white noise like a hair dryer or vacuum
- ❑ Put baby in front of a mirror to watch his own dramatic show
- ❑ Try a few drops of over-the-counter anti-gas simethicone, if you suspect painful gas

If the colic becomes too stressful to handle

- ❑ Call in a friend or family member for help
- ❑ If you are feeling out of control, put baby down in a crib, close the door, and let him cry in a safe place (for no more than a few minutes)
- ❑ Never shake your baby
- ❑ Know that this too, shall pass, as the colic should subside in 3–4 months

Sleep Guide: Newborn to Three Years

Newborn

- ❑ Expect newborns to sleep 16–18 hours per day
- ❑ Dress baby in a single layer cotton pajama and wrap in a tight swaddle using thin cotton blankets
- ❑ Place newborn to sleep in a crib or bassinet for as many naps as possible
- ❑ If you choose to bed-share, place baby between a guardrail and Mom, not between Mom and Dad
- ❑ Do not bed-share with a smoker, someone who drinks before bed, or someone who is taking medications

One month

- ❑ Most infants awaken every 2–4 hours for feedings
- ❑ Try to lengthen sleep periods by feeding baby every 2–3 hours during the day
- ❑ To prevent positional plagiocephaly (flat head) establish a daily tummy time routine and limit time in car seats
- ❑ Let baby sleep in a partially lit room for daytime naps and in a darker room at night
- ❑ At night, keep the lights off when baby wakes; use night-lights and dimmer switches instead
- ❑ Hang a blackout curtain to keep baby from waking with the sun

Two months

- ❑ Most infants are still waking every 3–4 hours, with highly variable sleep patterns
- ❑ Fight the urge to talk or play during nighttime feedings or diaper changes
- ❑ Wake baby for a late-night feeding that suits your sleep schedule
  - ▸ If baby goes to sleep at 7:00 p.m. and sleeps until 2:00 a.m., wake baby at 11:00 p.m. for an aspirational 5:00 or 6:00 a.m. wakeup

Four months

- ❑ Babies typically have developed a regular sleep pattern and have dropped most nighttime feedings
- ❑ Between 4–6 months, most babies are ready for sleep training and are capable of sleeping 5–6 hours through the night

Six months

- ❑ If baby sleeps for 9–10 hours at night, he's learned how to settle back to sleep
- ❑ If baby isn't sleeping 5–6 hours straight, you're not alone
- ❑ Nighttime feedings are no longer necessary after 6 months or so

Nine months

- ❑ Infants may resist going to sleep due to separation anxiety
- ❑ A favorite soft toy or transition object may be helpful
- ❑ It is not unusual for a child to awaken at night due to teething or developmental milestones
- ❑ After 1–2 hours of deep sleep, baby will move into a stage of lighter snoozing
- ❑ During lighter phases of sleep, baby may open eyes, look around, and cry; wait to see if baby can return to sleep
- ❑ If crying warrants attention, go to baby and touch him
- ❑ Reassure baby of your presence, but try not to pick him up

Twelve months

- ❑ Consolidate daytime sleep to one nap between twelve and eighteen months
- ❑ Never use television or screens for the bedtime routine
- ❑ Expect your child to wake earlier and earlier if he is handed an iPad when he wakes

Eighteen to thirty-six months

- ❑ Move from a crib to a big bed between eighteen and thirty-six months
- ❑ With two children close in age, don't feel rushed to move the elder sibling to a bigger bed
- ❑ Older child can sleep in a crib while newborn sleeps in a bassinet
- ❑ Borrow another crib if children are very close in age

Kim's sleep recommendations

- ❑ Check for any medical conditions affecting sleep
- ❑ Make baby tired with active play
- ❑ Establish clear play and tummy time guidelines for caregivers
- ❑ Maintain a regular feeding schedule
  - ▸ Every 2–3 hours in the first few months
- ❑ Establish a pleasant sleep environment
  - ▸ A darkened room
  - ▸ Room-darkening shades or curtains, especially for summertime
  - ▸ Soft music or white noise for drowning out household and street noise
- ❑ Establish a soothing bedtime routine
  - ▸ A warm bath
  - ▸ A massage with body lotion
  - ▸ A loving swaddle for newborns
  - ▸ Books, prayers, and/or songs
  - ▸ Hugs
  - ▸ Feeding
  - ▸ Rocking for younger babies
- ❑ Decide whether to feed before bedtime
  - ▸ Feed baby and then read a book before bed to disrupt direct association between sleep and feeding, if desired
- ❑ Wake baby up to top her off at your bedtime, with the hope of adding an extra 1–2 hours of sleep
  - ▸ Pump before bedtime and let your partner help out with nighttime feedings

- ❑ Skip nighttime diaper changes, unless baby has a rash, wet cloth, or significant bowel movement
- ❑ If diaper change is unavoidable at night, keep the lights dim and avoid interacting with baby
- ❑ Consider switching baby from a bassinet to a crib between 2–3 months
- ❑ Try not to use a swing as a nighttime sleeping crutch; baby is best on a firm flat surface (for his developing spine and oxygen flow)
- ❑ Use a portable crib or floor mattress if you want to keep baby in the room with you longer
- ❑ At 4–6 months, feed for nourishment before bedtime, but try not to feed in the middle of the night
- ❑ If baby wakes crying, soothe her with a gentle caress or soft lullaby
- ❑ If you must feed baby at night, keep the lights low and shorten nighttime feedings over time
- ❑ If baby still wakes to eat after 6 months, break the cycle with gentle sleep training
  - ▸ When baby has been fed and her diaper is clean, lay her in the crib
  - ▸ Let her "whimper it out" while checking in
  - ▸ If baby is inconsolable, cuddle and rock her for a few minutes
  - ▸ If you must feed during the night, keep it short and sweet
- ❑ Have your partner reassure baby if night weaning is a goal
- ❑ Do not expect night weaning to be successful during times of transition, travel, or sickness

Starting Solid Foods

Signs your baby is ready to start solid foods

- ❑ Baby is at least four months old with good head control and can sit up supported
- ❑ Baby shows interest in watching others eat
- ❑ Baby's tongue-pushing reflex has subsided
- ❑ Your pediatrician gives the OK to start solid foods

Signs your baby is not ready to start solid foods

- ❑ Baby is 4–6 months and sleeping through the night on breast milk or formula alone
- ❑ Baby cries or turns away from solid foods
- ❑ Baby spits out solid foods beyond the first few feedings
- ❑ Baby cannot sit up by himself supported, such as in a high chair

Four months

Cereals: oatmeal cereal

- ❑ If baby is thriving on breast milk or formula only, there is no need to start cereal
- ❑ If you choose to start solids, mix cereal with breast milk, formula, or water
- ❑ Start with oatmeal; use an organic brand cereal
- ❑ Use your finger as baby's first spoon, then work up to utensils
- ❑ Give cereal once per day. Pediatricians recommend mornings, but you may prefer evenings
- ❑ Feed one tablespoon the first day, increasing to three tablespoons per serving
- ❑ Wait 3–5 days before introducing a new type or brand of cereal
- ❑ Be patient; it can be messy and baby may only ingest a small amount
- ❑ Consider solid foods an "extra" to breast milk or formula at this time

Five months

Vegetables: sweet potatoes, squash, carrots, green beans, peas, avocados

- ❑ Puree your own vegetables with filtered water, or use "stage 1" prepared foods
- ❑ One serving is typically two to four ounces, or one-half to one full jar
- ❑ Add plenty of water when pureeing steamed vegetables and fruits
- ❑ Introduce new foods one variety at a time, waiting 3–5 days between each food

- ❑ Note any allergic reactions:
  - ▸ Severe gassiness
  - ▸ Red rash on the face
  - ▸ Red rash around the anus
  - ▸ Diarrhea
  - ▸ Runny nose
  - ▸ Watery eyes
  - ▸ Vomiting
- ❑ Try sweeter veggies first, like sweet potatoes and carrots

Six months

Fruits: apples, pears, bananas, prunes, peaches, berries, apricots

- ❑ Puree steamed or cooked fruits in a blender or grate them
- ❑ By six to eight months, some infants are eating two small meals per day
  - ▸ One meal of cereal and fruit in the morning
  - ▸ One meal of vegetables in the evening
- ❑ With fruit, introduce frozen plain bagels or teething biscuits, especially if baby is experiencing teething pain
- ❑ Let baby practice gnawing, chewing, and eating independently
- ❑ Introduce water in a sippy cup to aid digestion. Let baby practice drinking independently
- ❑ If baby is constipated, add pureed prunes, pears, or apricots to her cereal
- ❑ If baby's stools are runny, add a more binding fruit and cereal combo, like bananas and oatmeal
- ❑ If baby develops a new, unexplained diaper rash, assess the acidity level of fruits and adjust her diet

Seven to twelve months

Meats: turkey, lamb, chicken, pork, beef

Beans/legumes: lentils, chick peas, black beans, pinto beans

Processed dairy products: cheese, yogurt (Greek style), cottage cheese

Other protein sources: salmon, tofu, egg yolks

- ❑ At this age, blend baby's proteins and veggies together and try seasonings
- ❑ Stage 3 prepared foods are okay (though the preserved meat ones are disgusting)
- ❑ Baby is now typically eating 2–3 meals per day
- ❑ Typical formula or breast milk intake is 24 oz. or 3–4 feedings/day, or 50% of total caloric intake
- ❑ If baby is fussy while you steam her food, hand her a toy rather than a snack food
- ❑ Feed baby blended meet in stages
  - ▸ Easiest to digest: Lamb and turkey
  - ▸ Moderate to digest: Pork and chicken
  - ▸ Hardest to digest: Beef
- ❑ Allow plenty of soft finger foods, such as fresh fruit and steamed veggie pieces
- ❑ For convenience, feed baby ripe avocados and bananas, which require no prep
- ❑ Try organic frozen vegetables with a longer shelf life for convenience and cost savings
- ❑ For on-the-go snacks, use:
  - ▸ organic puffs
  - ▸ O-shaped cereal
  - ▸ freeze-dried fruit
  - ▸ yogurt melts
- ❑ Continue to give water in a sippy cup
- ❑ Hand baby his own spoon for distraction while you feed him
- ❑ Take a CPR and First Aid for Choking class for babies and infants through the American Red Cross (or watch a video online)

Starting solid foods: Allergy considerations

- ❑ Do not delay the introduction of allergenic foods. This may actually increase risk of food allergy or eczema. Be aware of these most common allergenic foods and look for reactions to them:
  - ▸ Milk
  - ▸ Eggs
  - ▸ Peanuts
  - ▸ Soy
  - ▸ Wheat
  - ▸ Tree nuts (pecans, walnuts, almonds)
  - ▸ Fish
  - ▸ Shellfish (shrimp, oysters, crab)
- ❑ Once an infant older than four months has tolerated several non-allergenic foods (e.g., oatmeal, sweet potatoes, bananas, and pears), parents can proceed with the introduction of more allergenic foods, one food at a time
- ❑ Introduce allergenic foods at home every three to five days to isolate triggers of an allergic reaction
- ❑ If you are pregnant or lactating, you do not have to avoid foods such as milk, eggs, and peanuts
- ❑ Do not introduce cow's milk until twelve months
- ❑ If you have allergies in your family history, talk to your doctor. She may recommend you avoid some common allergens while nursing

Starting solid foods: Serving tips

- ❑ Strain baby's first foods through a metal strainer or flour sifter
- ❑ Prepare only what baby needs
- ❑ Don't feed from a large blender container; put smaller portions into a separate feeding bowl
- ❑ Don't heat baby food in plastic; use small glass prep bowls for microwaving food
- ❑ Serve food no warmer than body temperature
- ❑ Add flavorful seasonings to baby's food, but do not add salt or sugar
- ❑ Do not sweeten baby's food with honey or corn syrup
- ❑ Store unused portions in the refrigerator and use within 2–3 days

- ❑ Do not leave food out of the fridge for more than two hours
- ❑ Make large batches of baby food and freeze into ice cube trays; then transfer cubes into an airtight freezer bag
  - ▸ Fruits and veggies can last 6–8 months in frozen cubes
  - ▸ Meat, poultry, and fish last 1–2 months in frozen cubes
- ❑ Use a clean brush to clean blender blades thoroughly
- ❑ Use bibs, a floor mat, a cordless sweeper, a bowl with a suction cup, and extra spoons to manage messy feedings
- ❑ For breastfeeding moms: solid foods may be easier for a caregiver to administer while you are at work so you can focus on breastfeeding in the evenings

Just for Mom

Breastfeeding Support

- ❑ Learn as much as possible before baby arrives. Popular resources are:
  - ▸ Online instructional videos
  - ▸ La Leche League International online portal
  - ▸ KellyMom.com
- ❑ If you are struggling in the beginning, it's totally normal
- ❑ Overcome challenges with a sense of purpose; the initial pain should subside in 2–4 weeks
- ❑ Overcome work schedule challenges with compromise and supplemental feedings, but keep giving what breast milk you can
- ❑ Assess baby's feedings one day at a time
- ❑ Get your partner on the breastfeeding team for support

Breastfeeding nutrition

- ❑ Talk to a doctor before taking supplements beyond a prenatal vitamin
- ❑ Continue taking prescription-level prenatal vitamin with DHA and at least 500 mcg of folic acid
- ❑ Drink plenty of water

- ❑ Eat foods high in omega-3 fatty acids (DHA and EPA)
- ❑ Enjoy sushi again but stay away from high mercury seafood
- ❑ Limit stimulants such as caffeine and chocolate
- ❑ Minimize overly spicy and gas-producing foods if they are affecting Mom and baby
- ❑ If you have celiac disease or are a gluten-free non-celiac, talk with your doctor about diet

Sensitive foods

If baby is consistently uncomfortable after feeding, restrict certain foods

- ❑ dairy products
- ❑ soy products
- ❑ coffee, tea, soda, and chocolate
- ❑ peanuts
- ❑ shellfish
- ❑ gas-producing vegetables, such as peppers, onions, broccoli, cabbage, and cauliflower
- ❑ acidic foods, such as tomatoes, citrus, berries
- ❑ stronger spices, such as garlic, chili pepper, and curry

Elimination diet

If baby is still uncomfortable, eat the least allergenic foods in each of the major food groups:

- ❑ turkey
- ❑ lamb
- ❑ potatoes
- ❑ sweet potatoes
- ❑ rice
- ❑ rice pasta
- ❑ pears
- ❑ zucchini
- ❑ yellow squash

If baby starts doing better, slowly add back in apples, bananas, avocado, asparagus, carrots, rolled oats, yogurt/kefir, chicken, and wild salmon

Motherhood and Isolation

- ❑ Get out of the house at least once a day
- ❑ After waking up, get dressed and ready to go out
- ❑ Establish a weekly schedule and assign chores to a specific day
- ❑ Use sitter time to socialize or work out
- ❑ Join a postpartum support group
- ❑ Join a local play group
- ❑ Join a list-serv or online parenting community
- ❑ Invite a friend for a stroller walk
- ❑ Visit a local gym or YMCA that offers child care
- ❑ Go to story time at a library
- ❑ Sign up for a movement or music class with baby
- ❑ Start a project during naptime
- ❑ Start a home business
- ❑ Sell a product that you like (jewelry, makeup, skincare, etc.)
- ❑ Start taking a night or online class
- ❑ Set aside quality time to spend with your child every day

Motherhood and Weight Gain

- ❑ Watch out for stress eating
- ❑ Limit grazing
- ❑ Limit processed foods
- ❑ Don't let breastfeeding justify too many extra calories
- ❑ Be aware that your body holds on to fat stores to breastfeed
- ❑ Find creative ways to exercise
- ❑ Embrace a little vanity
- ❑ Get your partner to support healthy eating and exercising

How to Dress Skinnier after Baby

- ❑ Wear long V-necks
- ❑ Stick with a single hue
- ❑ Vary dark colors: You don't have to wear all black

- ❑ Wear simple dark jeans
- ❑ Wear accessories
- ❑ Support your breasts properly
- ❑ Match your shoe color to your leg
- ❑ Wear heals with pointed toes
- ❑ Wear your hair up
- ❑ Wear clothes that fit; baggy is not better

Baby on the Go

Diaper Bag

Five essentials for the minimalist

- ❑ Wallet
- ❑ Keys
- ❑ Cell phone
- ❑ Diapers/wipes (and a wet bag for cloth diapers)
- ❑ Bottle or sippy cup with formula, breast milk, or water
- ❑ *Epi-Pen, or an epinephrine auto-injector (for treatment of acute allergic reactions), if required

Diaper bag for daily use

- ❑ Wallet
- ❑ Keys
- ❑ Cell phone
- ❑ Diapers/wipes/wet bag
- ❑ Bottle or sippy cup with formula, breast milk, or water
- ❑ Small bottle of hand sanitizer
- ❑ Small bottle of sunscreen
- ❑ Formula dispenser with pre-measured formula, if formula feeding
- ❑ Nursing cover, if breastfeeding
- ❑ 1–2 thin burp cloths
- ❑ Travel changing pad

- ❑ Change of clothes and socks (in a collapsible, reusable bag)
- ❑ Pacifiers with a cover or in a container
- ❑ If eating solids, baby food and a spoon or a pouch
- ❑ A bib
- ❑ Finger-sized snacks for your older baby
- ❑ Water and snacks for mom and dad
- ❑ Small toys
- ❑ Baby books (soft ones that crinkle and have sensory stimulation)
- ❑ *Epi-Pen, or an epinephrine auto-injector (for treatment of acute allergic reactions), if required

Car Travel with Baby

Sleeping

- ❑ Portable crib or travel crib
- ❑ Portable crib or travel crib sheets (2)
- ❑ Swaddle blankets, or a wearable blanket (1–2)
- ❑ Favorite stuffed animal, lovey, or blanket
- ❑ Thin, light paper books
- ❑ Baby monitor, if desired
- ❑ iPod and portable speaker, if desired
- ❑ Night light, if desired

Baby clothing

- ❑ Pajamas, shirts, pants, playsuits, shoes, and socks for duration of trip
- ❑ Special clothes for church, holidays, or photos, such as tights, hair bows, shoes, and bow ties
- ❑ Cold weather: coats, jackets, hats, gloves, winter bunting, stroller sack
- ❑ Warm weather: light jacket, sun hat, sun shirt, bathing suit, swim diapers

Diapering

- ❑ Diapers for the duration of your trip (8–12 per day, depending on baby's age)
- ❑ Wipes, at least one large pack for your suitcase and a travel pack for the diaper bag
- ❑ Travel changing pad
- ❑ Diaper cream

Bathing

- ❑ Baby washcloths (2–3)
- ❑ Baby soap or shampoo in a small travel bottle
- ❑ A few small bath toys (I put these inside a bendable rinsing cup)

Health and grooming items

Put in a reusable bag

- ❑ Thermometer
- ❑ Baby pain reliever and fever reducer (if you bring it, you won't need it)
- ❑ Saline drops and a suction bulb
- ❑ Nail clippers and files
- ❑ Baby lotion, if desired (in a small travel bottle)
- ❑ Hair brush, if desired
- ❑ Cold weather: lip balm or cream for chapped lips and faces
- ❑ Warm weather: baby sunscreen

Feeding

- ❑ Nursing pillow with slipcover, if desired
- ❑ Burp cloths (3–5, depending on length of stay)
- ❑ Breast pump and accessories, if breastfeeding, even if you don't pump much at home
- ❑ Formula, if formula feeding
- ❑ Bottles

- ❑ Bottle warmer, if desired
- ❑ Bibs (2)
- ❑ Feeding spoons (2–3)
- ❑ Extra sippy cups
- ❑ Extra pacifiers, if required
- ❑ Booster seat, or travel high chair

Playing

- ❑ Small, light car-friendly toys, such as a truck, train, doll, animal, hanging toy, etc.
- ❑ Bouncer seat, if desired
- ❑ Baby carrier, if desired

Just for Mom

- ❑ A regular purse (for outings without baby)
- ❑ Nursing bras (day and night)
- ❑ Nursing pads
- ❑ Nursing friendly clothing and nursing cover

For the car

- ❑ See: Diaper Bag Checklist
- ❑ Small towels, tissues, extra hand sanitizer, extra diapers, and a travel bag of wipes that stays in the car
- ❑ A small ditty bag of hanging toys, soft books, teething rings, spatulas, and other entertainment items
- ❑ Small books to read if there is an additional passenger to read from the back seat
- ❑ A battery pack for pumping milk while traveling, if desired
- ❑ A more structured, thicker blanket
- ❑ Optional: a DVD player or iPad for older siblings to let baby sleep

Car travel tips

- ❑ Add extra time for unplanned surprises and unexpected stops
- ❑ Be proactive in changing dirty diapers and anticipate diaper rashes while traveling
- ❑ Plan your travel around naptime or bedtime
- ❑ Plan gas stops when baby is awake, even if the tank is not empty
- ❑ If given a choice in routes, select the one with the most highway miles for sleeping
- ❑ Keep your diaper bag, extra clothing, snacks, bottles/sippy cups, and toy bag accessible
- ❑ Buy or borrow a rearview baby mirror to check on baby
- ❑ Bring relaxing music or audio books

Air Travel with Baby

Packing list for the plane

- ❑ One diaper for each hour of transit, plus extras
- ❑ A large travel pack of wipes
- ❑ Diaper rash cream
- ❑ Diaper-changing travel pad
- ❑ Small reusable wet bags or Ziploc-type plastic bags
- ❑ Sanitizing wipes
- ❑ Small bottles of hand sanitizer
- ❑ 2 thin receiving blankets
- ❑ 2 washcloths
- ❑ Tissues
- ❑ Extra pacifiers
- ❑ Old and new inexpensive toys
- ❑ Air travel toys
- ❑ 1–3 clothes changes, socks, and shoes. Put outfits in individual bags.
- ❑ Formula, water, and/or juice
- ❑ Baby food and snacks
- ❑ Extra bottle or sippy cup
- ❑ Breast pump
- ❑ A travel or inflatable nursing pillow

- ❑ Baby saline nose solution and a suction bulb
- ❑ Sling or front carrier
- ❑ Car seat
- ❑ Collapsible stroller
- ❑ Snacks and an empty water bottle for you
- ❑ Extra shirt for you
- ❑ Mesh packing cubes or ditty bags, if you travel often
- ❑ Cell phone and charger
- ❑ Headphones
- ❑ Diaper bag. Transfer to a rolling carry-on, if desired.
- ❑ Special treats for severe meltdowns
- ❑ *Epi-Pen, or epinephrine auto-injector, for treatment of acute allergic reactions, if required

Favorite baby and toddler apps for travel

- ❑ Scribble
- ❑ Baby Sign ASL
- ❑ Elmo Loves ABCs
- ❑ Bubbles
- ❑ Toddler Cards
- ❑ Nighty Night
- ❑ Peekaboo Barn
- ❑ Fish School
- ❑ Monkey Preschool Lunchbox
- ❑ Endless Alphabet

Air travel tips

- ❑ Consider whether you need to buy a separate seat for baby
- ❑ Make friends with airline employees and request a seat change for a full row, if possible
- ❑ Book an aisle seat if flying solo with baby
- ❑ To protect against turbulence, bring a car seat or FAA-approved restraint system and secure it in a purchased seat or hold a lap baby facing you while protecting the head

- ❑ Take a flight earlier in the day to avoid delays
- ❑ Take a flight during sleepy times with a younger baby
- ❑ Leave plenty of time to make connections during layovers
- ❑ Prepare children for air travel by involving them in trip planning and teaching them about flight
- ❑ Rent or borrow a car seat at your destination to avoid the hassle of checking one
- ❑ Dress comfortably but respectably
- ❑ If both parents are traveling, send one to board early and prepare seats while the other parent stays back at the gate with your child(ren)
- ❑ If one parent is traveling, board early to set up
- ❑ Use discretion if you breastfeed on the plane; bring a nursing cover to make it a non-issue
- ❑ Try to bring a car seat if using a taxi. If you are without a car seat, use a seat belt rather than holding a child in your arms
- ❑ If you are traveling in NYC, Philadelphia, or Washington DC, try Uber Family

Health, Safety, and Lifestyle

Autism Awareness

Signs of autism

A child with autism might...

- ❑ Not respond to their name by 12 months
- ❑ Not point at objects to show interest by 14 months
- ❑ Not play "pretend" games by 18 months
- ❑ Avoid eye contact and want to be alone
- ❑ Not look at objects when another person points at them
- ❑ Have trouble understanding other people's feelings or talking about their own feelings
- ❑ Have delayed speech and language skills
- ❑ Prefer not to be held or cuddled or might cuddle only when they want

- ❑ Repeat words or phrases over and over (echolalia)
- ❑ Give unrelated answers to questions
- ❑ Get upset by minor changes
- ❑ Have trouble adapting when a routine changes
- ❑ Have obsessive interests in single subjects, like cars or trains
- ❑ Flap their hands, rock their body, or spin in circles
- ❑ Have unusual reactions to the way things sound, smell, taste, look, or feel
- ❑ Lose skills they once had (for instance, stop saying words they were using previously)
- ❑ Have chronic bowel or gastrointestinal issues, such as diarrhea or chronic constipation

If you think your child has autism...

- ❑ Talk with your child's doctor and ask for a development screening
- ❑ Contact your local Early Intervention (EI) agency for children under three, or school system for three years and up

Toxins Suspected of Causing Autism, ADHD, and Other NDDs

- ❑ Lead
- ❑ Methylmercury
- ❑ Polychlorinated biphenyls (PCBs)
- ❑ Organophosphate pesticides
- ❑ Organochlorine pesticides
- ❑ Endocrine disruptors (ECDs), such as phthalates and bisphenol A (BPA)
- ❑ Automotive exhaust
- ❑ Polycyclic aromatic hydrocarbons (PAHs)
- ❑ Brominated flame retardants (polybrominated diphenyl ethers or PBDEs)
- ❑ Perfluorinated compounds (PFCs)
- ❑ Arsenic
- ❑ Toluene
- ❑ Manganese

- ❑ Fluoride
- ❑ Tetrachloroethylene

Vaccine Debate

Why I support vaccines

- ❑ Vaccines save lives
- ❑ Parents do not understand the risks when they choose not to vaccinate
- ❑ Parents do not understand community immunity or herd immunity
- ❑ Autism rates have continued to soar despite intense vaccine scrutiny
- ❑ The number of children dying or adversely affected by skipping vaccinations is undeniable

Why I question vaccines

- ❑ No medical intervention comes without risk
- ❑ Inquiries about vaccines and neurological disorders in children are completely reasonable, considering the unique vulnerabilities of this group
- ❑ The signs of autism develop at the same time that certain shots are administered, amplifying the need for rigorous scientific study

Food Allergies

Common food allergens in children

- ❑ Eggs
- ❑ Cow's milk
- ❑ Peanuts
- ❑ Tree nuts (walnuts, pecans, hazelnuts, almonds, cashews, and pistachios)
- ❑ Soy or soybeans (primarily in infants)
- ❑ Fish (like tuna, salmon, cod)

- ❑ Shellfish (shrimp, crab, lobster)
- ❑ Wheat

Common food allergens in adults

- ❑ Shellfish, such as shrimp, crayfish, lobster, and crab
- ❑ Peanut
- ❑ Tree nuts
- ❑ Fish

Symptoms of food allergies

Look out for these symptoms as you introduce foods to your baby:

- ❑ Swelling in the tongue and throat
- ❑ Tingling in the mouth
- ❑ Hives
- ❑ Eczema or an itchy rash
- ❑ Coughing or wheezing
- ❑ GI symptoms, such as abdominal pain, vomiting, or diarrhea
- ❑ Dizziness
- ❑ Loss of consciousness
- ❑ Anaphylaxis

Organic Foods

Organic definition

- ❑ Organic foods are produced without bioengineering or genetically modified organisms (GMOs), antibiotics, synthetic growth hormones, synthetic fertilizers, sewage sludge, ionizing radiation, and manmade pesticides

Prioritize organic animal products

Due to the combination of GMO feed, hormones, and antibiotics use organic:

- ❑ Dairy (milk, yogurt, butter, cheese)
- ❑ Eggs
- ❑ Beef
- ❑ Chicken
- ❑ Pork
- ❑ Fish

The Dirty Dozen plus

These fruits and vegetables are worth buying organic:

- ❑ Apples
- ❑ Strawberries
- ❑ Grapes
- ❑ Celery
- ❑ Peaches
- ❑ Spinach
- ❑ Sweet bell peppers
- ❑ Nectarines (imported)
- ❑ Cucumbers
- ❑ Cherry tomatoes
- ❑ Snap peas (imported)
- ❑ Potatoes
- ❑ Plus: Hot peppers and kale/collard greens for pesticides of special concern

The Clean Fifteen

Foods that are least likely to have pesticides and don't need to be organic on a tight budget:

- ❑ Avocados
- ❑ Sweet Corn
- ❑ Pineapples
- ❑ Cabbage
- ❑ Sweet Peas (frozen)

- ❑ Onions
- ❑ Asparagus
- ❑ Mangos
- ❑ Papayas
- ❑ Kiwi
- ❑ Eggplant
- ❑ Grapefruit
- ❑ Cantaloupe (domestic)
- ❑ Cauliflower
- ❑ Sweet Potatoes

Other organic, non-GMO priorities for kids (most popular foods):

- ❑ organic baby food
- ❑ organic peanut butter
- ❑ organic ketchup
- ❑ organic apples
- ❑ organic grapes
- ❑ organic potatoes
- ❑ organic dips and salad dressings (avoid cottonseed, corn, and soy-modified oils)
- ❑ 100% olive oil

Buying organic food on a budget

- ❑ Look beyond your conventional supermarket
- ❑ Search LocalHarvest.org to find local produce
- ❑ Buy a share in a Community-Supported Agriculture (CSA) program
- ❑ Join a co-op
- ❑ Buy organic fruits and vegetables in season
- ❑ Start a buying club with friends
- ❑ Take a trip through an area with farms and stock up
- ❑ Grow your own organic garden

How to reduce toxin exposure in conventional foods

If organics are still out of your budget

- ❑ For apples and pears, cut out the fruit's core, top, and bottom
- ❑ For strawberries, cut out the stalk and core
- ❑ For peaches and nectarines, peel the skin
- ❑ For grapes, avoid imported grapes during the winter months
- ❑ For bell peppers, buy red, yellow, and orange varieties rather than green peppers
- ❑ For leafy greens and lettuce, remove the outer layers
- ❑ For potatoes, scrub the surface and peel the skins for children
- ❑ For fish, beef, pork, and poultry, peel away the skins and extra fat

Green Cleaning

Low cost green cleaning supplies

- ❑ Plain liquid soap
- ❑ Baking soda
- ❑ 100% distilled white vinegar
- ❑ Lemon juice

Conventional cleaning products to avoid or minimize

- ❑ Drain cleaner, acidic toilet cleaner, oven cleaner, furniture polish, silver and metal polisher, bleach, and liquid cleaner with harsh chemicals, spot remover, and ammonia-based window cleaner
- ❑ Don't buy products labeled "danger," "poison," or "fatal if swallowed"
- ❑ Avoid the EWG's Hall of Shame or list of most toxic household cleaners

Going Green

Top five ways to reduce your carbon footprint

- ❑ Green your commute
- ❑ Be more energy efficient at home
- ❑ Choose green electricity
- ❑ Eat less meat, especially red meat
- ❑ Buy less stuff

Money-saving green tips

- ❑ Turn off lights, appliances, and computers when not in use
- ❑ Use a smart power strip
- ❑ Replace older incandescent bulbs with CFLs, LEDs, or halogens
- ❑ Replace aging appliances with new Energy Star appliances
- ❑ Turn your thermostat down in the winter and up in the summer
- ❑ Wash clothes in cold water
- ❑ Wash hands in cold water and turn down the water heater
- ❑ Eat at least one meatless meal per week
- ❑ Don't waste food
- ❑ Bring your lunch
- ❑ Skip bottled water and drink from a reusable bottle
- ❑ Keep reusable shopping bags handy
- ❑ Buy a more fuel efficient vehicle
- ❑ Downsize to one vehicle
- ❑ Use public transportation
- ❑ Combine errands into fewer trips and drive the speed limit
- ❑ Recycle electronics properly: search online databases like Greener Gadgets or Call2Recycle for drop-off locations
- ❑ Think before you buy new. Try consignment sales, yard sales, or Craigslist
- ❑ Compost at home to avoid and save on chemical fertilizers
- ❑ Visit your public library or use the Overdrive app to borrow ebooks
- ❑ Visit favorite green web sites for current news and information: Grist, TreeHugger, and WorldChanging

Top green mobile apps

- ❑ GoodGuide
- ❑ greenMeter
- ❑ GasHog
- ❑ HootRoot
- ❑ CarbonCalc
- ❑ Carbon Tracker
- ❑ Meter Readings
- ❑ Control4 MyHome
- ❑ iRecycle
- ❑ What's Fresh
- ❑ LocaVore
- ❑ Gorgeously Green Survival Guide
- ❑ Get Green

Financial Tips

- ❑ Set aside at least three months living expenses for emergencies
- ❑ Create a budget using budget software or an online tool
- ❑ Purchase life insurance for you and your spouse or increase current coverage
- ❑ Consider disability insurance
- ❑ Make a will
- ❑ Do your banking at a credit union, if possible
- ❑ Try these tips if you are buying a new home
    - ▸ Maximize your credit score before applying for a mortgage or loan
    - ▸ Never buy a mortgage from your bank
    - ▸ Look up wholesale mortgage rates online and compare rates from a number of banks, lenders, and mortgage brokers
    - ▸ Don't select a mortgage provider based on quotes offered online or over the telephone
    - ▸ If the home you are considering was recently a foreclosure or bargain snag fixed up by an investor, beware of inflated real estate appraisals
- ❑ Check your credit score regularly

- ❑ Try these tips for increasing your credit score, especially prior to applying for a mortgage or loan.
  - ▶ Dispute all errors
  - ▶ Negotiate past late payments
  - ▶ Ask to increase any available credit limits on existing accounts
  - ▶ Do not close any current credit card accounts
  - ▶ Pay your bills on time (35% of your score); set up auto-payments
  - ▶ Pay off any credit card balances before applying for a loan, even if you normally pay the balance month to month; any balance lowers your score
- ❑ Take advantage of child tax deductions, credits, and savings programs, such as:
  - ▶ Dependent exemption
  - ▶ Child Tax Credit
  - ▶ Child and Dependent Care Credit
  - ▶ Dependent Care Flexible Spending Account
  - ▶ Medical Flexible Spending Account
  - ▶ Affordable Care Act Tax Provisions for Individuals and Families
- ❑ Start saving for college

Top "must have" apps that make life better

- ❑ Personal finance: Mint
- ❑ Credit score and credit monitoring: Credit Karma
- ❑ Scanning tool (for receipts and documents): Turboscan
- ❑ Password manager: Last Pass
- ❑ Podcast downloader: Downcast
- ❑ E-books and audiobooks (from the public library): OverDrive
- ❑ Music (never buy a song again): Spotify
- ❑ Note taking: Evernote
- ❑ Shopping (nutrition): ShopWell
- ❑ Shopping (green product ratings): GoodGuide
- ❑ Maps: Google Maps
- ❑ Weather: Yahoo Weather

Top apps for new parents

- ❑ Travel with baby: Baby Monitor
- ❑ Medical for baby: WebMD Baby
- ❑ Breastfeeding (to track feedings): Baby Tracker
- ❑ Breastfeeding (to track pumping): Milk Maid
- ❑ Baby timers and trackers: Total Baby
- ❑ Nighttime feedings: Flashlight
- ❑ Colic: Baby Shusher
- ❑ Photos of baby: Qwiki and BabyCam
- ❑ Public restroom finder (for blowouts or nursing): SitOrSquat

Top apps for fitness

- ❑ Best for daily activity tracking: Fitbit or Argus
- ❑ Best for runners: Map My Run
- ❑ Best gradual approach: Couch-to-5K
- ❑ Best for yogis: Yoga Studio
- ❑ Best for dieters and calorie counters: Calorie Counter or Weight Watchers Mobile
- ❑ Best for toning a flabby body: Nike Training Club
- ❑ Best for busy parents: Hot5 (free 5-minute video workouts) or Johnson and Johnson 7 Minute Workout
- ❑ Best for distracting non-exercisers: Zombies, Run! Part interactive fitness trainer and part horror flick, this app guides you through interval training while fleeing from zombies

Save Money on Baby Costs

- ❑ Don't rush into upgrading your home
- ❑ Embrace hand-me-downs
- ❑ Breastfeed your baby
- ❑ Make homemade baby food
- ❑ Buy generic store-brand formula and disposable diapers
- ❑ Use coupons for diapers and formula
- ❑ Shop at warehouse stores with warehouse coupons

- ❑ Use cloth diapers and wash them yourself
- ❑ Buy expensive baby products online
- ❑ Research prices online before making purchases in a store
- ❑ Use deal sites to snag bargains and money-saving tips
- ❑ Ask family for free babysitting and offer acts of kindness in return
- ❑ Buy white or unisex-colored clothing
- ❑ Buy kids' clothing the next size up or two at the end of the season
- ❑ Turn everyday items into toys
- ❑ Use your library for free story time and parks for playtime
- ❑ Send "wish lists" with practical items to gift givers at holidays and birthdays
- ❑ Avoid purchasing food and baby supplies on the go

Cold and Flu Season

For newborns

- ❑ Do not allow people to hold your baby until they have washed their hands
- ❑ Avoid kissing baby on the face, especially if you have cold symptoms
- ❑ Keep away from crowds, especially indoors
- ❑ Don't let anyone smoke around baby
- ❑ Limit the time that high risk babies spend in a day care center

For older babies

- ❑ Children and caregivers should wash their hands for twenty seconds or more
- ❑ Wash your child's hands before eating and after leaving public places
- ❑ Use hand sanitizer if soap and water are unavailable
- ❑ In cold weather, bundle up children to go outside rather than going to densely-populated indoor areas
- ❑ If you know someone is sick, politely skip the visit, especially for younger babies
- ❑ Clean and disinfect highly-used surfaces

  - ▸ Telephones and cell phones
  - ▸ Keyboards (including iPads and your mouse)
  - ▸ Doorknobs
  - ▸ Refrigerator door handles
  - ▸ Light switches
  - ▸ Remote controls
  - ▸ Bathroom and kitchen faucets
  - ▸ Dishwasher handles
  - ▸ Sponges
  - ▸ Salt and pepper shakers
  - ▸ Toothbrushes
- ❑ If baby has a cold, wash plastic toys in soap and water and launder plush toys. Wrap stuffed animals in a pillowcase before washing
- ❑ Do not share or finish a child's uneaten food
- ❑ Do your best to keep siblings' toothbrushes separate, since as many as 10 million germs and bacteria can be found on a single toothbrush. The American Dental Association recommends replacing toothbrushes every three to four months
- ❑ During peak cold and flu season, detox after leaving day care or preschool
- ❑ Keep a sick child at home until at least twenty-four hours after a fever has subsided, and he/she has no yellow or green mucus in the nose
- ❑ Try a smart combination of remedies to treat minor illnesses at home
  - ▸ Plenty of fluids: soak baby's nose with saline drops and suction out mucus before feedings
  - ▸ Plenty of rest
  - ▸ Plenty of love and attention
  - ▸ A warm bath: the steam from the warm water should help clear congestion
  - ▸ A vaporizer or humidifier
- ❑ Be judicious with baby's first illnesses, but be aware of first time parent "fever phobia"
- ❑ Talk to your doctor about accurate medicine dosing and careful use of infant pain relievers
  - ▸ Use the medicine dispenser that came with your medicine

- Double check all labels and double check all labels and measurements
- Never use a kitchen utensil to dispense medicine to your child
- Follow through with all prescriptions
- Never give a child expired or unused medications
- Note your child's weight, since dosages for most nonprescription drugs are based on weight, not age
- Do not give medicine to a child under age 3 months
- Do not give ibuprofen to a child less than 6 months old

Appendix B: Infant Formula

Infant formula

Walking down the baby aisle of any grocery or big-box store can be overwhelming for a new parent. How many different cans of formula could a baby possibly need? The truth is that formula makers intentionally produce many different varieties of their formulas, such as hypoallergenic, sensitive, for fussiness and gas, for colic, with prebiotics and probiotics, etc. so that you never quite have an accurate price point for your formula. The goal is to raise prices above the cost of the additives.

To save money on formula costs, try these tips:

- ❑ **Buy generic and store brand formulas.** All formulas sold in the U.S. must meet basic nutrient requirements, including store brands from Walmart, CVS, Target, Sam's Club, Babies R' Us, Costco, BJ's, and Walgreens. Differences in formulas lie in the fillers. Store brand formulas, such as Walmart's Parent's Choice, can be up to 50% cheaper than leading name brands, such as Enfamil and Similac, saving parents $600–700 per year.
- ❑ **Buy formula at warehouse stores and through mass merchandisers.** A leading consumer magazine revealed that prices for one ounce of a popular name brand formula varied by almost 25%, with the lowest prices found at Costco and Walmart and the highest prices at retail drugstores like Walgreens and CVS. Babies R' Us, Target, and supermarkets were in between.
- ❑ **Collect formula coupons and carry them in your wallet.**
- ❑ **Save money on formula with an online subscribe and save program, such as Amazon Mom.**

- ❑ **If you meet income eligibility requirements, you may be able to receive assistance from the government for infant formula.** The Supplemental Nutrition Assistance Program (SNAP) for Women, Infants, and Children (WIC) provides federal grants to states for supplemental foods. WIC purchases over one-half of all U.S. infant formula, and most states allow you to apply online (http://www.fns.usda.gov/snap/apply).

Types of formula

Formula comes in three forms:

- **Ready-made.** This form is convenient, although it's also 20% more expensive than powdered formula.
- **Liquid concentrate.** This form requires mixing equal parts formula and water. It is more expensive than powdered formula because it makes less of a mess, and it is less expensive than ready-made because it requires mixing.
- **Powdered formula.** This is the most economical and environmentally friendly option. Powdered formula has a one-month shelf life after opening and must be mixed exactly as the manufacturer recommends. Moms with older children may warn you about BPA and formula cans; however, in July 2013, the FDA banned the use of BPA-based epoxy resins in the use of formula packaging.

Most infant formulas contain cow's milk whey and casein as a protein source, a blend of vegetable oils as the fat source, lactose or sugar from milk as a carbohydrate source, a vitamin and mineral mixture, and other filler ingredients, depending on the manufacturer.

- **Cow's milk based.** Most formula is made from cow's milk, although the milk protein is significantly altered for digestion. Most babies do well with this type of formula, which strives to mix the right amounts of protein, carbohydrates, and fat. Your baby will not be able to digest regular cow's milk until he is one year old.
- **Lactose-free.** This formula may be used if baby cannot digest the sugar naturally found in milk, which is rare.

- **Soy-based.** If you are a vegan or your baby cannot digest cow's milk, you may try a soy-based formula. However, soy-based formulas contain soy protein isolates, which are highly processed, chemically-altered soybeans that are not similar to breast milk. Some doctors also worry about the high concentration of plant-based estrogen (called phytoestrogens) in soy formula. About half of babies with milk allergies also have soy allergies. The American Academy of Pediatricians (AAP) notes that soy protein-based formulas are not designed for or recommended for preterm infants.[201]
- **With added probiotics or prebiotics.** A probiotic supplement is a food product that has enough tiny, active organisms to alter baby's microflora, while prebiotics are non-digestible ingredients that stimulate growth of indigenous probiotic bacteria. Breast milk has lots of prebiotics. You may consider formulas with these additives if your baby was born via C-section, or if baby has a high risk for asthma or eczema based on your family history.[202]
- **Extensively hydrolyzed.** In this formula, protein is broken down even further for digestion and may be used for babies with multiple allergies or preemies having difficulties absorbing nutrients. Extensively hydrolyzed formulas may be suggested for infants at high-risk for allergies who are not breastfed.[203]
- **Other specialty formulas.** These formulas are for babies requiring specialized nutrition, due to premature birth, diseases, or digestive disorders. Talk to your doctor before buying expensive "specialized" formulas.

Organic infant formula

I strongly recommend using organic formula, if possible. The question of whether to feed baby organic formula versus regular formula isn't about nutrients; it's about the chemicals and processes used to alter the ingredients.

Pros: Formula is derived from cow's milk. The USDA organic label for livestock verifies that producers did not use antibiotics or growth hormones, fed the cows 100% organic feed, and provided animals with access to the outdoors. Also, organic formula sweeteners and fatty oils are not Genetically Modified Organisms (GMOs).

Cons: The extra price tag for organic formula can add up ($5–10 more per 23 oz. can). Use coupons and buy in bulk to offset higher organic costs.

Organic infant formula ingredients

Read organic formula labels. Not all brands are the same. Similac Organic, the market-leader in organic formula, sweetens its more expensive organic formula with cane sugar, or sucrose, which is significantly sweeter than lactose sugar (extracted from milk). Babies need added sugars to help digest the protein in cow's milk. However, pediatricians warn that sucrose can harm tooth enamel faster than other sugars, and might lead to baby refusing less sweet formulas and foods in the future. Sucrose is banned in infant formula in the EU and Canada, except when ordered by a doctor. Similac Organic also contains other synthetic nutrients, such as lycopene and lutein, touted for health benefits in the U.S. Those two substances are banned in EU formulas, too.

Similac is not the only brand looking to lure customers with sweeter, cheaper ingredients. PBM Nutritionals (owned by private label health conglomerate Perrigo), makers of Earth's Best, 365/Whole Foods, Bright Beginnings, Parent's Choice, and Vermont Organics brand formulas are also transitioning to less or no lactose sugar, which mimics mother's milk best. To cut costs, PBM is replacing lactose with cheaper, plant-based sweeteners, such as "organic glucose syrup solids" (another name for "corn syrup solids") and "maltodextrins" (starch molecules derived from potatoes, rice, and corn). In 2007, Earth's Best organic formula contained only organic lactose, but by 2011, it contained both organic lactose and organic glucose syrup solids. Today organic lactose still remains in Earth's Best and Vermont's Organics formula but has disappeared altogether in Parent's Choice, Bright Beginnings, and Whole Foods' 365 organic formula brands.

Bottom line: Ingredients in organic formulas must meet USDA standards for no hormones, no antibiotics, and no GMOs, but that doesn't mean that organic formula makers aren't trying to sneak in other cheaper ingredients.

Sensitive infant formula

Talk to your doctor before switching to an expensive sensitive formula. Feeding sensitivities may be helped by something as simple as burping baby more often, switching bottle nipples, or holding baby upright for thirty minutes after feedings. Some parents switch formulas and then tout miraculous changes in their baby. However, keep in mind that colic often improves between four and six months, regardless of formula type. Also, more expensive, sensitive formulas are typically sweeter than basic formulas, and these companies are well aware that babies have more sweet taste buds than adults and are predisposed to having a "sweet tooth." This may explain why the first two ingredients of Similac Sensitive, labeled the number one formula for sensitive tummies, are corn syrup and sugar (sucrose). No wonder baby likes his sensitive formula! For a further look at the ingredients of leading brands, see Infant Formula Ingredients at the end of this section.

Soy infant formula

Ninety four percent of soy crops in the U.S. contain GMO soy, and the overwhelming majority are RoundUp Ready, or genetically engineered for resistance to Monsanto's glyphosate and Bayer Crop Science's glufosinate. In October 2014, *Consumer Reports* found "substantial amounts" of GMO soy in the following infant formulas: Enfamil ProSobee Soy Infant Formula, Gerber Good Start Soy, Similac Soy Isomil, and Similac Go & Grow Soy Infant formula.[204] Moreover, soy protein isolate is derived from a hexane extracting process (a toxic solvent derived from gasoline). Talk to your doctor before using or switching to a soy-based formula.

DHA-ARA in infant formula: a sticky topic

So how do oils extracted from fermented micro algae and lab-produced soil fungus mimic human fatty acids in breast milk? I have no idea. However, several studies support small but positive effects on visual and neural development with added DHA-ARA to infant formulas, and that is enough for health care providers and lawmakers to pay attention.[205] However, the DHA-ARA debate is not clear-cut. Other studies show no benefit at all, and policy makers and non-profits who advocate for moderate and low-income families are questioning whether companies wanting to add DHA-ARA, prebiotics, probiotics, lutein, and other additives are just trying to drive up costs.

Organic certification experts are also scratching their heads about infant formula additives since DHA-ARA oils are extracted using a synthetic technique. Dried, lab-made algae is blended with hexane in a continuous extraction process, which is typically an immediate disqualification for the USDA organic label (DHA-ARA is in organic formulas). After this process, synthetic preservatives, such as ascorbyl palmitate and beta-carotene, must be added to keep the algal oils from turning rancid.

The AAP has stayed conspicuously silent on DHA-ARA in infant formula, and the FDA approved its use because the additives are believed to be safe. Why not add DHA-ARA if it helps? The verdict is still out for determining whether the long term eye and brain benefits are worth the extra cost. If your baby has gastrointestinal upset, avoid DHA-ARA additives.

Infant formula buying guide with brand recommendations

To summarize, when comparing infant formulas, ask these questions:

- **Is the formula organic?** Conventional formula is likely to contain GMOs, milk with traces of antibiotics and growth hormones, and DHA-ARA.
- **Is the formula dairy or soy-based?** Soy-based formula should be an option reserved only for those who have talked to their doctor about family preferences or a dairy intolerance. Otherwise, soy formulas are filled with GMO ingredients.
- **Does the formula contain essential fatty acids (DHA and ARA)?** Are you okay with hexane-extracted DHA-ARA?
- **What else has been added?** Many parents will want to avoid synthetic added nutrients, such as lutein (hexane-extracted from marigolds), lycopene (created with the neurotoxin toluene), nucleotides (formed from chemically treated yeast), taurine (processed with cancer-causing sulfuric acid), and l-carnetine (banned from

organics, due to cancer-causing properties). Unfortunately, some of these ingredients are included in popular organic brands.

- **What sweetens the formula?** As mentioned previously, the sugar that most closely resembles breast milk is lactose. Unfortunately, formulas such as Parent's Choice, Bright Beginnings, Earth's Best, Whole Foods 365, and Vermont Organics are betting on public reassurance from organic milk and cutting costs by using cheaper plant-based carbohydrates including maltodextrin and glucose syrup solids (better known as corn syrup solids). If you see sucrose, sugar, or organic cane sugar, listed in your infant formula (e.g., Similac Organic, Similac Sensitive, Similac Soy, Gerber Soy), try another brand. In my opinion, these formulas are like baby milkshakes. Baby drinks the formula, triggering dopamine in the brain and making baby crave even more sugar and sweet tastes. Again, the point is not that sucrose is "safe" in infant formulas. It's that too much sugar is making our children obese.

Brand recommendations:

Conventional infant formula

- ❑ *Best Conventional Infant Formula:* If buying organic formula is not an option, leading consumer organizations and other pediatric groups recommend private label store brand formulas for cost savings, and I think their argument makes sense. If the differences only lie in filler ingredients, established name brand formulas, such as **Similac** and **Enfamil**, have no incentive to use high quality fillers. Look for infant formulas with the first two ingredients: nonfat milk and lactose.

Organic infant formula

- ❑ *Best Organic Infant Formula (for ingredients):* For GMO purists who do not desire synthetic DHA-ARA, I recommend **Nature's One Baby's Only Dairy Organic** (*$19 per 12.7 oz.*). Labeled as a toddler formula to promote breastfeeding, Baby's Only advertises superiority to other organic brands, using no organic corn syrup (or glucose syrup), no organic palm oils, and no hexane-produced DHA (an organic-compliant process extracts DHA-ARA from eggs). There are lingering questions about arsenic levels in Baby's Only, but the company has been using a process since 2012 to remove all heavy metals, including arsenic. Unfortunately, cost will prohibit most parents from using this formula. Note the smaller can size *($34.71 for 23.2 oz.)*

- ❑ *Best Value Organic Infant Formula:* My value choices for organic formulas include either **Earth's Best Organic Formula** *($27 per 23.2 oz.)*, or **Vermont Organics** *($27–30 per 23.2 oz.)*, which is now offered at Costco.
- ❑ *Best Imported Infant Formula:* Parents completely skeptical of U.S. organic brands may opt to import brands from Europe, such as Germany's **Holle Organic Infant Formula** *($30 per 400 g)*, although expect to pay hefty shipping costs.

Soy-based infant formula

- ❑ *Best Soy-based Infant Formula:* If your baby must use soy formula, I recommend **Nature's One Baby's Only Organic Soy Formula** *($9.99 for 12.7 oz.)*, due to non-GMO ingredients. Baby's Only is also the only soy formula on the market that doesn't use corn syrup (or glucose syrup) as its source of carbohydrate.

Infant Formula Ingredients

Conventional formula

Milk-based Formulas:

Similac Infant Formula
With Iron, Powder

Ingredients:
Nonfat Milk, Lactose, High Oleic Safflower Oil, Soy Oil, Coconut Oil, Whey Protein Concentrate, and less than 2% of: C. Cohnii Oil (Source of Docosahexaenoic Acid [DHA]), M. Alpina Oil (Source of Arachidonic Acid [ARA]), Potassium Citrate, Calcium Carbonate, Ascorbic Acid, Soy

Lecithin, Potassium Chloride, Magnesium Chloride, Ferrous Sulfate, Choline Chloride, Choline Bitartrate, Ascorbyl Palmitate, Sodium Chloride, Taurine, M-Inositol, Zinc Sulfate, Mixed Tocopherols, D-Alpha-Tocopheryl Acetate, Niacinamide, Calcium Pantothenate, L-Carnitine, Vitamin A Palmitate, Cupric Sulfate, Thiamine Chloride Hydrochloride, Riboflavin, Pyridoxine Hydrochloride, Folic Acid, Manganese Sulfate, Phylloquinone, Biotin, Sodium Selenate, Beta-Carotene, Vitamin D3, Cyanocobalamin, Calcium Phosphate, Potassium Phosphate, Potassium Hydroxide and Nucleotides (Adenosine 5'-Monophosphate, Cytidine 5'-Monophdsphate, Disodium Guanosine 5'-Monophosphate, Disodium Uridine 5'-Monophosphate).

Enfamil Infant Formula (Newborn)
Milk-based Infant Formula with Iron, Powder

Ingredients:
Nonfat Milk, Lactose, Vegetable Oil (Palm Olein, Coconut, Soy, and High Oleic Sunflower Oils), Whey Protein Concentrate, Galactooligosaccharides (a Type of Prebiotic), Polydextrose (a Type of Prebiotic), and less than 1% of: Mortierella Alpina Oil (a Source of Arachidonic Acid (ARA)), Crypthecodinium Cohnii Oil (a Source of Docosahexaenoic Acid (DHA)), Soy Lecithin, Vitamin A Palmitate, Vitamin D3, Vitamin E Acetate, Vitamin K1, Thiamin Hydrochloride, Riboflavin, Vitamin B6 Hydrochloride, Vitamin B12, Niacinamide, Folic Acid, Calcium Pantothenate, Biotin, Ascorbic Acid, Inositol, Calcium Carbonate, Calcium Phosphate, Magnesium Oxide, Ferrous Sulfate, Zinc Sulfate, Manganese Sulfate, Cupric Sulfate, Potassium Iodide, Sodium Selenite, Potassium Citrate, Choline Chloride, Potassium Chloride, Sodium Chloride, Nucleotides (Cytidine 5'-Monophosphate, Disodium Uridine 5'-Monophosphate, Adenosine 5'-Monophosphate, Disodium Guanosine 5'-Mono-Phosphate), Taurine, L-Carnitine.

Enfamil Infant Formula (LIPIL)
Milk-based Infant Formula with Iron, Powder

Ingredients:
Nonfat Milk, Lactose, Vegetable Oil (Palm Olein, Soy, Coconut, and High Oleic Sunflower Oils), Whey Protein Concentrate, and less than 1% of: Mortierella Alpina Oil (a Source of Arachidonic Acid [ARA]),

Crypthecodinium Cohnii Oil (a Source of Docosahexaenoic Acid [DHA]), Vitamin A Palmitate, Vitamin D3, Vitamin E Acetate, Vitamin K1, Thiamin Hydrochloride, Riboflavin, Vitamin B6 Hydrochloride, Vitamin B12, Niacinamide, Folic Acid, Calcium Pantothenate, Biotin, Ascorbic Acid, Choline Chloride, Inositol, Calcium Carbonate, Magnesium Oxide, Ferrous Sulfate, Zinc Sulfate, Manganese Sulfate, Cupric Sulfate, Potassium Chloride, Potassium Citrate, Potassium Hydroxide, Sodium Selenite, Taurine, L-Carnitine, Nucleotides (Adenosine 5'-Monophosphate, Cytidine 5'-Monophosphate, Disodium Guanosine 5'-Monophosphate, Disodium Uridine 5'-Monoposphate).

Gerber Infant Formula (gentle)
Milk-based Powder With Iron

Ingredients:
Whey Protein Concentrate (from Cow's Milk, Enzymatically Hydrolyzed, Reduced in Minerals), Vegetable Oils (Palm Olein, Soy, Coconut, and High-Oleic Safflower or High-Oleic Sunflower), Corn Maltodextrin, Lactose, Galacto-Oligosaccharides (a Prebiotic Fiber Sourced from Milk), and less than 2% of: Potassium Citrate, Potassium Phosphate, Calcium Chloride, Calcium Phosphate, Sodium Citrate, Magnesium Chloride, Ferrous Sulfate, Zinc Sulfate, Sodium Chloride, Copper Sulfate, Potassium Iodide, Manganese Sulfate, Sodium Selenate, M. Alpina Oil (a Source of Arachidonic Acid [ARA]), C. Cohnii Oil (a Source of Docosahexaenoic Acid [DHA]), Sodium Ascorbate, Inositol, Choline Bitartrate, Alpha-Tocopheryl Acetate, Niacinamide, Calcium Pantothenate, Riboflavin, Vitamin A Acetate, Pyridoxine Hydrochloride, Thiamine Mononitrate, Folic Acid, Phylloquinone, Biotin, Vitamin D3, Vitamin B12, Taurine, Nucleotides (Cytidine 5'-Monophosphate, Disodium Uridine 5'-Monophosphate, Adenosine 5'-Monophosphate, Disodium Guanosine 5'-Monophosphate), Ascorbyl Palmitate, Mixed Tocopherols, L-Carnitine, Soy Lecithin.

Parent's Choice Infant Formula
Newborn

Ingredients:
Nonfat Milk, Lactose, Vegetable Oils (Palm Olein, Soy, Coconut, High Oleic (Safflower Or Sunflower) Oil), Whey Protein Concentrate,

Galacto-Oligosaccharid (Gos), and less Than 1% of: Mortierella Aplina Oil*, Crypthecodinium Cohnii Oil**, Soy Lecithin, Vitamin A Palmitate, Vitamin D3, Vitamin E Acetate, Vitamin K, Thiamine Hydrochloride, Riboflavin, Vitamin B6 Hydrochloride, Vitamin B12, Niacinamide, Folic Acid, Calcium Pantothenate, Biotin, Ascorbic Acid, Choline Bitartrate, Inositol, Calcium Carbonate, Calcium Chloride, Calcium Hydroxide, Magnesium Chloride, Ferrous Sulfate, Zinc Sulfate, Manganese Sulfate, Cupric Sulfate, Potassium Bicarbonate, Potassium Iodide, Potassium Hydroxide, Potassium Phosphate, Sodium Selenite, Sodium Citrate, Taurine, L-Carnitine, Beta-Carotene, Mixed Tocopherol Concentrate, Ascorbyl Palmitate, Monoglycerides, Nucleotides (Adenosine-5'-Monophosphate, Cytidine-5'-Monophosphate, Disodium Guanosine-5'-Monophosphate, Disodium Uridine-5'-Monophosphate). Contains Milk and Soy Ingredients. *A Source of Anachidonic Acid (Ara). **A Source of Docosahexaenoic Acid (DHA).

Sensitive milk-based formulas (for fussiness and gas):

Similac Sensitive Infant Formula:
With Iron for Fussiness & Gas, Powder

Ingredients:

Corn Syrup, Sugar, Milk Protein Isolate, High Oleic, Safflower Oil, Soy Oil, Galacto-Oligosaccaride, and less Than 2% of: C. Cohnii Oil, M. Alpina Oil, Beta-Carotene, Lutein, Lycopene, Calcium Phosphate, Potassium Citrate, Potassium Chloride, Sodium Citrate, Magnesium Phosphate, Ascorbic Acid, Calcium Carbonate, Choline Chloride, Ferrous Sulfate, Magnesium Chloride, Ascorbyl Palmitate, Choline Bitartrate, Taurine, M-Inositol, D-Alpha-Tocopheryl Acetate, Zinc Sulfate, Mixed Tocopherols, L-Carnitine, Niacinamide, Calcium Pantothenate, Vitamin A Palmitate, Cupric Sulfate, Thiamine Chloride Hydrochloride, Riboflavin, Pydroxide Hydrochloride, Folic Acid, Manganese Sulfate, Potassium Iodide, Phylloquinone, Biotin, Sodium Selenate, Vitamin D3, Cyanocobalamin, Potassium Hydroxide And Nucleotide (Adenosine 5'monophosphate, Cytide 5'-Monophosphate, Disodium Guanosine 5'-Monophosphate, Disodium Uridine 5'-Monophosphate). Galacto-Oligosaccharides Are Sourced from Milk (Gos). C. Cohnii Oil Is A Source of DHA. M. Alpina Oil Is A Source of Ara.

Enfamil Infant Formula (Gentlease)
For Fussiness & Gas

Ingredients:
Corn Syrup Solids, Partially Hydrolyzed Nonfat Milk and Whey Protein Concentrate Solids (Soy), Vegetable Oil (Palm Olein, Soy, Coconut, and High Oleic Sunflower Oils), and less than 2% of: Mortierella Alpina Oil (a Source of Arachidonic Acid (ARA)), Crypthecodinium Cohnii Oil (a Source of Docosahexaenoic Acid (DHA)), Vitamin A Palmitate, Vitamin D3, Vitamin E Acetate, Vitamin K1, Thiamin Hydrochloride, Riboflavin, Vitamin B6 Hydrochloride, Vitamin B12, Niacinamide, Folic Acid, Calcium Pantothenate, Biotin, Ascorbic Acid, Choline Chloride, Inositol, Calcium Carbonate, Calcium Phosphate, Magnesium Phosphate, Ferrous Sulfate, Zinc Sulfate, Manganese Sulfate, Cupric Sulfate, Sodium Selenite, Sodium Citrate, Potassium Chloride, Taurine, and L-Carnitine.

Soy-based formulas:

Similac Infant Formula
Isomil Soy for Fussiness & Gas with Iron, Powder

Ingredients:
Corn Syrup Solids (39%), Soy Protein Isolate (15%), High Oleic Safflower Oil (11%), Sugar (10%), Soy Oil (8%), Coconut Oil (8%), and less than 2% of: C. Cohnii Oil, M, Alpina Oil, Beta-Carotene, Lutein, Lycopene, Fructooligosaccharides, Calcium Phosphate, Potassium Citrate, Potassium Chloride, Magnesium Chloride, Salt, Ascorbic Acid, Choline Chloride, L-Methionine, Taurine, Ascorbyl Palmitate, Ferrous Sulfate, M-Inositol, Mixed Tocopherols, Zinc Sulfate, D-Alpha Tocopheryl Acetate, L-Carnitine, Niacinamide, Calcium Pantothenate, Cupric Sulfate, Thiamine Chloride Hydrochloride, Vitamin A Palmitate, Riboflavin, Pyridoxine Hydrochloride, Folic Acid, Potassium Iodide, Potassium Hydroxide, Phylloquinone, Biotin, Sodium Selenate, Vitamin D3 and Cyanocobalamin. C. Cohnii is a Source of DHA. M. Alpina Oil is a Source of ARA.

Enfamil Infant Formula (ProSoBee)
Soy, Iron Fortified, Powder

Ingredients:
Corn Syrup Solids (55 %), Vegetable Oil (Palm Olein, Soy, Coconut, and High Oleic Sunflower Oils) (27 %), Soy Protein Isolate (15 %), and less

Than 1% of: Vitamin A Palmitate, Vitamin D3, Vitamin E Acetate, Vitamin K1, Thiamin Hydrochloride, Riboflavin, Vitamin B6 Hydrochloride, Vitamin B12, Niacinamide, Folic Acid, Calcium Pantothenate, Magnesium Phosphate, Ferrous Sulfate, Zinc Sulfate, Cupric Sulfate, Potassium Hydroxide, Potassium Chloride, Sodium Citrate, Sodium Selenite, L-Methionine, Taurine, L-Carnitine.

Gerber Infant Formula
With Iron Soy, Powder

Ingredients:
Corn Maltodextrin, Vegetable Oils (Palm Olein, Soy, Coconut, and High-Oleic Safflower or High-Oleic Sunflower), Enzymatically Hydrolyzed Soy Protein Isolate, Sucrose, and less than 2% of: Calcium Phosphate, Potassium Citrate, Sodium Citrate, Calcium Citrate, M. Alpina Oil (A Source of Arachidonic Acid [ARA]), C. Cohnii Oil (A Source of Docosahexaenoic Acid [DHA]), Magnesium Chloride, Calcium Chloride, Potassium Chloride, Ferrous Sulfate, Zinc Sulfate, Copper Sulfate, Potassium Iodide, Sodium Selenate, Soy Lecithin, Sodium Ascorbate, Choline Chloride, Inositol, Alpha-Tocopheryl Acetate, Niacinamide, Calcium Pantothenate, Vitamin A Acetate, Riboflavin, Thiamine Mononitrate, Pyridoxine Hydrochloride, Folic Acid, Biotin, Phylloquinone, Vitamin 03, Vitamin B12, Ascorbyl Palmitate, Mixed Tocopherols, L-Methionine, Taurine, L-Carnitine.

Organic formula

Earth's Best Infant Formula
Milk Based With Iron, Powder

Ingredients:
Organic Lactose, Organic Nonfat Milk, Organic High Oleic Sunflower Oil, Organic Coconut Oil, Organic Soy Oil, Organic Whey Protein Concentrate, and less Than 1% of each of the following: Soy Lecithin, Vitamins: (Vitamin A Palmitate, Vitamin D3, dI-Alpha-Tocophero, Phytonadione, Thiamin Hydrochloride, Riboflavin, Pyridoxine Hydrochloride, Vitamin B12, Niacinamide, Folic Acid, Calcium Pantothenate, Biotin, Sodium Ascorbate, Ascorbic Acid, Ascorbyl Palmitate, Choline Chloride, Inositol), Minerals: (Calcium Phosphate, Calcium Citrate,

Magnesium Chloride, Ferrous Sulfate, Zinc Sulfate, Manganese Sulfate, Cupric Sulfate, Potassium Iodide, Potassium Citrate, Potassium Chloride, Potassium Hydroxide, Sodium Hydroxide, Sodium Selenite), L-Carnitine, Taurine, Nucleotides: (Adenosine 5' Monophosphate, Cytidine 5 Monophosphate, Disodium Guanosine 5' Monophosphate, Disodium Uridine 5' Monophosphate).

Earth's Best Infant Formula
Soy Infant Formula with Iron, Powder

Ingredients:
Organic Corn Syrup, Organic Soy Protein, Organic High Oleic Sunflower Oil, Organic Coconut Oil, Organic Soy Oil, and less than 1% of: Soy Lecithin, Vitamins: (Vitamin A Palmitate, Vitamin D3, Dl-Alpha-Tocopherol, Phytonadione, Thiamin Hydrochloride, Riboflavin, Pyridoxine Hydrochloride, Vitamin B12, Niacinamide, Folic Acid, Calcium Pantothenate, Biotin, Sodium Ascorbate, Ascorbic Acid, Ascorbyl Palmitate, Choline Chloride, Inositol), Minerals: (Calcium Phosphate, Calcium Citrate, Magnesium Chloride, Ferrous Sulfate, Zinc Sulfate, Cupric Sulfate, Potassium Iodine, Potassium Citrate, Potassium Chloride, Potassium Phosphate, Sodium Chloride, Sodium Hydroxide, Sodium Selenite), L-Carnitine, Taurine, Methionine, Lipids: DHA (Docosahexaenoic Acid), ARA (Arachidonic Acid).

Baby's Only Organic Toddler Formula
Dairy Iron Fortified

Ingredients:
Organic Brown Rice Syrup, Organic Nonfat Milk, Organic High Oleic Sunflower and/or Organic High Oleic Safflower Oil, Organic Soybean Oil, Organic Coconut Oil, Calcium Phosphate, Calcium Ascorbate (Vit. C), Organic Soy Lecithin, Calcium Citrate, Choline Bitartrate, Organic Vanilla, Taurine, Ferrous Sulfate, Inositol, Natural Vitamin E Acetate, Zinc Sulfate, Niacinamide, Vitamin A Palmitate, Calcium Pantothenate, Thiamin Hydrochloride (Vit. B1), Copper Sulfate, Riboflavin (Vit. B2), Pyridoxine Hydrochloride (Vit. B6), Folic Acid, Phylloquinone (Vit. K1), Potassium Iodide, Sodium Selenate, Biotin, Vitamin D3, Cyanocobalamin (Vit. B12). Gluten free.

Baby's Only Organic Toddler Formula
Soy Iron Fortified

Ingredients:

Organic Brown Rice Syrup, Organic Soy Protein Concentrate, Organic High Oleic Sunflower and/or Organic High Oleic Safflower Oil, Organic Coconut Oil, Organic Soybean Oil, Calcium Phosphate, Organic Vanilla, Organic Soy Lecithin, Potassium Phosphate, Magnesium Sulfate, Calcium Carbonate, Calcium Ascorbate (Vit. C), Sodium Chloride, Potassium Chloride, Calcium Citrate, Choline Bitartrate, L-Methionine, Taurine, Ferrous Sulfate, Inositol, Zinc Sulfate, D-Alpha Tocopheryl Acetate (Vit. E), L-Carnitine, Niacinamide, Calcium Pantothenate, Vitamin A Palmitate, Thiamin Hydrochloride (Vit. B1), Riboflavin (Vit. B2), Pyridoxine Hydrochloride (Vit. B6), Copper Sulfate, Folic Acid, Phylloquinone (Vit. K1), Potassium Iodide, Sodium Selenate, Biotin, Vitamin D3, Cyanocobalamin (Vit. B12). Gluten free.

Similac Organic Infant Formula

Ingredients:

Organic Nonfat Milk, Organic Maltodextrin, Organic Sugar from Evaporated Cane Juice, Organic High Oleic Sunflower Oil, Organic Soy Oil, Organic Coconut Oil, and less than 2% of: C. Cohini Oil (Source of Docosahexaenoic Acid [DHA]), M. Alpina Oil (Source of Arachidonic Acid [ARA]), Potassium Citrate, Soy Lecithin, Calcium Carbonate, Ascorbic Acid, Magnesium Chloride, Sodium Chloride, Ferrous Sulfate, Choline Chloride, Choline Bitartrate, Ascorbyl Palmitate, Taurine, M-Inositol, Zinc Sulfate, Mixed Tocopherol, D-Alpha-Tocopheryl Acetate, Niacinamide, Calcium Pantothenate, L-Carnitine, Vitamin A Palmitate, Cupric Sulfate, Thiamine Chloride Hydrochloride, Riboflavin, Pyridoxine Hydrochloride, Folic Acid, Manganese Sulfate, Phylloquinone, Biotin, Beta-carotene, Sodium Selenate, Vitamin D3, Cyanocobalamin, Potassium Hydroxide and Nucleotides (Cytodyne 5'-Monophosphate, Disodium Guanosine 5'-Monophsopahte, Disodium Uridine 5'-Monophosphate, Adenosine 5'-Monophosphate).

Appendix C: Diapers

Disposable Diapers

The key to choosing the right disposable diaper for your baby is balancing per diaper cost with fit and minimal leaks. Newborns will typically go through 10 to 12 diapers per day, while older babies use closer to six to eight per day.

How many diapers will you need in the first year? An average eight to 10 diapers per day = 2920 to 3650 diapers a year. If each diaper takes approximately two minutes to change, changing nine diapers per day for one year equals 109.5 hours, or 4.5 days of diaper changing!

Brand recommendations for disposable diapers:

Best disposable diapers for newborns

- ❑ First choice: any private label brand that doesn't leak or irritate your newborn's skin.
- ❑ **Pampers Swaddlers**
  $0.28 each ($1022 per year, using 10 diapers per day)
  These are softer than Huggies, with a long runway of soft material up the back vs. an elastic band and a pocket to "catch" runny messes.

  Pros:

  - Swaddlers are what many hospitals use (in the green and yellow pack)
  - Three sizes fit babies up to 18 pounds

- Extra padding in back (great for inactive "back is best" babies)
- Has a fold-down section for navel area in newborn size
- Sign up on the company web site for digital coupons, or for coupons to be sent to your home

Cons:

- More expensive than store-brand or private label diapers
- Not available in larger sizes
- Some parents do not like the powdery smell of Pampers
- Signing up for coupons comes with the price of sharing your personal information

❑ **Huggies Little Snugglers**
$0.28 each ($1022 per year)
These can be helpful for bigger eaters and leakers. However, test different brands for fit. You may love one brand for your first child and then figure out that another brand is better for the next.

Pros:

- Little Snugglers are designed to "catch" runny messes with a pocket
- Elastic strap in back tries to keep in the "runny mess"
- Huggies are more available in big-name warehouse stores
- Sign up on the company web site for digital coupons, or for coupons to be sent to your home

Cons:

- More expensive than store-brand diapers
- May not mold as well around the legs as softer Pampers
- The elastic band in back may irritate sensitive skin
- Signing up for coupons comes with the price of sharing your personal information

Best disposable diapers for older babies

❑ *Conventional brands:* **Pampers Cruisers** *$0.25–0.27 each ($913–986 per year)*, **Pampers Baby Dry** *$0.23–0.26 each ($840–949 per year)*, or **Huggies Snug and Dry** *$0.22–0.28 each ($803–1022 per year)*. The best brand depends on fit with your baby.

- ❑ *Budget Choice*: **Kirkland Signature Supreme** *$0.15–0.19 each ($548–694 per year)* diapers from Costco or any private label that fits your baby, such as **Parent's Choice** *$0.12–0.14 each ($438–511 per year)*
- ❑ *Hybrid Choice (part reusable, part disposable)*: **gDiapers with gPants** *$18-22 gPants/cover + $4.75/cloth insert + $0.39/disposable insert ($1423 per year for inserts)*. gPants are colorful, reusable diaper covers that you use with gDiapers disposable inserts.

Best overnight diapers or 12-hour disposables

- ❑ **Huggies Overnites** *$0.32–0.45 each ($117–164 per year)*. Want to decrease your chances of waking in the middle of the night with a leak? Bring on the Overnites, which are well worth their cost.
- ❑ **Pampers Baby Dry** *$0.23–0.26 each ($84–95 per year)*. These diapers are really thin, yet 10–12 hours later your baby's diaper remains packed, but not leaky. The tabs on these diapers are also very flexible, expanding and contracting as baby sleeps.

Best eco-friendlier disposable diapers

- ❑ **Bambo Nature Diapers** *$0.45–0.51 each ($1643–1862 per year)*. This brand receives praise for excellent construction and performance from an eco-diaper, in addition to stricter adherence to eco-friendly practices.

  Pros:

  - The company claims they are 80% compostable.
  - They have less SAP; it is replaced with wheat starch and acrylic polymers.
  - Least amount of SAP among popular eco-diapers
  - No phthalates, heavy metals, chlorine, or AZO-pigments
  - Excellent overnight absorbency

  Cons:

  - They are twice the cost of regular diapers.
  - The back of the diaper is not stretchable.
  - These diapers use sodium polyacrylate (SAP) for absorption.

- ❑ **Earth's Best TenderCare Chlorine Free Diapers** *$0.31–0.45 each ($1132–1643 per year)*. This is the Best Value eco-brand of choice for pediatrician-owned BabyGearLab, and it is available in most mainstream stores. Earth's Best are also a more affordable eco-brand across all sizes.

  Pros:

  - They arc latex, dye, and perfume free.
  - Some parents prefer to support companies trying to be sustainable.
  - One of the more affordable eco-brands
  - These receive some of the best reviews for not leaking among eco-brands.

  Cons:

  - There are reports of rashes among multiple review sources.
  - These diapers contain corn and wheat, which can be allergens for some babies.
  - These diapers use sodium polyacrylate (SAP) for absorption.

Eco-friendlier disposables (needs improvement)

- ❑ **Seventh Generation Free and Clear Diapers** *$0.31–0.42 each ($1132–1533 per year)*. This well-known, widely available green brand has a track record from parent reviewers and diaper testers that is less than stellar, due to complaints of leaks, low absorption, and a reformulation of the brand.

  Pros:

  - The wood pulp used in these diapers is harvested from sustainably managed forests.
  - No fragrances, latex, petroleum-based lotions, or chlorine processing
  - Excellent brand recognition and availability
  - Reasonably priced for an eco-diaper

  Cons:

  - These diapers are dyed a brownish-tan color to make consumers think they are all natural or biodegradable in appearance. Seventh Generation states on its website, "We use brown pigments to help distinguish Seventh Generation Chlorine Free Diapers from others in the marketplace that are bleached with chlorine-containing substances." Note: The actual color of diapers is translucent like a milk jug.

- Parent reviews are scathing to mixed for absorption and leaks.
- These diapers use sodium polyacrylate (SAP) for absorption.

Cloth Diapers

You may also be considering cloth diapers as an eco-friendly, chemical-free alternative to disposables, or landfill diapers. To help you think through this decision, first ask yourself "How much poop do I want to touch?" Then analyze some of the other pros and cons of cloth diapers.

Pros:

- Better for the environment
- Healthier for baby: There are no chemicals against baby's skin, such as dioxin (a by-product of the bleaching process with chlorine), tributyltin (a toxin linked to hormonal problems in humans and animals), and sodium polyacrylate or SAP (this supposedly non-toxic gel found in nearly all diapers was removed from tampons, due to a link to Toxic Shock Syndrome).[206]
- No more pins: cloth diapers now come in cute colors with Velcro straps or snaps.
- Cloth diapers are more affordable and more convenient than ever.
- If you do not enjoy washing diapers, you can have a service do it for you, although it nullifies the cost and energy savings of cloth.
- A diaper sprayer that attaches to your toilet plumbing can make cleaning the mess off cloth diapers doable.

Cons:

- Cloth diapers with stool must be rinsed in the toilet. Disposable users should actually do this too, although few do.
- Parents must be okay with regular laundry duty.

- Parents must be okay with poop on their hands and in the washing machine.
- Many day cares do not allow cloth diapers.
- Travel is more difficult because you must carry soiled diapers with you.
- Runny stool can be messy with cloth, if fit is an issue.

Types of cloth diapers

- ❑ *Best for frugal parents/most economical:* **Prefolds + diaper covers**

  These diapers must be changed as soon as baby gets wet. You may place a stay dry liner, usually made of fleece, on top of the prefold to keep baby drier between changes.

- ❑ *Best for parents reluctant to try cloth, best for day care, easiest to use:* **All-in-one diapers**

  All-in-one cloth diapers are perhaps your best argument for a day care center to accept cloth diapers–no stuffing required. AIO diapers have absorbent material already sewn into the waterproof cover, and they can essentially be treated like a disposable diaper (with the one difference that the diaper is tossed in a wet bag to wash later rather than disposed in the trash). The downside to this convenience is cost, although they do come in one-size varieties with adjustable snaps.

- ❑ *Most popular/most convenient:* **Pocket diapers**

  Pocket diapers, or stuffing diapers, are the most popular type of cloth diapers today because no extra cover is required, and they are more affordable than all-in-one diapers. A pocket diaper has an opening (located along the edge that touches baby's back) that allows an absorbent pre-cut insert or foldable diaper to be placed in a pocket between the diaper's waterproof outer shell and an inner layer that touches baby's skin. A pocket diaper may be a one-size diaper or one that comes in different sizes (newborn, S/M/L); it also comes with Velcro or snap closures. For nighttime, you can add superabsorbent hemp inserts for extra protection.

Compromise: using cloth and eco-diapers

If you find yourself stuck in the middle of the cloth debate (caring about the environment and health of your baby, but not ready to commit to 100% cloth), there is a compromise solution. Do a mix of both: use cloth diapers at home and eco-friendly alternatives, such as hybrid diapers or eco-diapers, for travel and day care. Note: Hybrid diapers are biodegradable, flushable inserts that fit into an outer diaper cover, such as gDiapers and Kushies. Inserts with stool on them get flushed down the toilet, while wet ones can be flushed or added to a compost pile. However, reviews from parents say the inserts clog the toilet.

Cost: cloth vs. disposables

It can be difficult to assess the true cost of cloth vs. disposable diapering since many variable factors go into these calculations, such as cost of supplies, laundry service, electricity, water, etc. For example, if you're a style-conscious parent buying limited print all-in-one cloths, such as bumGenius' Albert or Audrey diapers (inspired by Albert Einstein and Audrey Hepburn), you're not going to save $2,000 cloth diapering, as favorite eco-websites claim. Therefore, in a cost-benefit analysis for one child, the cloth vs. disposable debate may be "a wash" on dollar cost, with the long-term environmental savings going to cloth. Pass a full set of cloth diapers and inserts on to a younger sibling, and the scale tips to cloth.

Bottom line: Disposable diapers are easy to toss, and they're convenient. That's why 90–95% of U.S. parents use them. However, with the option of all-in-one diapers, flushable inserts, and eco-diapers for travel and day care, cloth diapers can work for busy, environmentally conscious parents.

Brand recommendations for cloth diapers:

Best cloth diapers

The best advice for cloth diapers is to never buy too many of one kind up front. Try a sample of different brands because they all fit differently.

- ❑ **bumGenius One Size Pocket Diaper** *($15–25/diaper)*

  Pros:

  - ▸ Fits from birth to potty training
  - ▸ Adjustable enough to be used with siblings in diapers
  - ▸ Snap-down front to adjust size (most parents prefer the longevity of snaps to Velcro)
  - ▸ Diapers are bundled with two inserts: a newborn insert and a one-size insert for older babies up to 35 pounds

  Cons:

  - ▸ Fasteners wear out over time
  - ▸ May not work for heavier babies
  - ▸ You may need separate newborn diapers for babies under seven pounds

- ❑ **Rumparooz G2 One Size Pocket Diaper** *($16–26/diaper)*

  Pros:

  - ▸ One diaper for four sizes
  - ▸ Fits birth to potty training (6–35 lb)
  - ▸ Winner of numerous awards for cloth diapers
  - ▸ Dual inner gussets (inner row of elastic for leaks)

  Cons:

  - ▸ Double gusset can be bulky
  - ▸ Elasticity can wear out over time
  - ▸ More expensive up front

Best hybrid cloth diapers

- ❑ **gDiapers** (reusable gPants cover with option to use prefolds, cotton inserts, or disposable inserts)

  Price: $18-22 gPants/cover + $4.75/cloth insert + $0.39/disposable insert ($1423 per year for inserts)

  Pros:

  - ▸ Style and versatility
  - ▸ Easy for multiple caregivers to use because they fasten like disposables

- Product is widely available online and in mainstream stores, such as Walmart, Target, and BRU

Cons:

- Marketed for convenience, but the shell, pouch and inserts should be washed separately
- You can't put the liner in the dryer so the diaper must be disassembled.
- Diapers do not come with inserts (must buy separately)
- Diapers must be purchased for each size. Try **Flip** diapers for a hybrid one size.
- Disposable inserts are expensive.

Appendix D: Vaccines

Vaccine-Preventable Diseases and the Vaccines that Prevent Them

Disease	Vaccine	CDC Vaccine Schedule
Chickenpox	Varicella vaccine protects against chickenpox.	1st dose: 12 to 15 months, 2nd dose: 4 to 6 years
Diphtheria	DTaP* vaccine protects against diphtheria.	5 doses at 2 months, 4 months, 6 months, 15 to 18 months, 4 to 6 years
Hib	Hib vaccine protects against Haemophilus influenza type b.	1st dose: 2 months, 2nd dose: 4 months, 3rd dose: 6 months (if needed, depending on brand), 4th dose: 12 to 15 months
Hepatitis A	HepA vaccine protects against hepatitis A.	1st dose: 12 to 23 months, 2nd dose: 6 to 18 months after 1st dose
Hepatitis B	HepB vaccine protects against hepatitis B.	1st dose: birth, 2nd dose: 1 to 3 months, 3rd dose: 6 to 18 months, 4th dose (if needed, talk to your doctor)
Flu	Flu vaccine protects against influenza.	every year for everyone 6 months or older***
Measles	MMR** vaccine protects against measles.	1st dose: 12 to 15 months, 2nd dose: 4 to 6 years (before school)
Mumps	MMR** vaccine protects against mumps.	1st dose: 12 to 15 months, 2nd dose: 4 to 6 years (before school)
Pertussis	DTaP* vaccine protects against pertussis (whooping cough).	5 doses at 2 months, 4 months, 6 months, 15 to 18 months, 4 to 6 years
Polio	IPV vaccine protects against polio.	4 doses at 2 months, 4 months, 6 to 18 months, 4 to 6 years
Pneumococcal	PCV vaccine protects against pneumococcus.	4 doses at 2 months, 4 months, 6 months, 12 to 18 months
Rotavirus	RV vaccine protects against rotavirus.	1st dose: 2 months, 2nd dose: 4 months, 3rd dose: 6 months (if needed)
Rubella	MMR** vaccine protects against rubella.	1st dose: 12 to 15 months, 2nd dose: 4 to 6 years (before school)
Tetanus	DTaP* vaccine protects against tetanus.	5 doses at 2 months, 4 months, 6 months, 15 to 18 months, 4 to 6 years

* DTaP combines protection against diphtheria, tetanus, and pertussis.

** MMR combines protection against mumps, measles, and rubella.

*** Two doses at least four weeks apart are recommended for children aged 6 months through 8 years who are getting a flu vaccine for the first time.

Source: Centers for Disease Control and Prevention, American Academy of Family Physicians, American Academy of Pediatrics

Disease symptoms	Disease complications
Rash, tiredness, headache, fever	Infected blisters, bleeding disorders, encephalitis (brain swelling), pneumonia (infection in the lungs)
Sore throat, mild fever, weakness, swollen glands in the neck	Swelling of the heart muscle, heart failure, coma, paralysis, death
May be no symptoms unless bacteria enter the blood	Meningitis (infection of the covering around the brain and spinal cord), intellectual disability, epiglottis (life-threatening infection that can block the windpipe and lead to serious breathing problems), pneumonia (infection of the lungs), death
May be no symptoms, fever, stomach pain, loss of appetite, fatigue, vomiting, jaundice (yellowing of skin and eyes), dark urine	Liver failure, arthralgia (joint pain), kidney, pancreatic, and blood disorders
May be no symptoms, fever, headache, weakness, vomiting, jaundice (yellowing of skin and eyes), joint pain	Chronic liver infection, liver failure, liver cancer
Fever, muscle pain, sore throat, cough, extreme fatigue	Pneumonia (infection in the lungs)
Rash, fever, cough, runny nose, pinkeye	Encephalitis (brain swelling), pneumonia (infection in the lungs), death
Swollen salivary glands (under the jaw), fever, headache, tireness, muscle pain	Meningitis (infection of the covering around the brain and spinal cord), encephalitis (brain swelling), inflammation of testicles or ovaries, deafness
Severe cough, runny nose, apnea (a pause in breathing in infants)	Pneumonia (infection in tho lungs), death
May be no symptoms, pneumonia (infection in the lungs)	Paralysis, death
May be no symptoms, sore throat, fever, nausea, headache	Bacteremia (blood infection), meningitis (infection of the covering of the brain and spinal cord), death
Diarrhea, fever, vomiting	Severe diarrhea, dehydration
Children infected with rubella virus sometimes have a rash, fever, swollen lymph nodes	Very serious in pregnant women-can lead to miscarriage, stillbirth, premature delivery, birth defects
Stiffness in neck and abdominal muscles, difficulty swallowing, muscle spasms, fever	Broken bones, breathing difficulty, death

Recommended Immunizations for Children from Birth Through Six Years Old

Birth	1 month	2 months	4 months	6 months	12 months	15 months	18 months	19-23 months	2-3 years	4-6 years
HepB	HepB				HepB					
		RV	RV	RV						
		DTaP	DTaP	DTaP		DTaP				DTaP
		Hib	Hib	Hib	Hib					
		PCV	PCV	PCV	PCV					
		IPV	IPV		IPV					IPV
						Influenza (Yearly)*				
					MMR					MMR
					Varicella					Varicella
						HepA$^{\phi}$				

Is your family growing? To protect your new baby and yourself against whooping cough, get a DTaP vaccine in the third trimester of each pregnancy. Talk to your doctor for more details.

Shaded boxes indicate the vaccine can be given during shown age range.

Note: If your child misses a shot, you don't need to start over, just go back to your child's doctor for the next shot. Talk with your child's doctor if you have questions about vaccines.

Immunization schedule published by CDC, 2014.

Footnotes: *Two doses given at least four weeks apart are recommended for children aged 6 months through 8 years of age who are getting a flu vaccine for the first time and for some other children in this age group.

ϕ Two doses of HepA vaccine are needed for lasting protection. The first dose of HepA vaccine should be given between 12 months and 23 months of age. The second dose should be given 6 to 18 months later. HepA vaccination may be given to any child 12 months and older to protect against HepA. Children and adolescents who did not receive the HepA vaccine are at high-risk, should be vaccinated against HepA.

If your child has any medical conditions that put him at risk for infection or is traveling outside the United States, talk to your child's doctor about additional vaccines that he may need.

Appendix E: Recommended Resources

"Be awesome! Be a book nut!" –Dr. Seuss

Baby care

- ❑ *Caring for Your Baby and Young Child: Birth to Age 5* by the American Academy of Pediatrics
- ❑ *Mayo Clinic Guide to Your Baby's First Year* by Mayo Clinic
- ❑ *The Baby Book: Everything You Need to Know About Your Baby from Birth to Age Two* by William, Martha, Robert and James Sears
- ❑ *Baby 411: Clear Answers and Smart Advice for Your Baby's First Year* by Denise Fields and Ari Brown

Breastfeeding

- ❑ *The Womanly Art of Breastfeeding* by La Leche League International
- ❑ *Ina May's Guide to Breastfeeding* by Ina May Gaskin
- ❑ *Breastfeeding Made Simple: Seven Natural Laws for Nursing Mothers* by Nancy Mohrbacher and Kathleen Kendall-Tackett
- ❑ *The Nursing Mother's Companion* by Kathleen Huggins

Postnatal nutrition and baby food cookbooks

- ❑ *Expect the Best: Your Guide to Healthy Eating Before, During, and After Pregnancy* by Elizabeth Ward and American Dietetic Association
- ❑ *Trim Healthy Mama* by Pearl Barrett and Serene Allison

- ❑ *Cooking for Baby: Wholesome, Homemade, Delicious Foods for 6 to 18 Months* by Lisa Barnes
- ❑ *Top 100 Baby Purees* by Annabel Karmel

Crying and colic

- ❑ *The Happiest Baby on the Block* by Harvey Karp

Sleep-training

- ❑ *Healthy Sleep Habits, Happy Child* by Marc Weissbluth
- ❑ *Solve Your Child's Sleep Problems* by Richard Ferber
- ❑ *The No-Cry Sleep Solution: Gentle Ways to Help Your Baby Sleep Through the Night* by Elizabeth Pantley

Depression and postpartum depression

- ❑ *Feeling Good: The New Mood Therapy* by David D. Burns
- ❑ *The Pregnancy and Postpartum Anxiety Workbook: Practical Skills to Help You Overcome Anxiety, Worry, Panic Attacks, Obsessions, and Compulsions* by Kevin Gyoerkoe and Pamela Wiegartz

The developing brain

- ❑ *Brain Rules for Baby: How to Raise a Smart and Happy Child from Zero to Five* by John Medina
- ❑ *Mind in the Making: The Seven Essential Life Skills Every Child Needs* by Ellen Galinsky
- ❑ *The Whole-Brain Child: 12 Revolutionary Strategies to Nurture Your Child's Developing Mind* by Daniel Siegel and Tina Payne Bryson

Health and lifestyle

Personal transformation

- ❑ *Daring Greatly: How the Courage to Be Vulnerable Transforms the Way we Live, Love, Parent, and Lead* by Brene Brown
- ❑ *The Gifts of Imperfection: Let Go of Who You Think You're Supposed to Be and Embrace Who You Are* by Brene Brown
- ❑ *The 7 Habits of Highly Effective People: Powerful Lessons in Personal Change* by Stephen Covey
- ❑ *The Happiness Project* by Gretchen Rubin

General nutrition and food science

- ❑ *The Omnivore's Dilemma: A Natural History of Four Meals* by Michael Pollan
- ❑ *Food Rules: An Eater's Manual* by Michael Pollan
- ❑ *Grain Brain: The Surprising Truth about Wheat, Carbs, and Sugar–Your Brain's Silent Killers* by David Perlmutter
- ❑ *Wheat Belly: Lose the Wheat, Lose the Weight, and Find Your Path Back to Health* by William Davis
- ❑ *The China Study: The Most Comprehensive Study of Nutrition Ever Conducted and the Startling Implications for Diet, Weight Loss, and Long-term Health* by Thomas Campbell and T. Colin Campbell

Popular psychology

- ❑ *Learned Optimism: How to Change Your Mind and Your Life* by Martin Seligman
- ❑ *David and Goliath, Blink, Tipping Point, and Outliers* by Malcolm Gladwell
- ❑ *Predictably Irrational, Revised and Expanded Edition: The Hidden Forces That Shape Our Decisions* by Dan Ariely
- ❑ *Thinking, Fast and Slow* by Daniel Kahneman

Relationships and Marriage

- ❑ *The Five Love Languages: The Secret to Love that Lasts* by Gary Chapman
- ❑ *Love and Respect* by Emerson Eggerichs
- ❑ *How to Win Friends & Influence People* by Dale Carnegie

Parenting

- ❑ *How to Talk So Kids Will Listen and Listen So Kids Will Talk* by Adele Faber and Elaine Mazlish
- ❑ *How Children Succeed: Grit, Curiosity, and the Hidden Power of Character* by Paul Tough
- ❑ *The Secrets of Happy Families: Improve Your Mornings, Rethink Family Dinner, Fight Smarter, Go Out and Play, and Much More* by Bruce Feiler

Notes

• • • • • • •

Baby Care

1. La Leche League International, *Is My Baby Getting Enough Milk?* New Beginnings, 2008. 25(5): p. 44-45.
2. Hamosh, M., and others, *Breastfeeding and the working mother: effect of time and temperature of short-term storage on proteolysis, lipolysis, and bacterial growth in milk.* Pediatrics, 1996. 97(4): p. 492-8.
3. Academy of Breastfeeding Medicine (ABM), *Academy of Breastfeeding Medicine (ABM) clinical protocol #8: human milk storage information for home use for full-term infants* Breastfeed Med, 2010. 5(3): p. 127-30.
4. Jones, F. and M. Tully, *Best practice for expressing, storing and handling human milk in hospitals, homes and child care settings.* 2005, Raleigh, NC: The Human Milk Banking Association of North America (HMBANA).
5. Sears, W. *Thrush.* Ask Dr. Sears 2015; Available from: http://www.askdrsears.com/topics/health-concerns/childhood-illnesses/thrush.
6. American Academy of Pediatrics. *Nonnutritive Sucking: Pacifiers.* April 28, 2014; Available from: http://www2.aap.org/ORALHEALTH/pact/ch8_sect1b.cfm.
7. Dube, R. *Mom survey says: three is the most stressful number of kids.* Today Moms (Today.com) April 25, 2014; Available from: http://www.today.com/moms/mom-survey-says-three-most-stressful-number-kids-6C9774150.
8. Bureau of Labor Statistics. *Employment Characteristics of Families 2013.* 2014; Available from: http://www.bls.gov/news.release/famee.nr0.htm.
9. Shamir, R., and others, *Infant crying, colic, and gastrointestinal discomfort in early childhood: a review of the evidence and most plausible mechanisms.* J Pediatr Gastroenterol Nutr, 2013. 57 Suppl 1: p. S1-45.
10. Medical Letter on Drugs and Therapeutics, *Simethicone for gastrointestinal gas.* Med Lett Drugs Ther, 1996. 38(977): p. 57-8.
11. Metcalf, T.J., and others, *Simethicone in the treatment of infant colic: a randomized, placebo-controlled, multicenter trial.* Pediatrics, 1994. 94(1): p. 29-34.

12. Shelov, S.P. and American Academy of Pediatrics, *Caring for your baby and young child: birth to age 5*. New & rev. 5th ed. 2009, New York: Bantam xxxvi, p. 160.
13. Kattan, J., R. Cocco, and K. Jarvinen, *Milk and soy allergy*. Pediatr Clin North Am, 2011. 58(2): p. 407-426.
14. Karp, H., *"Happy baby doctor" calms colic crying*, M. Falcon, Editor. 2002: USA Today.
15. Stamatas, G.N., and others, *Infant skin microstructure assessed in vivo differs from adult skin in organization and at the cellular level*. Pediatr Dermatol, 2010. 27(2): p. 125-31.
16. Child Welfare Information Gateway. *Understanding the Effects of Maltreatment on Brain Development* November 2009; Available from: http://www.childwelfare.gov/pubs/issue_briefs/brain_development/brain_development.pdf.
17. Shonkoff, J., D. Phillips, and National Research Council (U.S.) Committee on Integrating the Science of Early Childhood Development, *From neurons to neighborhoods : the science of early child development*. 2000, Washington, D.C.: National Academy Press. xviii, p. 182-218.
18. Frank, M.G., N.P. Issa, and M.P. Stryker, *Sleep enhances plasticity in the developing visual cortex*. Neuron, 2001. 30(1): p. 275-87.
19. Mindell, J.A., *Sleeping through the night : how infants, toddlers, and their parents can get a good night's sleep*. Rev. ed. 2005, New York: HarperResource. vi, p. 22-32.
20. Moon, R.Y. and Task Force on Sudden Infant Death Syndrome, *SIDS and other sleep-related infant deaths: expansion of recommendations for a safe infant sleeping environment*. Pediatrics, 2011. 128(5): p. 1030-9.
21. Sears, W., The baby book: everything you need to know about your baby—from birth to age two. 2nd ed. 2003, Boston: Little, Brown and Company, p. 340-350.
22. Centers for Disease Control and Prevention. *Sudden Unexpected Infant Death and Sudden Infant Death Syndrome*. 2014; Available from: http://www.cdc.gov/sids/aboutsuidandsids.htm.
23. Palfrey, J., *Safe Sleep: Tips for Avoiding Sudden Infant Death Syndrome*, in *Health Issues*. 2013, Boston Children's Hospital.
24. Halpin, D., *Nine Months - Sleeping*. 2012, Northern Virginia Pediatrics: Falls Church, VA.
25. Ferber, R., *Solve your child's sleep problems*. New, revised, and expanded ed. 2006, New York: Fireside Book. xxi, 440 p.
26. Ferber, R., *Important Tips to Help Your Child Sleep Well*, in *Boston Children's Hospital*. 2013.
27. Ezzo, G. and R. Bucknam, *Baby wise : how 100,000 new parents trained their babies to sleep through the night the natural way*. 1995, Sisters, OR: Multnomah Books. 198 p.

28. Aney, M., *'Babywise' advice linked to dehydration, failure to thrive*, in *AAP News*. 1998. p. 21.
29. Karp, H., *The happiest baby on the block : the new way to calm crying and help your baby sleep longer*. 2002, New York, N.Y.: Bantam Books. xv, 267 p.
30. Sears, W. *What AP is: 7 Baby B's*. Ask Dr Sears 2014; Available from: http://www.askdrsears.com/topics/parenting/attachment-parenting/what-ap-7-baby-bs.
31. Ahnert, L., and others, *Transition to child care: associations with infant-mother attachment, infant negative emotion, and cortisol elevations*. Child Dev, 2004. 75(3): p. 639-50.
32. Transparency Market Research. *Baby Diaper Market Projected to Reach USD 52.2 Billion Globally by 2017: Transparency Market Research*. 2012; Available from: http://www.transparencymarketresearch.com/baby-diapers-market.html.
33. Procter & Gamble. *Pampers: The Birth of P&G's First 10-Billion-Dollar Brand*. 2012; Available from: http://news.pampers.com/about/history.
34. Kelly, S., *Data warehousing : the route to mass customization*. Updated and expanded. ed. 1996, Chichester ; New York: Wiley. xiii, p. 192.
35. Environmental Protection Agency (EPA). *Municipal Solid Waste Generation, Recycling, and Disposal in the United States: Table 15*. 2014; Available from: http://www.epa.gov/epawaste/nonhaz/municipal/pubs/2012_msw_dat_tbls.pdf.
36. National Park Service Mote Marine Lab. *Time it takes for garbage to decompose in the environment*. 2014; Available from: http://des.nh.gov/organization/divisions/water/wmb/coastal/trash/documents/marine_debris.pdf.
37. Blum, N.J., B. Taubman, and N. Nemeth, *Why is toilet training occurring at older ages? A study of factors associated with later training*. J Pediatr, 2004. 145(1): p. 107-11.
38. Smith, M.V., and others, *Diaper need and its impact on child health*. Pediatrics, 2013. 132(2): p. 253-9.

Just for Mom

39. Center for Disease Control and Prevention, *Breastfeeding Report Card: United States 2014*. 2014, National Center for Chronic Disease Prevention and Health Promotion.
40. DiSanto, J. *Breast or Bottle?* KidsHealth.org, 2012.
41. Christakis, D.A., *Breastfeeding and cognition: Can IQ tip the scale?* JAMA Pediatr, 2013. 167(9): p. 796-7.

42. Brion, M.J., and others, *What are the causal effects of breastfeeding on IQ, obesity and blood pressure? Evidence from comparing high-income with middle-income cohorts.* Int J Epidemiol, 2011. 40(3): p. 670-80.
43. Varendi, H., and others, *Soothing effect of amniotic fluid smell in newborn infants.* Early Hum Dev, 1998. 51(1): p. 47-55.
44. DeCasper, A.J. and W.P. Fifer, *Of Human Bonding: Newborns Prefer their Mothers' Voices.* Science, 1980. 208(4448): p. 1174-1176.
45. Wolfberg, A.J., and others, *Dads as breastfeeding advocates: results from a randomized controlled trial of an educational intervention.* Am J Obstet Gynecol, 2004. 191(3): p. 708-12.
46. Li, R., and others, *Why mothers stop breastfeeding: mothers' self-reported reasons for stopping during the first year.* Pediatrics, 2008. 122 Suppl 2, S69-76 DOI: 10.1542/peds.2008-1315i.
47. Wagner, E.A., and others *Breastfeeding concerns at 3 and 7 days postpartum and feeding status at 2 months.* Pediatrics, 2013. 132, e865-75 DOI: 10.1542/peds.2013-0724.
48. Guthmann, R.A., J. Bang, and J. Nashelsky, *Combined oral contraceptives for mothers who are breastfeeding.* Am Fam Physician, 2005. 72(7): p. 1303-4.
49. Kennedy, K.I. and C.M. Visness, *Contraceptive efficacy of lactational amenorrhoea.* Lancet, 1992. 339(8787): p. 227-30.
50. Eidelman, A.I., *Breastfeeding and the use of human milk: an analysis of the American Academy of Pediatrics 2012 Breastfeeding Policy Statement.* Breastfeed Med, 2012. 7(5): p. 323-4.
51. Mennella, J.A., C.P. Jagnow, and G.K. Beauchamp *Prenatal and postnatal flavor learning by human infants.* Pediatrics, 2001. 107, e88.
52. Seligman, M.E.P., *Learned optimism : how to change your mind and your life.* 1st Vintage Books ed. 2006, New York: Vintage Books, p. 284-6.
53. Livingston, G. and D.V. Cohn. *Record Share of New Mothers are College Educated.* Pew Research Social & Demographic Trends 2013; Available from: http://www.pewsocialtrends.org/2013/05/10/record-share-of-new-mothers-are-college-educated/.
54. U.S. Department of Labor (Bureau of Labor Statistics). *America's Young Adults at 27: Labor Market Activity, Education, and Household Composition: Results From a Longitudinal Survey Summary.* Available from: http://www.bls.gov/news.release/nlsyth.nr0.htm.
55. Noble, R.E., *Depression in women.* Metabolism, 2005. 54(5 Suppl 1): p. 49-52.
56. Dietz, P.M., and others, *Clinically identified maternal depression before, during, and after pregnancies ending in live births.* Am J Psychiatry, 2007. 164(10): p. 1515-20.
57. Heinrichs, M., and others, *Selective amnesic effects of oxytocin on human memory.* Physiol Behav, 2004. 83(1): p. 31-8.

58. Ko, J.Y., and others, *Depression and treatment among U.S. pregnant and non-pregnant women of reproductive age, 2005-2009.* J Womens Health 2012. 21(8): p. 830-6.
59. Beck, C.T., *A meta-analysis of predictors of postpartum depression.* Nurs Res, 1996. 45(5): p. 297-303.
60. Muscat, T., and others, *Beliefs About Infant Regulation, Early Infant Behaviors and Maternal Postnatal Depressive Symptoms.* Birth, 2014. 41(2): p. 206-213.
61. Oppo, A., and others, *Risk factors for postpartum depression: the role of the Postpartum Depression Predictors Inventory-Revised (PDPI-R). Results from the Perinatal Depression-Research & Screening Unit (PNDReScU) study.* Arch Womens Ment Health, 2009. 12(4): p. 239-49.

Health, Safety, and Lifestyle

62. Centers for Disease Control and Prevention. *Autism Spectrum Disorder (ASD): Data & Statistics.* April 17, 2014; Available from: http://www.cdc.gov/ncbddd/autism/data.html.
63. National Institute of Neurological Disorders and Stroke. *Autism Fact Sheet.* April 14, 2014; Available from: http://www.ninds.nih.gov/disorders/autism/detail_autism.htm.
64. Lemcke, S., and others, *Early signs of autism in toddlers: a follow-up study in the Danish National Birth Cohort.* J Autism Dev Disord, 2013. 43(10): p. 2366-75.
65. Gaugler, T., and others, *Most genetic risk for autism resides with common variation.* Nat Genet, 2014. 46(8): p. 881-5.
66. Wong, C.C., and others, *Methylomic analysis of monozygotic twins discordant for autism spectrum disorder and related behavioural traits.* Mol Psychiatry, 2014. 19(4): p. 495-503.
67. LaSalle, J.M., *A genomic point-of-view on environmental factors influencing the human brain methylome.* Epigenetics, 2011. 6(7): p. 862-9.
68. Hallmayer, J., and others, *Genetic heritability and shared environmental factors among twin pairs with autism.* Arch Gen Psychiatry, 2011. 68(11): p. 1095-102.
69. Reichenberg, A., and others, *Advancing paternal age and autism.* Arch Gen Psychiatry, 2006. 63(9): p. 1026-32.
70. Idring, S., and others, *Parental age and the risk of autism spectrum disorders: findings from a Swedish population-based cohort.* Int J Epidemiol, 2014. 43(1): p. 107-15.
71. Schieve, L.A., and others, *Population attributable fractions for three perinatal risk factors for autism spectrum disorders, 2002 and 2008 autism and*

developmental disabilities monitoring network. Ann Epidemiol, 2014. 24(4): p. 260-6.

72. Schendel, D. and T.K. Bhasin, *Birth weight and gestational age characteristics of children with autism, including a comparison with other developmental disabilities*. Pediatrics, 2008. 121(6): p. 1155-64.
73. Shelton, J.F., and others, *Neurodevelopmental Disorders and Prenatal Residential Proximity to Agricultural Pesticides: The CHARGE Study*. Environ Health Perspect, 2014. 122(10): p. 1103-9.
74. Landrigan, P.J., *What causes autism? Exploring the environmental contribution*. Curr Opin Pediatr, 2010. 22(2): p. 219-25.
75. Volk, H.E., and others, *Residential proximity to freeways and autism in the CHARGE study*. Environ Health Perspect, 2011. 119(6): p. 873-7.
76. Schmidt, R.J., and others, *Maternal Intake of Supplemental Iron and Risk of Autism Spectrum Disorder*. Am J Epidemiol, 2014. 180(9): p. 890-900.
77. Carlo, G.L. and R.S. Jenrow, *Scientific progress - wireless phones and brain cancer: current state of the science*. MedGenMed, 2000. 2(3): p. 40.
78. Rutter, M., *Incidence of autism spectrum disorders: changes over time and their meaning*. Acta Paediatr, 2005. 94(1): p. 2-15.
79. Taylor, B., *Vaccines and the changing epidemiology of autism*. Child Care Health Dev, 2006. 32(5): p. 511-9.
80. Stoner, R., and others, *Patches of disorganization in the neocortex of children with autism*. N Engl J Med, 2014. 370(13): p. 1209-19.
81. Grandjean, P. and P.J. Landrigan, *Neurobehavioural effects of developmental toxicity*. Lancet Neurol, 2014. 13(3): p. 330-8.
82. Landrigan, P.J., L. Lambertini, and L.S. Birnbaum, *A research strategy to discover the environmental causes of autism and neurodevelopmental disabilities*. Environ Health Perspect, 2012. 120(7): p. 258-60.
83. Grandjean, P. and P.J. Landrigan, *Developmental neurotoxicity of industrial chemicals*. Lancet, 2006. 368(9553): p. 2167-78.
84. Jusko, T.A., and others, *Blood lead concentrations < 10 microg/dL and child intelligence at 6 years of age*. Environ Health Perspect, 2008. 116(2): p. 243-8.
85. Hillyer, M.M., and others, *Multi-technique quantitative analysis and socioeconomic considerations of lead, cadmium, and arsenic in children's toys and toy jewelry*. Chemosphere, 2014. 108: p. 205-13.
86. Oken, E., and others, *Maternal fish intake during pregnancy, blood mercury levels, and child cognition at age 3 years in a US cohort*. Am J Epidemiol, 2008. 167(10): p. 1171-81.
87. Winneke, G., *Developmental aspects of environmental neurotoxicology: lessons from lead and polychlorinated biphenyls*. J Neurol Sci, 2011. 308(1-2): p. 9-15.
88. Weaver, D.E., *Contaminant levels in farmed salmon*. Science, 2004. 305(5683): p. 478.

89. Fleming, L., and others, *Parkinson's disease and brain levels of organochlorine pesticides.* Ann Neurol, 1994. 36(1): p. 100-3.
90. Eskenazi, B., and others, *Pesticide toxicity and the developing brain.* Basic Clin Pharmacol Toxicol, 2008. 102(2): p. 228-36.
91. Braun, J.M., and others, *Impact of early-life bisphenol A exposure on behavior and executive function in children.* Pediatrics, 2011. 128(5): p. 873-82.
92. Perera, F.P., and others, *Prenatal airborne polycyclic aromatic hydrocarbon exposure and child IQ at age 5 years.* Pediatrics, 2009. 124, e195-202 DOI: 10.1542/peds.2008-3506.
93. Herbstman, J.B., and others, *Prenatal exposure to PBDEs and neurodevelopment.* Environ Health Perspect, 2010. 118(5): p. 712-9.
94. Stapleton, H.M., and others, *Identification of flame retardants in polyurethane foam collected from baby products.* Environ Sci Technol, 2011. 45(12): p. 5323-31.
95. Stein, C.R. and D.A. Savitz, *Serum perfluorinated compound concentration and attention deficit/hyperactivity disorder in children 5-18 years of age.* Environ Health Perspect, 2011. 119(10): p. 1466-71.
96. Consumer Reports. *Arsenic in your food: Our findings show a real need for federal standards for this toxin.* 2012; Available from: http://consumerreports.org/cro/magazine/2012/11/arsenic-in-your-food/index.htm.
97. Woolf, A., and others, *A child with chronic manganese exposure from drinking water.* Environ Health Perspect, 2002. 110(6): p. 613-6.
98. Wright, R.O., and others, *Neuropsychological correlates of hair arsenic, manganese, and cadmium levels in school-age children residing near a hazardous waste site.* Neurotoxicology, 2006. 27(2): p. 210-6.
99. Crinella, F.M., *Does soy-based infant formula cause ADHD? Update and public policy considerations.* Expert Rev Neurother, 2012. 12(4): p. 395-407.
100. Cockell, K.A., G. Bonacci, and B. Belonje, *Manganese content of soy or rice beverages is high in comparison to infant formulas.* J Am Coll Nutr, 2004. 23(2): p. 124-30.
101. Choi, A.L., and others, *Developmental fluoride neurotoxicity: a systematic review and meta-analysis.* Environ Health Perspect, 2012. 120(10): p. 1362-8.
102. Environmental Protection Agency (EPA). *Fact Sheet on Perchloroethylene, also known as Tetrachloroethylene.* 2012; Available from: http://www.epa.gov/oppt/existingchemicals/pubs/perchloroethylene_fact_sheet.html.
103. Godlee, F., J. Smith, and H. Marcovitch *Wakefield's article linking MMR vaccine and autism was fraudulent.* BMJ, 2011. 342, c7452 DOI: 10.1136/bmj.c7452.
104. Bonanni, P., *Demographic impact of vaccination: a review.* Vaccine, 1999. 17 Suppl 3: p. S120-5.

105. Honda, H., Y. Shimizu, and M. Rutter, *No effect of MMR withdrawal on the incidence of autism: a total population study.* J Child Psychol Psychiatry, 2005. 46(6): p. 572-9.
106. Centers for Disease Control and Prevention. *Timeline: Thimerosal in Vaccines (1999-2010).* Vaccine Safety 2014 Available from: http://www.cdc.gov/vaccinesafety/concerns/thimerosal/thimerosal_timeline.html.
107. Bartholomous, D. *Anti-Vaccine Body Count.* 2014; Available from: http://www.jennymccarthybodycount.com/Anti-Vaccine_Body_Count/Home.html.
108. Branum, A.M. and S.L. Lukacs, *Food allergy among U.S. children: trends in prevalence and hospitalizations.* NCHS Data Brief, 2008(10): p. 1-8.
109. Jackson, K.D., L.D. Howie, and L.J. Akinbami, *Trends in allergic conditions among children: United States, 1997-2011.* NCHS Data Brief, 2013(121): p. 1-8.
110. Gupta, R.S., and others, *The prevalence, severity, and distribution of childhood food allergy in the United States.* Pediatrics, 2011. 128, e9-17 DOI: 10.1542/peds.2011-0204.
111. Sicherer, S.H., and others, *US prevalence of self-reported peanut, tree nut, and sesame allergy: 11-year follow-up.* J Allergy Clin Immunol, 2010. 125(6): p. 1322-6.
112. Gupta, R., and others, *The economic impact of childhood food allergy in the United States.* JAMA Pediatr, 2013. 167(11): p. 1026-31.
113. Sicherer, S.H., and others, *The US Peanut and Tree Nut Allergy Registry: characteristics of reactions in schools and day care.* J Pediatr, 2001. 138(4): p. 560-5.
114. National Institute of Allergy and Infectious Disease, *Food Allergy: An Overview.* July 2007, NIH Publication No. 07-5518.9: Bethesda, MD.
115. Lynch, S.V., and others, *Effects of early-life exposure to allergens and bacteria on recurrent wheeze and atopy in urban children.* J Allergy Clin Immunol, 2014.
116. Holbreich, M., and others, *Amish children living in northern Indiana have a very low prevalence of allergic sensitization.* J Allergy Clin Immunol, 2012. 129(6): p. 1671-3.
117. Stefka, A.T., and others, *Commensal bacteria protect against food allergen sensitization.* Proc Natl Acad Sci U S A, 2014. 111(36): p. 13145-13150.
118. Herman, E.M., *Genetically modified soybeans and food allergies.* J Exp Bot, 2003. 54(386): p. 1317-9.
119. Asthma and Allergy Foundation of America. *Adverse Reactions to Food Additives.* November 13, 2014; Available from: http://asthmaandallergies.org/food-allergies/adverse-reactions-to-food-additives/.
120. Shek, L.P., and others, *A population-based questionnaire survey on the prevalence of peanut, tree nut, and shellfish allergy in 2 Asian populations.* J Allergy Clin Immunol, 2010. 126(2): p. 324-31.

121. Allen, K.J., and others, *Vitamin D insufficiency is associated with challenge-proven food allergy in infants.* J Allergy Clin Immunol, 2013. 131(4): p. 1109-16.
122. World Health Organization. *Children Are Not Little Adults: Children's Health and the Environment.* [WHO Training Package for the Health Sector] 2008; Available from: http://www.who.int/ceh/capacity/Children_are_not_little_adults.pdf.
123. Environmental Protection Agency (EPA). *Supplemental guidance for assessing susceptibility from early-life exposures to carcinogens.* EPA Risk Assessment Forum 2005; Available from: http://www.epa.gov/ttn/atw/childrens_supplement_final.pdf.
124. Halbert, T. and E. Ingulli, *Law & ethics in the business environment.* Eighth edition. ed. 2014, Stamford, CT: Cengage Learning. xv, p.240.
125. Rakotoarisoa, M., M. Iafrate, and M. Paschali, *Why has Africa become a Net Food Importer?* 2012, Food and Agricultural Organization of the United Nations (FAO): Rome, Italy.
126. Pollan, M., *The omnivore's dilemma : a natural history of four meals.* 2006, New York: Penguin Press. p. 123-238.
127. Epstein, S.S. and B. Leibson, *Good clean food : shopping smart to avoid GMOS, rBGH, and other products that may cause cancer.* 2013, New York: Allworth Publishing.
128. Biro, F.M., and others, *Pubertal assessment method and baseline characteristics in a mixed longitudinal study of girls.* Pediatrics, 2010. 126, e583-90 DOI: 10.1542/peds.2009-3079.
129. Stoll, B.A., *Western diet, early puberty, and breast cancer risk.* Breast Cancer Res Treat, 1998. 49(3): p. 187-93.
130. U.S. Food and Drug Administration (FDA). *Steroid Hormone Implants Used for Growth in Food-Producing Animals.* October 15, 2014; Available from: http://www.fda.gov/AnimalVeterinary/SafetyHealth/ProductSafetyInformation/ucm055436.htm.
131. Clifford, J. *Hearing on Antibiotic Use in Animals.* House Committee on Energy and Commerce's Subcommittee on Health 2010; Available from: http://democrats.energycommerce.house.gov/sites/default/files/documents/Testimony-Clifford-HE-Antibiotic-Resistance-Animal-Agriculture-2010-7-14.pdf.
132. Roberts, J.R., C.J. Karr, and Council On Environmental Health. *Pesticide exposure in children.* Pediatrics, 2012. 130, e1765-88 DOI: 10.1542/peds.2012-2758.
133. Bouchard, M.F., and others, *Attention-deficit/hyperactivity disorder and urinary metabolites of organophosphate pesticides.* Pediatrics, 2010. 125, e1270-7 DOI: 10.1542/peds.2009-3058.

134. Rauh, V., and others, *Seven-year neurodevelopmental scores and prenatal exposure to chlorpyrifos, a common agricultural pesticide*. Environ Health Perspect, 2011. 119(8): p. 1196-201.
135. Zahm, S.H. and M.H. Ward, *Pesticides and childhood cancer*. Environ Health Perspect, 1998. 106 Suppl 3: p. 893-908.
136. Environmental Working Group. *EWG's 2014 Shopper's Guide to Pesticides in Produce*. 2014; Available from: http://www.ewg.org/foodnews/.
137. Mueller, T., *Extra virginity : the sublime and scandalous world of olive oil*. 1st ed. 2011, New York: W. W. Norton & Co., p. 125-126.
138. U.S. Department of Agriculture Economic Research Service. *Adoption of Genetically Engineered Crops in the U.S.* 2014; Available from: http://www.ers.usda.gov/data-products/adoption-of-genetically-engineered-crops-in-the-us/recent-trends-in-ge-adoption.aspx.
139. Kingston, H. *64 countries around the world label GE food*. Sound Consumer 2013; Available from: http://www.pccnaturalmarkets.com/sc/1305/countries_label_ge.html.
140. U.S. Department of Agriculture Agricultural Marketing Service (AMS). *National Organic Program*. Updated October 17, 2012; Available from: www.ams.usda.gov.
141. Oak Ridge National Laboratory (ORNL). *Predicting Light-Duty Vehicle Fuel Economy as a Function of Highway Speed*. 2014; Available from: http://www.fueleconomy.gov/feg/driveHabits.jsp.
142. Steinfeld, H., and others, *Livestock's long shadow : environmental issues and options*. 2006, Rome: Food and Agriculture Organization of the United Nations. xxiv, 390 p.
143. Scarborough, P., and others, *Dietary greenhouse gas emissions of meat-eaters, fish-eaters, vegetarians and vegans in the UK*. Climatic Change, 2014. 125(2): p. 179-192.
144. Rodale Institute. *Regenerative Organic Agriculture and Climate Change: A Down to Earth Solution to Global Warming*. 2014; Available from: http://rodaleinstitute.org/assets/RegenOrgAgricultureAndClimateChange_20140418.pdf.
145. Hall, K.D., and others, *The progressive increase of food waste in America and its environmental impact*. PLoS One, 2009. 4, e7940 DOI: 10.1371/journal.pone.0007940.
146. Harvard Food Law and Policy Clinic and N.R.D. Council. *The Dating Game: How Confusing Food Date Labels Lead to Food Waste in America*. 2013; Available from: http://www.nrdc.org/food/files/dating-game-report.pdf.
147. Environmental Protection Agency (EPA). *Composting at Home*. Updated April 29, 2014; Available from: http://www.epa.gov/waste/conserve/tools/greenscapes/pubs/compost-guide.pdf.

148. Lyons, L. and Gallup. *Last Wishes: Half of Americans Have Written Wills.* 2005; Available from: http://www.gallup.com/poll/16660/Last-Wishes-Half-Americans-Written-Wills.aspx.
149. Mattioli, D. *On Orbitz, Mac Users Steered to Pricier Hotels.* Technology at wsj.com August 23, 2012; Available from: http://online.wsj.com/articles/SB10001424052702304458604577488822667325882.
150. Child Care Aware. *Choosing Child Care.* 2013 April 11, 2014; Available from: http://childcareaware.org/parents-and-guardians/child-care-101/choosing-child-care.
151. Zero to Three: National Center for Infants Toddlers and Families. *Choosing Quality Child Care.* 2014; Available from: http://www.zerotothree.org/early-care-education/child-care/choosing-quality-child-care.html.
152. Sullivan, J.E., and others, *Fever and antipyretic use in children.* Pediatrics, 2011. 127(3): p. 580-7.
153. Yin, H.S., and others,*Unit of measurement used and parent medication dosing errors.* Pediatrics, 2014. 134, e354-61 DOI: 10.1542/peds.2014-0395.
154. Tough, P., *How children succeed : grit, curiosity, and the hidden power of character.* 2012, Boston: Houghton Mifflin Harcourt, p. xi-xxiii, 73-76.
155. Caspi, A., and others, *Moderation of breastfeeding effects on the IQ by genetic variation in fatty acid metabolism.* Proc Natl Acad Sci U S A, 2007. 104(47): p. 18860-5.
156. Belfort, M.B., and others, *Infant feeding and childhood cognition at ages 3 and 7 years: Effects of breastfeeding duration and exclusivity.* JAMA Pediatr, 2013. 167(9): p. 836-44.
157. Grant, A.M., *Give and take : a revolutionary approach to success.* 2013, New York, N.Y.: Viking. 305 p.
158. Achor, S., *Before happiness : the 5 hidden keys to achieving success, spreading happiness, and sustaining positive change.* 2013, New York: Crown Business. xviii, 252 pages.
159. Kim, S.Y., and others, *Does "Tiger Parenting" Exist? Parenting Profiles of Chinese Americans and Adolescent Developmental Outcomes.* Asian Am J Psychol, 2013. 4(1): p. 7-18.
160. Medina, J., *Brain rules : 12 principles for surviving and thriving at work, home, and school.* 1st ed. 2008, Seattle, WA: Pear Press, p. 65.
161. Gunderson, E.A., and others, *Parent praise to 1- to 3-year-olds predicts children's motivational frameworks 5 years later.* Child Dev, 2013. 84(5): p. 1526-41.
162. Hart, B. and T.R. Risley, *Meaningful differences in the everyday experience of young American children.* 1995, Baltimore: P.H. Brookes. xxiii, 268 p.
163. Dupere, V., and others, *Understanding the positive role of neighborhood socioeconomic advantage in achievement: the contribution of the home, child care, and school environments.* Dev Psychol, 2010. 46(5): p. 1227-44.

164. Trelease, J., *The read-aloud handbook*. 6th ed. 2006, New York: Penguin Books. xxvi, 340 p.
165. Carson, B. and C. Murphey, *Gifted Hands: The Ben Carson Story*. 1996, Grand Rapids, MI: Harper Collins/ Zondervan, 224 p.
166. Landry, R.G., *A Comparison of Second Language Learners and Monolinguals on Divergent Thinking Tasks at the Elementary School Level*. The Modern Language Journal, 1974. 58(1-2): p. 10-15.
167. Garfinkel, A. and K.E. Tabor, *Elementary School Foreign Languages and English Reading Achievement: A New View of the Relationship*. Foreign Language Annals, 1991. 24(5): p. 375-382.
168. Carpenter, J. and J. Torney, *Beyond the Melting Pot*, in *Childhood and Intercultural Education: Overview and Research*, P. Maloney, Editor. 1973: Washington DC.
169. Steele, C., *Whistling Vivaldi : and other clues to how stereotypes affect us*. 1st ed. Issues of our time. 2010, New York: W.W. Norton & Company. xii, 242 p.
170. Vedantam, S., *The hidden brain : how our unconscious minds elect presidents, control markets, wage wars, and save our lives*. 2010, New York: Spiegel & Grau. x, 270 p.
171. Carr, P.B. and C.M. Steele, *Stereotype threat affects financial decision making*. Psychol Sci, 2010. 21(10): p. 1411-6.
172. Steele, C.M. and J. Aronson, *Stereotype threat and the intellectual test performance of African Americans*. J Pers Soc Psychol, 1995. 69(5): p. 797-811.
173. Suzuki, S., *Ability development from age zero*. 1981, Secaucus, N.J. xi, 96 p.
174. Dunning, D., *Self-insight : roadblocks and detours on the path to knowing thyself*. Essays in social psychology. 2005, New York: Psychology Press. xiv, 225 p.
175. Svenson, O., B. Fischhoff, and D. MacGregor, *Perceived driving safety and seatbelt usage*. Accid Anal Prev, 1985. 17(2): p. 119-33.
176. Cross, K.P., *Not can, but will college teaching be improved?* New Directions for Higher Education, 1977. Spring(17): p. 1-15.
177. Odean, T., *Volume, Volatility, Price, and Profit When All Traders Are Above Average*. Journal of Finance, 1998. 53(6): p. 1887-1934.
178. Christakis, D.A., and others, *Early television exposure and subsequent attentional problems in children*. Pediatrics, 2004. 113(4): p. 708-13.
179. Healy, J.M., *Your child's growing mind : brain development and learning from birth to adolescence*. 3rd ed. 2004, New York: Broadway Books. xvii, 409 p.
180. Brown, A. and Council on Communications and Media, *Media use by children younger than 2 years*. Pediatrics, 2011. 128(5): p. 1040-5.
181. Lillard, A.S. and J. Peterson, *The immediate impact of different types of television on young children's executive function*. Pediatrics, 2011. 128(4): p. 644-9.
182. Gladwell, M., *The tipping point : how little things can make a big difference*. 1st Back Bay pbk. ed. 2002, Boston: Back Bay Books. xii, 301 p.

183. Martins, N. and K. Harrison, *Racial and Gender Differences in the Relationship Between Children's Television Use and Self-Esteem: A Longitudinal Panel Study.* Communication Research, 2011. 39(3).
184. Brown, C.B., *The gifts of imperfection : let go of who you think you're supposed to be and embrace who you are.* 2010, Center City, Minn.: Hazelden. xvii, p. 70.
185. Fradkin, J. *Prenatal Monitoring and Care: Q & A National Institutes of Health.* National Healthy Mothers, Healthy Babies Coalition 2014 March 3, 2014; Available from: http://www.hmhb.org/virtual-library/interviews-with-experts/gestational-diabetes/.
186. Brown, W.J., T. Pavey, and A.E. Bauman *Comparing population attributable risks for heart disease across the adult lifespan in women.* Br J Sports Med. DOI: 10.1136/bjsports-2013-093090.
187. Mayo Clinic, *Mayo Clinic Guide to Alternative Medicine*, ed. B. Bauer. 2010, New York, NY: Time Home Entertainment, Inc.
188. Bowman, S.A., and others, *Effects of fast-food consumption on energy intake and diet quality among children in a national household survey.* Pediatrics, 2004. 113(1 Pt 1): p. 112-8.
189. Burton, S., and others, *Attacking the obesity epidemic: the potential health benefits of providing nutrition information in restaurants.* Am J Public Health, 2006. 96(9): p. 1669-75.
190. Duffey, K.J. and B.M. Popkin, *High-fructose corn syrup: is this what's for dinner?* Am J Clin Nutr, 2008. 88(6): p. 1722-1732.
191. United States Department of Agriculture (USDA). *High fructose corn syrup: estimated number of per capita calories consumed daily, by calendar year*. 2014, Available from: http://www.ers.usda.gov/data-products/sugar-and-sweeteners-yearbook-tables.aspx.
192. Kleinman, R.E., and others, *A research model for investigating the effects of artificial food colorings on children with ADHD.* Pediatrics, 2011. 127, e1575-84 DOI: 10.1542/peds.2009-2206.
193. Dowd, J. and D. Stafford, *The vitamin D cure.* 2008, Hoboken, N.J.: John Wiley & Sons. xi, 260 p.
194. Environmental Protection Agency (EPA). *Questions About Your Community: Indoor Air.* 2014; Available from: http://www.epa.gov/region1/com munities/indoorair.html.
195. Meattle, K. *How to Grow Your Own Fresh Air: Kamal Meattle.* in *TED (Technology, Entertainment, Design) Conference.* 2009. Long Beach, CA: TED.com.
196. Wolverton, B.C., *How to grow fresh air : 50 houseplants that purify your home or office.* 1997, New York, N.Y.: Penguin Books. 144 p.
197. Twenge, J.M., J.D. Miller, and W.K. Campbell, *The narcissism epidemic: commentary on modernity and narcissistic personality disorder.* Personal Disord, 2014. 5(2): p. 227-9.

198. Brown, S.L. and C.C. Vaughan, *Play : how it shapes the brain, opens the imagination, and invigorates the soul*. 2009, New York: Avery. 229 p.
199. Seligman, M.E.P., *Flourish : a visionary new understanding of happiness and well-being*. 1st Free Press hardcover ed. 2011, New York: Free Press. xii, 349 p.
200. Pew Research Group. *"Nones" on the rise*. Pew Research Religion & Life Project May 3, 2014; Available from: http://www.pewforum.org/2012/10/09/nones-on-the-rise/.
201. Waite, L.J. and E.L. Lehrer, *The Benefits from Marriage and Religion in the United States: A Comparative Analysis*. Popul Dev Rev, 2003. 29(2): p. 255-276.
202. Blanchflower, D.O. and A.J. Oswald, *Money, Sex, and Happiness: An Empirical Study*. Scandinavian Journal of Economics, 2004. 106(3): p. 393-415.

Appendices

203. Bhatia, J., F. Greer, and American Academy of Pediatrics Committee on Nutrition, *Use of soy protein-based formulas in infant feeding*. Pediatrics, 2008. 121(5): p. 1062-8.
204. Thomas, D.W., and others, *Probiotics and prebiotics in pediatrics*. Pediatrics, 2010. 126(6): p. 1217-31.
205. Greer, F.R., and others, *Effects of early nutritional interventions on the development of atopic disease in infants and children: the role of maternal dietary restriction, breastfeeding, timing of introduction of complementary foods, and hydrolyzed formulas*. Pediatrics, 2008. 121(1): p. 183-91.
206. Consumer Reports. *Where GMOs hide in your food: New Consumer Reports' tests find genetically modified organisms in many packaged foods—including those labeled 'natural'*. 2014; Available from: http://www.consumerreports.org/cro/2014/10/where-gmos-hide-in-your-food/index.htm.
207. Simmer, K., S.K. Patole, and S.C. Rao, *Long-chain polyunsaturated fatty acid supplementation in infants born at term*. Cochrane Database Syst Rev, 2008(1): p. CD000376.
208. Armstrong, L. and A. Scott, *Whitewash: Exposing the Health and Environmental Dangers of Women's Sanitary Products and Disposable Diapers, What You Can Do About It*. 1993, New York: Harper Collins, 194 p.
209. Centers for Disease Control and Prevention. *Vaccine-Preventable Diseases and the Vaccines that Prevent Them*. 2015; Available from: http://www.cdc.gov/vaccines/parents/downloads/parent-ver-sch-0-6yrs.pdf.
210. Centers for Disease Control and Prevention. *2015 Recommended Immunizations for Children from Birth Through 6 Years Old*. 2015; Available from: http://www.cdc.gov/vaccines/parents/downloads/parent-ver-sch-0-6yrs.pdf.

Photo Credits

Cover Photo: © iStock/dolgachov and © Thinkstock/Photodisc

Author Photo: © Dawnielle Westerman All These Years Photography

Pages 4–5, Breastfeeding positions © Fotolia-DPC/ono

Pages 126–135, Toxin illustrations © Jackie Lay

Page 167, Carbon Diet pyramid © CarbonDiet.ca

Index

Made in the USA
Charleston, SC
12 September 2015